Cultural Globalization and Music

Cultural Globalization and Music

African Artists in Transnational Networks

Nadia Kiwan
University of Aberdeen, UK

Ulrike Hanna Meinhof
University of Southampton, UK

First published 2011 by
PALGRAVE MACMILLAN

Palgrave Macmillan in the UK is an imprint of Macmillan Publishers Limited, registered in England, company number 785998, of Houndmills, Basingstoke, Hampshire RG21 6XS.

Palgrave Macmillan in the US is a division of St Martin's Press LLC, 175 Fifth Avenue, New York, NY 10010.

Palgrave Macmillan is the global academic imprint of the above companies and has companies and representatives throughout the world.

Palgrave® and Macmillan® are registered trademarks in the United States, the United Kingdom, Europe and other countries.

ISBN 978–0–230–22129–1   hardback

This book is printed on paper suitable for recycling and made from fully managed and sustained forest sources. Logging, pulping and manufacturing processes are expected to conform to the environmental regulations of the country of origin.

A catalogue record for this book is available from the British Library.

Library of Congress Cataloging-in-Publication Data

Kiwan, Nadia.
Cultural globalization and music : African artists in transnational networks / Nadia Kiwan, Ulrike Hanna Meinhof.
    p. cm.
    Includes index.
    ISBN 978–0–230–22129–1 (alk. paper)
1. Popular music—Social aspects—Africa.   2. Music and transnationalism—Europe.   3. Music and transnationalism—Africa.   I. Meinhof, Ulrike Hanna.   II. Title.
ML3917.A4K59 2011
780.89'92761—dc22   2011004140

10   9   8   7   6   5   4   3   2   1
20   19   18   17   16   15   14   13   12   11

Printed and bound in Great Britain by
CPI Antony Rowe, Chippenham and Eastbourne

Contents

List of Illustrations

List of Maps

Acknowledgements

This book bears the fruits of a rich and rewarding collaboration between its authors, which began in 2003, when we started working together on the EU-funded 5th Framework Project, directed by Ulrike Hanna Meinhof: *Changing City Spaces: New Challenges to Cultural Policy in Europe*. We would therefore like to express our sincere thanks to the European Commission for funding the *City Spaces* project. When *City Spaces* came to an end in 2005, we decided to continue working together in this area and extend our work on music in migration contexts to a research project on musicians' transnational networks (*Diaspora as Social and Cultural Practice: A Study of Transnational Networks across Europe and Africa* or TNMundi for short). Our own earlier work had hinted that artists in the diasporic 'hubs' of capital cities interlink with cultural and social 'movements' in their originating countries for various artistic, economic, social, political and ecological reasons. But it was only with TNMundi that we were able to study the underlying dynamics that bind artists and cultural agents from such cultural movements in translocal and transnational networks of similar motivations way beyond the reach of capital cities. For this opportunity to extend our work on music and migration, we are extremely grateful to the UK Arts and Humanities Research Council (Diaspora, Migration and Identities programme) for the generous three-year funding which allowed us to conduct our research across Europe, Morocco and Madagascar. In particular, we would like to thank the DMI programme director, Professor Kim Knott, for her guidance and enthusiasm throughout our project's duration. We would like to express our warmest thanks to Dr Marie-Pierre Gibert for being an outstanding project research assistant in every way. Her energetic professionalism and friendship made our partnership an extremely positive experience. We would particularly like to thank Marie-Pierre Gibert for her research on the North African networks in the UK and for her valuable assistance in the fieldwork conducted in France, the Netherlands and Morocco. We would also like to thank the project consultant and musician Zafimahaleo Rasolofondraosolo – Dama – for his sharp expertise, insight and companionship throughout both the *City Spaces* and TNMundi projects. Dama's involvement as consultant, musician and artistic director of the many cultural events which arose out of these two projects has facilitated and enriched much of our empirical and theoretical work, especially the research on Madagascar, and for this we are greatly indebted to him. Furthermore, we extend our thanks to Professor Taieb Belghazi for his consultancy in relation to the Moroccan dimension of the project. We also want to thank Ricky Olombelo for accompanying some parts of the fieldwork in Madagascar and in supporting the selection and interviewing of some of the local artists. Our project secretaries, Natacha Borrel and Amanda Elvines, did amazing work over the duration of the project and we are particularly grateful for their patient and efficient transcribing of many of the interviews which feature in this book. Our deepest thanks go to the musicians, cultural producers, members of NGOs and cultural institutions who so sincerely embraced the spirit of our project by giving so generously of their time and letting us into their worlds to conduct our research. Their involvement was so fundamental to our work and to this book that we would like to thank at least some of them by name here, though they represent many others who cannot be named individually: from North Africa Adlane Defouad, Amel Abou el aazm, Badr Defouad, Badre Belhachemi, Otmane and the band members from Shabka, Fez City Clan, Hatim and Othmane from H-Kayne, Ali Faiq, Momo Merhari, Hicham Bahou, Hicham Bajjou, Hocine Boukella, Taoufik Mimmouni, Karim Chaya, Karim Ziad, Hichem Takaoute, Mohand Haddar, DJ Awal, Seddik Zebiri, Yazid Fentazi, Karim Dellali, Farid Nainia, Hicham El-Kebbaj, Kasba (Khalid), Salah Edin, Karine aka Sista K from Watcha Clan, Elsa, Nassim Kouti, Abdelati Loaoufi, Aïcha Lebga, Skander Besbes, Oum, Khansa Batma, Ali Faraoui, Ousso, Hiba Mansour, Bigg, Majid Bekkas, Safaa Kaddioui, DJ Amina, Claire Le Goff, Khalid Moukdar, Mounir Kabbaj. From Madagascar Bekoto, Charle, Dadah, Dama, Fafa, Nono, and Raoul from the group Mahaleo; Ricky Olombelo, Régis Gizavo, Justin Vali, Erick Manana, Marius Fontaine, HAJAMadagascar, Rachel Ratsizafy and Olivier Roman-Garcia, Edgar Ravahatra, Mamiso (Senge), Mbasa (Salala), Mfa Kera (Black Heritage), Fassio, the group Mavana, Seheno, Carson, Hughes Modeste, Lolo sy ny Tariny, Jaojaoby, Hanitra from Tarika, Rakapo, Remanindry, Tsiliva, Teta, the group Sandratsy (Anna, Mamy, Dimby, Mauritus), the groups Antsiva, Tsivarioky, Lazan'Anosy, Briant, Good look, Tsy kivy an'i Nosibe, Goala, Berikely, Biba. Apart from the musicians, we would also especially like to thank Eckehart Olszowski (CGM, Tana), Marie-Clemence and Cesar Paes (Laterit), Lova Ramisamanana (Kanto Productions), Jaobarison (Media Consulting), Josielle Randriamandranto (Jakaranda), Anne and Erich Raab (Freunde

Madagascars), Brett Masoud (Azafady), Familie Pesendorfer (Verein Baobab), Heribert Ableidinger (Welthaus Linz), Diana Spiegelberg (Serious), Leah Zakks (British Council), Simon Broughton (Songlines), Werner Fuhr (WDR) and Jenny Fuhr (the latter for sharing her passion and insights into Malagasy music with us).

The TNMundi cultural events in Antananarivo, Rabat and Southampton were co-funded by the Goethe Cultural Institute (CGM Antananarivo), Vazimba productions (Antananarivo), the Institut français (Rabat), British Council Morocco and the Arts Council South-East (UK) and we would like to extend our gratitude to them and to the many other sponsors who supported these events.

We would also like to thank our colleagues and institutions for their support throughout the research project and the writing of this book, in particular for the periods of research leave granted to Nadia Kiwan by the University of Aberdeen and to Ulrike Meinhof by the University of Southampton.

The team at Palgrave Macmillan have been very supportive throughout this project and we are very grateful to them for their enthusiasm and guidance from the outset.

Finally, we would like to express our warmest thanks to our families (Marc, Charlotte, Angela, Mageed and Frank, Leander, Munna, Onni) for their love, support and patience throughout the writing of this book. The years of researching for and writing this book saw the beginning of a new life when Nadia's daughter Charlotte was born in February of 2009, and it sadly also saw the decline and eventual end of one, when Ulrike's husband Frank Gloversmith passed away in August 2009. It is to them and to all the artists who shared their life stories with us that this book is dedicated.

Introduction: Networks and Transnational Movements: A Theoretical and Methodological Challenge to Migration Research

This is a book about South–North, North–South relations between Africa and Europe, seen through the alternative prism of artists from North Africa (mainly Morocco and Algeria) and Madagascar, and of their complex networks within and across African, European and wider global spaces: a decidedly 'bottom-up' view, which privileges the voices of people 'on the move'. Our study presents and analyses the personal narratives and practices of such musicians in different locations across Africa and Europe, and those of the people who constitute their networks within the wider artistic, cultural and civil society milieus of global or globalizing societies.

We suggest that artists who create or enter such networks follow a different logic of translocal and transnational links than is normally associated with diaspora and migration research on music. Thus we are widening the scope from 'bi-focal', ethnically and spatially defined communities in sending and originating countries to the more complex and fluid flows and networking of individuals. We are thus extending the groundbreaking work of ethnomusicologists such as Guilbault (1993), who have studied the movements of musicians between two locations, in her case the Antilles and France, by a multi-sited ethnographic model based on the networking of key individuals. While recently there has been a plethora of research which theorizes networks and flows in many different disciplines across the humanities and the social sciences, little empirical research has as yet emerged which studies these in closer empirical detail (see Holton 2005 for a review of some of the network literature). By contrast, our work offers original case-study material collected through ethnographic observation and narrative interviews with musicians and their associates. This will allow us to challenge established approaches to diasporas, while substantiating cutting-edge theories of transnationalism and translocalism through empirical data.[1]

1

Of particular significance in our study is a new perspective on migration, which focuses on migrant musicians in their new countries of residence. But although this obviously constitutes an important aspect of our study, we do not purely engage with transnational movements between country of origin and country of residence. Instead, our contention is that many phenomena associated with migration and diasporas cannot be fully understood unless we analyse the processes of movement and interconnections within so-called 'sending' countries as well. Such initial moves often create country-internal movements and circuits of people which in turn underpin the first steps towards transnational migration, which in turn become part of transnational circular movements. Our network model thus embraces a much wider set of interconnections than is usually the case in migration studies.

This Introduction offers three main themes. First of all, we will present a theoretical framework for our translocal and transnational network model with four key parameters and show their methodological consequences for fieldwork design. Secondly, we will relate these debates to the more specific groups of musicians of Malagasy and North African origin, providing a rationale for the choice of these particular groups. Here we will also draw on a new theoretical concept, which we previously defined as 'transcultural capital' (Meinhof and Triandafyllidou 2006). Transcultural capital theory combines and integrates in one framework theories of different types of social and cultural 'capital', familiar since Bourdieu's and his associates' seminal work (for example Bourdieu and Wacquant 1992), with the notion of 'social remittances' from migration studies (for example Levitt 1998, 2001). This will be explained in more detail below. Thirdly, we will give a chapter-by-chapter overview of the entire book, its aims, procedures and key arguments. In conclusion the Introduction will also show why a study of this kind challenges traditional approaches to diasporas and migration while complementing more contemporary but largely theoretical discussions of transnationalism by new empirical findings.

Transnational networks

Our main departure from existing network models (Becker 1982; Bunnell 2007; Castells 1996; Collins 1998; Holton 2008; Landolt 2001; Latour 1999, 2005; Li 1998; Pizzorno 1991; Russell and Tuite 2002; Smith and Guarnizo 1998; van de Veer 2002; Zhou and Tseng 2001) lies with our mapping of four interconnecting multi-dimensional, multi-directional parameters. Borrowing a metaphor from electronic circuit designs we define these as 'hubs' with specific properties. These are *human* hubs, *spatial* hubs, *institutional* hubs and – somewhat tongue in cheek – *accidental* hubs. Let us now explore this in more detail.

Human hubs

We begin with human hubs since these represent the key motivation for integrating the other three. Why this emphasis on specific individuals? There are different entry points into migration research which all have consequences. One of the most obvious problems for diaspora and migration research stems from the circularity of researching dense diasporas in specific locations, which seemingly reinforce the notion of diasporas as spatially defined, self-defining or even isolated and ghettoized communities. Wimmer and Glick Schiller (2003) have critiqued this approach as 'methodological nationalism', which reinforces the view of diasporas as displaced, 'neo-communitarian' people whose identities are formed by retention of ethnic ties to their 'homeland' and ethnic concentration at new place of residence. In our own work with African[2] musicians in a previous project on capital cities (www.citynexus.soton.ac.uk) we could easily find places, spaces and discourses which answered to this pattern. However, by pursuing individual artists across their different spaces of engagement, with different types of audiences, and by engaging them in long conversations about their life histories, it quickly emerged that ethnicity is only one, albeit powerful form of identification, sitting alongside more globalized cosmopolitan tendencies. This led us to suggest that musicians' identities were constructed through multiple discourses which simultaneously comprised registers depending on the context of the narrative (see Meinhof and Triandafyllidou 2006; Meinhof 2009). This analysis led us to a redesign of our subsequent work, where specific individuals rather than preconfigured spaces provided the entry point. Timothy Rice (2003) in addressing similar issues from the point of view of an ethnomusicologist promotes a 'subject-centred musical ethnography' as a way to create 'narrative coherence'.

> One of the goals of modelling these ethnographies would be to bring some narrative coherence to the complex and seemingly fragmented world that many social theorists, cultural critics, and ethnomusicologists are writing about. That coherence would be situated in subjects' biographies and in the interaction of people occupying slightly different subject positions but interacting in time and place. (Rice 2003: 156–7)

Rice subsequently develops a three-dimensional model for his ethnographic work, with the parameters of location, time and musical metaphor as a way of capturing what he calls 'musical experience' (Rice 2003: 158ff.; see also Fuhr forthcoming). Our own model shares with Rice the notion of the multi-dimensional context-dependent space, but follows a different logic by insisting on specific and highly significant musicians and cultural organizers as an entry point to these multiple spaces. Hence 'human hubs', as we would like to call them, differ from other less well-connected musicians in that they are the key nodes which link all the other parameters in our network model. They are the main agents who provide the focus for everyone in the network and it is they who know and are known by everyone, even though the other members of the network will not all be familiar with one another. Importantly, it is in the nature of 'human hubs' that their social networks cross over and link very different geographic spaces across sending and receiving countries as well as different types of social spaces in a variety of cultural, institutional, professional and other kinds of contexts. Gaining access to the life histories and live practices of such 'human hubs' redresses any danger of methodological nationalism, or 'ethnoaesthetics' (Erlmann 1993: 6, also quoted in Rice 2003: 156).

Examples for such key individuals in extensive transnational networks without having left their country of origin are for Madagascar, among others, the musicians from the group Mahaleo, most notably their eponymous founder Dama (Zafimahaleo Rasolofondraosolo), Ricky Olombelo and Rajery, and in the North Africa context, the Boulevard des jeunes musiciens founders and activists, Momo Merhari and Hicham Bahou. Through their activities some translocal and transnational networks not only remain rooted in the capital cities of the South, but they also create South < > North circuits for migrant musicians. By contrast, the Paris-based Malagasy musicians Justin Vali and Régis Gizavo and the music promoter and director of Kanto Productions Lova Ramisamanana equally fulfil the role of transnational human hubs but now from the perspective of the North. The Algerian musician Hocine Boukella (aka Cheikh Sidi Bémol) and the Louzine artists' collective in Paris, the Algerian music promoter Mohand Haddar and his New Bled label and production company are just some of the North African examples which represent human diasporic hubs in the North. Chapters 2 and 3 in particular will present such artists and organizers and their networking in more detail.

Spatial hubs

From the discussion of human hubs it has already emerged that the analysis of specific individuals' movements leads us to a multiplicity of translocal and transnational routes across geographically dispersed spaces. While the unprecedented scale of physical global movements together with the explosion of virtual technologies allow networks to exist across locales of any kind, number or size, from the smallest village to the capital city, there are nevertheless spatial hubs which have a similar function to human hubs in that they bundle and focalize these flows. The important role of capital and metropolitan cites in the North such as Paris and London, Rome, Berlin or Vienna as key nodes for migration flows and migrant cultures has been amply discussed, our own work included (for just some examples of the extensive literature on urban globalization see Smith 2001 and the different city chapters by Kiwan and Kosnick, Aksoy, Robins, Kosic and Triandafyllidou, Busch and Böse, in Meinhof and Triandafyllidou 2006). However, the pivotal roles which capital and/or metropolitan cities in the South play as hubs for cultural and transcultural networking is far less obvious from the cultural/artistic research literature. This may partly be due to a more pronounced focus on so-called 'traditional' (music) cultures (for example Rice 2003 offers examples from Bulgarian, Baily 2008 from Afghan, and Schmidhofer 1994 from Malagasy traditional music), which are more easily located in village life than in the bustle of big cities. (The extensive research on global hip-hop provides the main exception to this.) Yet cities in the South play similar roles to those in the North for both the translocal movements of artists within their nations and the transnational multi-directional movements between North and South.

Transnational migration begins in the country of origin and is often preceded by translocal migration to the major or capital cities, often in repeated cycles of to-and-fro movements. These cities through their infrastructures and the concentration of 'human' and 'institutional hubs' within them can offer national recognition to aspiring musicians, function as hub for translocal touring and offer the potential to access the national and transnational music industry, and act as international jumping board and nodes for returnees. Antananarivo and Casablanca, alongside many sub-Saharan cities such as Dakar, Cape Town and Johannesburg, are hubs in their own right, linking musicians in the South as well as between North and South through migration, return migration and cyclic migration flows (see, for example, Hegasy 2007; Lemanski 2007). Once again, multi-sited ethnography on the nodes created by 'human hubs' provides a privileged vantage point for studying these spatially defined interconnections in a more systematic way. We will return in Chapter 2 to this relatively new role of African cities in the directing and redirecting of artistic energy.

Institutional hubs

A third parameter which links human and spatial hubs in a multi-layered way is provided by particular key institutions and organizations that either help organize or are themselves integrated into artists' networks. Here we need to distinguish between three quite different but significant layers of artistic support: firstly, there are cultural institutions from the North located in the South, whose primary goal it is to engage with cultural dissemination. This first group is highly influential in both Madagascar and Morocco. The low priority of creating an effective cultural policy at national and governmental level in Madagascar for example has turned foreign cultural institutions, most importantly the Cercle germano-malgache/Goethe Cultural Centre, the Alliance française, the Centre culturel Albert Camus and cultural wings of some foreign embassies located there into the most important supporters of local and transnational migrant artists. In Morocco there is a similar dynamic in that many foreign cultural institutes (and particularly the network of French Institutes across the country) provide much needed performance and rehearsal space for musicians outside the highly visible festival circuit. Very many musicians in and from Madagascar and Morocco had their first opportunities of performing or touring at one of these 'institutional hubs'. Local cultural centres suffering from shortage of funds for their activities are often directly co-supported by these institutions from allied countries. Secondly, there is a plethora of expatriate associations in the North organized locally, nationally or globally via the internet as support organizations for the diaspora, and thus indirectly also for 'their' artists. Malagasy examples to be further explored in Chapter 6, include among others diaspora organizations in Toulouse and Nantes. North African examples include Mosaik Production in Geneva, Éclats de lune in Marrakesh and ASIDD in Tassemmitt (Morocco), all of which represent differing models of South–North mutual support. And finally there is the almost completely unresearched interconnection between artists and civil society movements devoted primarily to developmental causes of aid but which in some important instances interact with artists (see also Gibert and Meinhof 2009). All three types will be discussed in detail later, and their role in interconnection with our 'human hubs' further analysed.

Accidental hubs

Accidental hubs are those where we as researchers are implicated in building up the very network structures that we are researching. The anthropological literature on the 'observer paradox' is substantial, and differing solutions have been offered by major writers in the field (see among many others the various publications by Marcus, such as Fisher and Marcus 1986, Clifford and Marcus 1986, Marcus 1998 and Armbruster 2008 for an overview), all involving the need for self-reflexivity in the approach to the collection and analysis of data. In working with professional or aspiring artists, the chance of our turning into accidental hubs is arguably even stronger than in the anthropology of everyday practices. Artists by definition seek out any opportunity for practising and supporting their arts, and we as researchers of the arts also come with our own interconnections in academic, media and other artistic fields. Hence researchers such as ourselves, who come with an agenda of pursuing individuals in networks, cannot but involve artists in our own networking across the hubs identified. This may seem an irresolvable dilemma for constructing sufficiently independent scientific research methods. However, given the continuing links between ourselves and certain key artists and the involvement of some artists in our own research practices as co-interviewers, consultants, mediators and curators of events for disseminating and demonstrating what we are finding out (see Chapter 5), we decided to make positive use of these interactions in our network design, and turn ourselves into conscious and self-reflexive insiders wherever possible. Such 'friendship' or collaborative models for ethnographic research are not a recipe for all and every kind of research, and would certainly not work in cases where researchers do not share the ideologies, values or aims of those researched (for a discussion of this dilemma see Meinhof and Galasinski 2005). Their application in the field depends on a transparent and shared ethical agenda, and a continuous awareness of the need for self-reflexive and critical self-assessment. But they do offer a unique opportunity for more in-depth and personalized research than would otherwise be feasible. Hence, in our research practices, all new links created by our interactions with the artists were positively embraced and subsequently researched, leading to a chain of continuing networking which supported the artists as well as ourselves in about as equal a 'gift exchange' (Mauss 1997) between ourselves and the artists as one could envisage. And it is not only between ourselves and the artists we worked with that we noted this equality in gift and counter-gift, but this extended equally to some of the relations we have researched between

NGOs and artists, subject of Chapter 6.[3] Such exchanges between North and South were a topic that we have frequently discussed with some of those musicians that we encountered more frequently during the different stages of our fieldwork and who became friends rather than simply interviewees. Raoul, a doctor in Tamatave, brother of Dama and one of the four singer-songwriters of Mahaleo, described his relation to the NGOs as follows:[4]

> You know, we musicians, we are idealists. And I am very attached to the earth ... So I would like to put into practice in the country-side what I'm singing, what I'm composing. And fortunately, we found partners to help us realize our dreams. The idea is that there is a lot to do in the South and a lot of money in the North. How to make the link? So I think, well, if the South can find serious partners in the North, and the North can find serious partners in the South, then you can talk about development ... This is not help to make us dependent but to give a little push in the right direction. [1][5] (Meinhof's and Gibert's interview with members of the Mahaleo group, June 2007, Paris)

Transcultural capital and transnational artists

Transcultural capital theory was first introduced by Meinhof and Triandafyllidou (2006) in order to capture the highly integrated inter-action of different types of capital in the lives of transnational artists. Starting with Bourdieu's seminal writing (see especially Bourdieu and Wacquant 1992), cultural or symbolic capital, contained for example in linguistic, artistic or intellectual skills, and social capital (see also Halpern 2005; Putnam 2000), contained for example in forms of social networks, represent powerful resources for those who possess them, comparable to the more traditional view of capital as an economic resource. Building on these insightful ideas, the concept of a *trans*cultural capital has the advantage of showing the interdependencies of these forms of capital in the lives of the migrant artists we have studied, and creates a frame for analysis where other notions from within diaspora and migration research, most notably that of social remittances (Levitt 1998), can be integrated. Transcultural capital is thus a heuristic concept to enable interpretation and analysis of resources typically associated with trans-national migrants who retain substantive links between country of origin *and* country/ies of settlement and who activate the continuing interdependencies between them in various flows and cycles of migration, return and re-return. It is thus not an essentializing concept through which artists are frozen into their ethnic niches, but rather a strategic one, which enables us to describe the ways in which artists use the valuable resources acquired in their countries and cultures of origin to underwrite and develop their art *and* at the same time underwrite and support their commercial appeal to different publics.

In the case of migrant musicians, substantive cultural capital is brought from the country of origin to the new country of settlement. All interviewed artists from North Africa and Madagascar alike drew substantively on the musical and linguistic resources of, and were inspired in their lyrics by, the natural, social and cultural environment of their countries or regions of origin. The creativity unleashed by these continuing links is well understood by the artists themselves and was frequently articulated in their conversations with us (see also Chapter 3). This 'imported' cultural capital underpins the connection of migrant artists to their respective diasporas who in many cases constitute the artists' primary *social* capital through extensive infrastructures of physical and virtual means of communication and dissemination, which very often take place on the margins or completely 'under the surface' of mainstream society and its music industry. This is the case for the French Malagasy and the (Parisian) Algerian diaspora; but it is less evident for the Moroccan musicians in France and other European countries who constitute a less dense network. In that way the interaction between cultural and social capital creates the economic capital, which in turn enables artists to fully professionalize and gain a living from their art. The diasporas' retention of substantive links back to their country of origin in turn adds a cyclical and multi-dimensional element to transcultural capital, enabling artists who never before had left their country of origin to tour in Europe, and to join up with those who have taken up residence, and vice versa. We will discuss these interconnections especially in Chapters 2 and 3. The continuing movements from the South to the North and back again can be seen for example in the trajectories of musicians such as Dama and the other musicians from the Mahaleo group, or of Ricky Olombelo, Rajery or Jaojoaby, who never left Madagascar in spite of their frequent touring, or of Majid Bekkas, H-Kayne and Darga in the North African case. They complement similar cycles whereby first- or in many cases also second- or even third-generation musicians move from the North to the South and back again: Hindi Zahra and also Watcha Clan are typical examples here. In each scenario it is the transcultural capital of musicians which motivates and provides the key for understanding these continuing cycles. Hence transcultural capital theory allows for a more dynamic and complex cross-fertilization between South and North and North and South than does Levitt's notion of social remittances. The latter captures very well the influence of the new understanding, values and know-how gained by migrants in their new societies which is flowing back to the country of origin through the continuing networking with people 'back home'. However, it ignores the ways in which migrants themselves have already imported substantive transcultural capital to their new countries of residence, so that anything flowing back has already emerged from such interaction (Levitt 1998, 2001, but see Levitt and Lamba-Nieves 2011 for a more updated account that takes note of this interchange). It also ignores the impact which people in the South who never left their country of origin can assert on migrants who come back to resource themselves (for example the story of DJ Amina and the influence of the Casablanca Boulevard des jeunes musiciens movement on her activities in Geneva; and various comments made by Justin Vali and Erick Manana) or on other members of societies in the North, such as those civil society activists who will be discussed in Chapter 6. We therefore propose an integration of social remittances into the more multi-directional scope of transcultural capital. Finally, as we will show in Chapter 1, transcultural capital theory also applies at the translocal level to the relations within a country of origin. Hence a musician such as Rakapo from the south-western Malagasy town of Toliara refers to his regular visits to the villages around Toliara which includes his own home village as the source from where he draws his inspiration when composing the music for his eponymous group. Translocally a group such as Rakapo links countryside with town, and through connections with other local musicians such as Teta, who are now working in Tana, with the capital city as well. Yet as the brother of Damily who has migrated to France with his French wife and who is much discussed in Julien Mallet's work (Mallet 2002, 2009), Rakapo also gains artistic and economic support through his frequent tours in France where he 'searches for the good grass' in playing with the group Damily ('chercher des bonnes herbes').[6] Many musicians rely on such combinations of translocal and transnational networking. We will discuss this in much more detail in the chapters to follow.

Transnationalism through the prism of 'African' musicians

Apart from its theoretical ambitions our study has a very specific empirical basis. For several years we have followed the trajectories of individuals and groups of artists from the huge Indian Ocean island of Madagascar off the south-eastern shores of Africa on the one hand, and from the countries of the Maghreb, especially Morocco and Algeria, on the other. Whereas these countries are geographically assigned to Africa, neither the Malagasy nor the North Africans tend to identify themselves as such. The majority of Malagasies by origin, linguistic and cultural affiliation share more with their Polynesian ancestors than they do with their nearest sub-Saharan neighbours, whereas the majority of the people of the Maghreb identify more with transnational and local Arab and Berber (Amazigh) cultures. Living on the edges of Africa their cultural idiosyncracies are very striking. Our choice of these two regions was further influenced by their shared French colonial past, their strong diasporic presence in France and their global transnational networks. And, finally, the contrast between them is very striking indeed. Whereas the North African diaspora in France in particular extends several generations back, has high visibility and is often negatively identified, the Malagasy diaspora is mainly first- or early second-generation and remains largely invisible in public and unrepresented in the media.[7]

In this book we want to tell the stories of artists of North African or Malagasy origin who lead very distinctive but nevertheless representative lives. Their stories will throw light on the changing face of migration in a global context where physical and virtual interconnectivity has multiplied to such an extent that it is now possible to talk about transnational communities which are not geographically adjacent (Vertovec 2009) but which nevertheless sustain themselves by extensive networking.

In the first part of the book – in Chapters 1 and 2 – we introduce musicians who live in Madagascar and North Africa, but who move on different types of translocal and transnational circuits in pursuit of their art. This offers the perspective of those musicians who live in the 'South' but for whom moving 'North' is already either part of their imaginary or their professional practice. To begin a study on migration with musicians who never left their country may seem counterintuitive but makes good sense for several reasons. Most importantly, transnational migration – that is moving from one country to another – is only part and parcel of a much more fundamental form of migration – that of moving from one place to another. To move for example from a village in the south of Madagascar or a Moroccan mountain village or one in the Saharan desert to the nearest town, and from there to a big metropolitan centre, undoubtedly transcends more frontiers of modern life than the move from Casablanca or Antananarivo to Paris. For many of our migrant musicians that first move to the city was the precondition of their eventual move to Europe. But even for those who remain in their villages, the knowledge of others who left or of others who came and visited already creates a consciousness which places their art in a translocal and potentially transnational (imaginary) space. As we will show in Chapter 1, this arouses both desire and fear. Provincial towns also create their own dynamics. Minor but nevertheless emergent opportunities for musicians offered up by cultural agents and institutions in provincial towns are stepping stones for rural musicians who may get the occasional contract to perform and meet up with the more urban artists who live in those towns. They in turn have often established connections with better-known artists from the big city/ies who pass there. Musicians are often caught between a wish to develop their local music industry where they can record, practise, perform and make a living as an artist, and the enormous pull of the capital city and its promise of an international career. One cannot overestimate the enormous significance which metropolitan centres in the South have as hubs in the networks of artists within their own countries. In Chapter 1 we will introduce artists who represent different stages in the migration story – moving across the translocal connections between village, town and metropolis or in some cases back again.

But those who never left also offer another quite different aspect to the story as well. In Chapter 2 we will introduce artists who live in the metropolitan cities of the South, making use of its emergent cultural industries – recording studios, media, cultural institutions, performance sites – and the transnational connections that affords, so as *not* to leave. Artists such as Mahaleo tour frequently in Europe and worldwide but resist any temptation to leave. At their most successful, these artists utilize all the facilities of global interconnections while remaining firmly rooted in their country of origin. Their role for the networks we are describing in this book is pivotal, since they are key nodes not only for the rural and provincial artists in their own countries, but also for those who have migrated but who want to retain creative connections.

Hence even though the emphasis in Part 1 is on artists in the southern hemisphere from and between village, town and city, they are already part and parcel of a globalizing world, however remote they may seem. Their perspective on the North[8] is multifaceted and ambivalent. Metropolitan cities such as Antananarivo and Casablanca are for many as distant or as relatively close as any city in Europe. When Remanidry from Toliara joins the Justin Vali Orkestra to tour Madagascar, and then goes on to perform in Europe, however briefly, what matters is his access to a world beyond the traditional circuit of ceremonies of burial, circumcision, birth, marriage, to a very different (potential) public. This is one end of the spectrum. The young musicians from Fort Dauphin who take a leap to Tana, or the artists from Fez, Meknes or Agadir in Morocco who want to succeed nationally and internationally are another part of it. For them as for many of the most successful artists we will discuss in the other sections, Antananarivo and Casablanca is the *passage obligé*. This is another point of the scale. But when Mahaleo or the Boulevard activists decide to resist the pull of abroad and instead invest their energy in building and sustaining local, translocal and transnational connections for themselves and many other musicians, their view of the relation between North and South once more adds another dimension.

While Chapter 2 thus looks at networking and moving from the perspective of the South to the North, Chapter 3 reverses this and looks at the South from the perspective of the North. In both chapters the underlying theoretical thinking arises from current understanding about global cities and cultural globalization. Whereas with Chapter 2, and mainly basing ourselves on our own empirical observations and analyses, we are tracing the still underrated major significance of global cities as major 'hubs' in the southern hemisphere, Chapter 3 investigates metropolitan cities in the North. Here the theoretical discussion is well established and largely complementary to our own thinking and empirical work. Because of our concern with artists from former French colonies, the main city that we will focus on in the northern hemisphere is Paris, for most migrating artists a *passage obligé* in various ways: as home to the largest clusters of migrants, as a centre for cultural activities and opportunities, and as the focal point for individual migrants' diasporic networks. However, we will not neglect the role of other capital cities, especially London, which, apart from being its own post-imperial centre for artists from former British colonies, is also attracting artists from all over the world. Hence the role of London, and to a lesser extent of Amsterdam, especially for North African artists will also be discussed in Chapter 3. Whereas Chapter 3 thus foregrounds the global cities in the North as spatial hubs, Chapter 4 uses the transnational movements of individual migrants outside the capital cities and their diasporic cluster as its lens. It is here where the methodological innovation of following the path of individual artists across their networks rather than researching preconfigured centres of settlement or artistic performance pays off.

In Chapter 4 we pursue a series of multi-sited individuals or groups who are simultaneously located in metropolitan cities and provincial towns, straddling different regions in Europe, or across Europe and their countries of origin, and including those who embark on circles of migration as well as those who have returned 'home'. What Chapter 4 will add to the already highly complex picture of migration is an even more multi-layered picture where mono- or even bi-directional notions about migration have to give way to a much more multi-directional space. Whereas Chapters 1 and 2 already make the case for an interconnection between translocal and transnational movements and a continuum between internal and international migration, Chapter 4 shows that seemingly clear-cut notions such as transnational migration to and return migration from a specified place need to be equally complexified. Chapter 4 concludes the second part of the book. In both parts it was the artists themselves who were our main concern.

Part 3 focuses on the vital support structures that underpin artistic performances and networking and without whom most of the artists discussed in this book could not survive. Chapter 5 introduces what we have called key 'institutional hubs', official organizations funded by the wealthy nations of the North that are located in the South and which play a major role in cultural networking, not only transnationally between the North to the South, but also, and perhaps more surprisingly, also translocally in the South. In our interviews with artists, by observing the cultural activities in Madagascar and North Africa during our times there and through the internet links, we were easily able to identify the respective key players. In Chapter 5 we will discuss the most significant of these in Madagascar and North Africa, namely the Institut français/ Alliances françaises/Centre culturel Albert Camus, the Goethe-Institut/ Goethe-Centres/Cercle germano-malgache and the British Council, and their respective links to French, German and British cultural policy. If Chapter 5 highlights the institutional support for artists by agencies financed by governments and acting more or less in line with the cultural missions of their funders, Chapter 6 moves beyond the governmental or public sector into the larger or smaller associations of civil society movements and activists. We have already mentioned that our discovery of multi-layered, multi-sited networks of artists – the subject of Chapter 4 – owed a great deal to our person-centred research design and – thanks to the funding from the AHRC's DMI programme – our own ability to empirically pursue this across transnational spaces. Understanding the nature of the connections between civil society and artists depended even more on this research strategy. Chapter 6 analyses examples of mutual support that exist between artists and civil society actors, from the diasporic or ethnically defined groupings and their aims to those that are not primarily related to the arts at all, but who in collaboration with artists have gained powerful mediators for their own objectives and purposes. The final part of the book thus challenges the more usual perspective of the rich North that gives and the poor South that receives, and allows a more optimistic outlook to equal relations between the North and the South, based on mutual support for each other's concerns – with the artists centre stage.

Part 1
The View from the South

1
Translocal Networking in Madagascar and Morocco

The main focus of our book is on migrant musicians whose main residence is at present in Europe. However, in this first part we start at the point of origin. More specifically, in this chapter we begin with the artists from the provinces, who live in or come from some of the rural regions and provincial towns of Madagascar and Morocco, and in Chapter 2 we add those in the countries' metropolitan cities.

Such an unusual perspective in migration studies has several good reasons. First of all, many artists whom we will encounter in this book have as the first stage of their departure for Europe a prior departure from village to town, and/or from town to capital. By inverse, artists who live in the metropolitan cities will in many cases be the hubs for artists in the more remote regions as well as for those who have migrated abroad. Thus if we want to understand the movements of artists across geographical spaces and the networking at physical or at virtual level that underpins and enables it – what Featherstone *et al.* have described as the 'spatialities of transnational networks' (Featherstone *et al.* 2007: 383) – we need to take note of the complex relationships that migrant artists have with their places of origin, the specificities of their local cultures and the enormous step that moving from the provinces to the metropolitan centres implies. Why do people leave home in the first place? Why do they settle where they do? What kinds of movements do they engage in? What kinds of networks enable and sustain these movements? And how and at what points of their careers does a translocal mobility – and by this we mean the movements from and between particular places in the same country – become a transnational jump away from their country of origin to Europe or North America? The distance – geographical and social – between rural villages in some parts of Africa, where people may live in small self-made huts of clay

19

without electricity or water, to the nearest towns which often comprise village-like quarters next to more modern down-town shopping streets, and further on to the metropolitan cities, is so much greater than the one between metropolitan cites such as Casablanca or Antananarivo to Paris. And yet many musicians span these distances on a regular basis, so that even in remote rural regions the effects of translocal and transnational networks are felt, creating a consciousness of conflict and desire but also a range of opportunities.

To give a flavour of these interconnections we will describe in a bit more detail one of the Malagasy provinces where we conducted our fieldwork and interviews with artists, and which was the original home for many of the artists whom we will encounter later on in this chapter as well as in subsequent chapters.[1]

The province of Toliara

The former province of Toliara – until the referendum of April 2007 one of six first-level administrative units of Madagascar – stretches along the coastal lands of Madagascar from the mid-west to the furthest south (Map 1.1).[2] With its capital located in the town that gives the province its name, Toliara province also comprises two other small but major towns: Morondava which lies 219 air miles (353 km) north of the town of Toliara on the northern edge of the province, and Fort Dauphin or – to use its Malagasy name Toalagnaro – 236/379 air miles/km south-east of Toliara town on a peninsula in the furthest south-east. All of these towns can be reached by expensive Air Madagascar internal flights that connect each to the capital city and via Toliara town with one another. However, not one of the three towns is interconnected with the others by an easily accessible direct road. Only dirt tracks that are impassable for large parts of the year and, even at best, only an option for the most hardy or adventurous provide an alternative to the – in mileage much longer but in time much shorter – indirect routes that connect with the great north <> south axis of the national route RN7. Thus the direct 'taxi brousse'[3] connection from Morondava to Toliara along the coast-line takes approximately two days for roughly 285 miles/458 km,[4] and is only passable in the dry season of the southern winter, whereas that between Fort Dauphin and Toliara takes between two and three days for its 378 miles/609 km and has a similar expedition character. But most traffic and most long-distance taxi brousse routes use the system of the asphalted major roads, which are in reasonable or not so reasonable condition. Heading north-east from Toliara on the RN7 the road is in

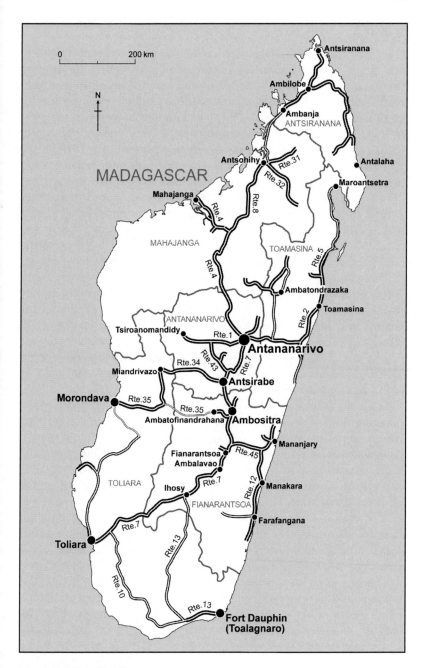

Map 1.1   Map of Madagascar

good condition and much frequented by local, national and tourist traffic alike.

To reach Morondava from that route, the most comfortable option is to go up from Toliara as far as Antsirabe (c. 350 miles/563 km) and then turn west on the RN34 to Miandrivazo (c. 154 miles/248 km), and from there on south-west (c. 76 miles/122 km) till joining the RN35 for a further 114 miles/184 km, a journey of altogether approximately 694 miles/1117 km. Even on this major national route, the enormous potholes of the last decades are only gradually being repaired. The more adventurous option is the old RN35 – heading west from Ambositra and descending down from the mountains after Ambatofinandrahana, a taxi brousse ride of c. 289 miles/465 km which Dama (Mahaleo) has memorialized in 'RN35', the title of one of his recent songs, and which starts with the line: 'There it is, road number 35, still an A road, but forgotten by the people.'[5] To reach Fort Dauphin from Toliara it is again the national route RN7 that provides part of the more comfortable answer, covering the 160 miles/257 km distance to Ihosy. However, the south-east turn in Ihosy off the RN7 onto the RN13 makes for a very bumpy ride even after the road-building programme of the Ravalomanana years, and is better measured in days rather than hours for the c. 306 miles/492 km. Hence it is not only the geographical distance to the capital city of Antananarivo which makes Morondava, Fort Dauphin and Toliara seem remote and far-apart places, but equally the difficulty of reaching across from one to the other.

Culturally, the province is home to quite distinct ethnicities with different forms of rituals, 'fady' (taboos), music, dance and local dialects. However, the overarching Malagasy language in spite of substantial dialectal variation does provide a certain unity,[6] and many popular forms of music and dance have a regional hybrid rather than a distinctive ethnic flavour (see Mallet 2009: 151).[7] In relation to the capital city of Antananarivo, all coastal regions have a long tradition of more or less subdued animosity which time and again is being exploited for political reasons by incumbent or ousted presidents and their national and international supporters (for an excellent account of successive crises in Madagascar see the International Crisis Group's *Rapport Afrique* No. 156 from 18 March 2010). The sense in the provinces of being politically, culturally and economically marginalized and dominated by the power of the capital city and its elites creates a bond for identification at regional level, which may or may not be expressed in corresponding ethnic terms. Yet, as we shall see, the capital city with its open-air and indoor concert venues, clubs, media, recording studios, cultural institutes and the sheer concentration of musicians and music promoters from all over Madagascar is the measure against which success or failure is pitched. For Malagasy musicians Antananarivo is a place of fear and desire, jealousy and triumph – and the *passage obligé* for all but a few musicians en route for transnational migration. The testimonies of artists in the latter part of this chapter will underline the ways in which the cultural geography of Madagascar enters the musicians' everyday discourse.

So far we have only discussed the distance between regional towns and the capital city. But even if towns are far away and difficult to reach, they are nevertheless part of global transport networks, attracting transnational industries and international tourism. Fort Dauphin, whose adjacent virgin forests grow on one of the largest depositories of the much coveted ilmenite mineral,[8] underwent a much discussed and highly controversial transformation in the past few years from an – albeit very poor – emerging tourist town with a local lobster fishing industry and small-scale agriculture to one of the largest ilmenite mining sites in the world. A subsidiary of the Canadian-owned Rio Tinto group, QIT Madagascar Minerals invested millions in this development during the years of the Ravalomanana regime, bringing thousands of largely South African construction engineers and miners to the region to oversee the construction of mines, and to build a new harbour in Ehoala at the edge of one of the most beautiful bay areas of Madagascar. Segregated housing facilities on the outskirts of town were built to house the mine's employees and the town's hotels burst out of their seams. With its foreign engineers now departed and the road building and new housing facilities completed, the local and – as far as mining is concerned – unskilled former peasants and fishermen are largely left unemployed. Tourism has declined, rural communities are threatened by the advance of the mines as is river and marsh-land fishing, and an increase in the hitherto rare AIDS/HIV and syphilis is already worrying health officials. For a very moving portrait of the testimonies of people from the rural areas affected, see *Madagascar, Voices of Change, Oral Testimony of the Antanosy People,*[9] which echoes little of the upbeat tone of Rio Tinto's own publications about the positive financial impact of QIT and its environmental and cultural programme.[10]

In our effort to see the work of local musicians we visited villages untouched by the mining industry and thus not in the vicinity of the miles of asphalted roads linking the mining areas to the town and the harbour. One of these, the village of Nosybe – not to be mistaken for its namesake, the famous tourist island off the north-western coast of

Madagascar – is connected to its nearest town, Fort Dauphin, by a red-soil dirt road, passable in the dry season by cars and in the rainy season by four-wheel-drive vehicles only. The villagers themselves take their goods to the markets in Fort Dauphin by bicycle or on long walks. In spite of its prefix Nosy, which means island in the Malagasy language, Nosybe today lies in the middle of hills and fields where the famous zebu cattle graze. Water needs to be fetched from afar, cooking is done by wood and twigs, and light is provided by petroleum lamps and candles – few and far between. It is places such as these which exemplify our earlier assertion that the social distance between rural Madagascar and its capital city is greater than the transnational distance between Antananarivo and European cities such as Paris – *point final* or *passage obligé* for most artists from Francophone countries.

Have you come to take our songs?

Yet even at these remote places, artists are aware of the potential and pitfalls of connecting themselves to the outside world, from Fort Dauphin to Antananarivo and beyond. One typical example is the ambivalence with which incoming artists – be they visitors or returnees from the capital city – or those who depart from the village for the capital are perceived. Musicians are acutely aware of the opportunities but also of the threats of translocal or transnational connections. These find expression in the hope that incoming artists may bring with them opportunities to have their music heard outside the village or even to enable their own move to the capital city and beyond. But there is also genuine fear that local musicians who depart from home, or visiting musicians who turn up, could unwittingly or purposefully take songs with them that are deemed 'traditional' but are in fact authored by locals who do not get any credit for them.[11] Most rural musicians have no or very minor literacy skills. Neither music nor lyrics are written down but are remembered and passed on through performance. Registration of authored or performed music with OMDA, the Malagasy equivalent though far less effective version of MCPS (Mechanical-Copyright Protection Society) and PRS (Performing Rights Society), is no realistic option for local musicians. Indeed, as we shall see later, one of the many important roles which Brett Massoud, former director of the Malagasy branch of the NGO Azafady in Fort Dauphin, played for those musicians he took under the wing of his organization was to register their music with OMDA. But this is a rare example of good practice, which largely depends on the mediation of knowledgeable outsiders. Hence uncertainty and fear of music thefts cloud the otherwise startling hospitality extended to every visitor.

One of the local artists from the group Nosibe Tsykivy told us of his surprise to find on his visit to a group of local Tanosy musicians – now working in Antananarivo – with whom he had previously played and who were starting to get national recognition, that they had adapted one of his songs and were performing it under their own name. And even our own research team was not beyond suspicion since apart from Ulrike it also comprised our local mediator Daday, director of the cultural programme of QIT and himself a musician, and musicians Dama Mahaleo and Ricky Olombelo from Antananarivo. On our arrival in Nosybe in December 2009, we were treated with utmost hospitality and friendliness, and the enthusiastically received welcome songs by Ricky and Dama were responded to by a wonderful display of music and dance from the group Nosibe Tsykivy (Figure 1.1). However, at one point one of the hundred or more villagers who came to watch this impromptu event asked us publically: 'Have you come to take our songs?' Dama and Ricky later explained that our visit, intended by the research team as a purely information-seeking and interview mission, had aroused some suspicion, as well as great expectations that they in their role as nationally and internationally known musicians would now do something for the local groups.

Figure 1.1 Nosybe musicians, with Dama on the right

Hence to summarize: the reasons for beginning a discussion of transnational migration with stories far away from the metropolitan cities lies in the enormous significance which migration away from provincial homes holds, even if their trajectory does not transcend international boundaries. Given the enormous difference in lifestyles between countryside and the city these initial steps require extraordinary motivation and courage. Furthermore, the continuing pertinence of translocal and transnational networking long after the initial departure from home, makes an awareness of the local points of origin essential. Many of those artists who are now living in the capital cities of their home countries or who have migrated to Europe are continuously returning – both physically in the form of frequent visits and symbolically in their life narratives, their musical creations and their lyrics. As with all out-migration, the point of arrival and new settlement of migrations offer never more than part of a much fuller story. Departures and return visits to villages and small towns by those who left have great impact on the perception of those who stay behind or who fail in their attempt to leave.[12] Understanding the full trajectories of musicians on the move gives us a much deeper sense of the implications of translocal and transnational networking at all the nodal points of interconnection: village, town, metropolitan city in the south and places overseas.

In the next section we will investigate the nature of translocal networks from the point of view of those who left their villages and regional towns, and re-examine the notion of transcultural capital introduced in the Introduction by exploring it in its translocal dimension.

Translocal networks and translocal capital

Before turning our attention to the nature of translocal networks and its associated translocal capital, we need to briefly justify our reasons for limiting in this study the use of the term 'translocal' to the interconnections between people and spaces within a country and that of 'transnational' to those that transcend national borders. We are fully aware that this is an unorthodox differentiation, since the translocal or the transnational normally references a shift in perspective rather than any material difference between intra- or international connections. There is a great deal of overlap – as well as confusion – in the contemporary terminology regarding these terms, which is to some extent inevitable. Both have arisen from the same discourse of globalization which created other neologisms for the complex relations existing between the local and the global, such as the somewhat awkwardly named neologism 'glocal' which also attempts to capture the aspect of locality within the global (for example Robertson 1994, 1995). Especially in literature emerging from the virtual world of technological globalization and networking, the distinction between a transnational or a translocal network is largely irrelevant since it does not capture any material distinction: both exist simultaneously. A reference to translocality foregrounds the multiplicity of local nodes in a virtual and, at the same time, potentially global system of interconnections. In virtual networks where no actual material movements across geopolitical borders are involved, the national easily loses its identificatory strength and point of reference. From the perspective of the internet user, any network of interconnecting people is by definition translocal and at the same time potentially transnational or global.

By contrast, writers with a more specific interest in the *physical* migration of people and in the formation of 'diasporas' in new host countries tend to prefer a transnational terminology, since migration research usually foregrounds the actual physical movements or displacement of people from one nation to the other. Here the dimension of the national retains its currency in the shape of citizenship laws and the associated travel and residence permits or restrictions. However, since people in 'diasporas' are not only movers across national boundaries but also people who have left a specific locality and moved to another, any difference between transnational and translocal perspectives again blurs (see for example Smith 2001; Levitt *et al.* 2003; Vertovec 2009). For us this creates a fuzziness at the heart of our work since we want to thematize, and differentiate between the movements and the material and virtual networking of musicians within *originating* countries and localities on the one hand, and between localities in *different* countries on the other. We therefore propose a more materially grounded distinction, restricting the translocal to those physical or symbolic movements that remain within national boundaries, and referencing as transnational those that transcend them. The advantage of this distinction will become obvious when we discuss translocal and transnational capital.

In the Introduction we introduced the concept of transcultural capital as the combination and interaction of cultural, social and economic capital. In this chapter we want to highlight its translocal specificities within the country of origin. By focusing on a few selected examples of Malagasy musicians originating mainly but not exclusively from three sub-regions of Toliara province – Fort Dauphin, Toliara and Morondava – we shall demonstrate the ways in which the cultural and social capital, accrued by virtue of the musicians' ethnic and regional origin, can enable and sustain their careers translocally and can even be strategically employed as a marketing device at transnational level.

The cultural dimension of translocal capital

The cultural dimension of translocal capital arises from the local styles and rhythms, the knowledge of local scenes, customs, rituals and dialects of musicians in their home regions, and captures their continuing pertinence once they have moved away. In the case of Madagascar, different regions and ethnic identities are associated with specific styles of music and rhythms. These 'musics' accompany the various rites of passage of everyday life, such as birth, circumcision, marriage, burial and, for the people of the Highlands, the Famadihana or reburial ceremonies. But such music is equally present at more mundane functions – such as concerts to celebrate end of school terms, music festivals, sports events, open-air concerts or so-called 'cabarets'.

Fassio, a young musician who left Fort Dauphin after having married an Italian woman, and whom we met while they were living in London for several years, describes this as follows:

> But when I sing, I think that I sing in the traditional sense. It is traditional in the sense that the song that really inhabits your bloodstream, that is what traditional means to me, that it's original to you. It is something original because that's where you show your soul and sometimes it is also something someone has done before ... So if you are Antandroy, you sing banaiky, if you are Antanosy, you sing mangaliba ... Salegy comes from the north, the centre has hira gasy and tsapiky, that's Tulear, that's the tradition in Tulear, that's the way it is. So I do traditional music as a bit of a mixture, I take two, I do mangaliba and also jihe, it's similar to the beko rhythm that I have composed with a guitar and I did it so as to feel good with the music. [1] (Meinhof's and Gibert's interview, October 2007, London)

The ethnomusicologist Julien Mallet, who spent several years studying what he describes as 'the young music' of tsapiky and its practitioners, argues that tsapiky is the key identification for the Tulear region, connecting the town with the villages and the villages with the town: 'This identity process accompanies the double movement of tsapiky from the city to the countryside and from the countryside to the city' (Mallet 2009: 15, Meinhof's translation). [2]

Equally popular for ceremonial as well as for more purely entertainment functions, Mallet sees tsapiky as a symbol both of modern life and of more traditional ritualistic practices:

> Tsapiky unifies the landscape of the city. It transcends ordinary time and gives meaning to the different festive events: sports, concerts, 'dust' dances [*bals poussières*] and ceremonies. As a musical practice, it is inseparable from dance and singing. As a shared language, it's a reflection of the violence and the misery. (Mallet 2009: 126, Meinhof's translation) [3]

Similar points could be made for other distinctive sounds and rhythms of Madagascar: for salegy in the north, mangaliba from the region of Fort Dauphin or beko of the deep south. It is this overlap between continuously evolving musical practices across urban and rural settings in Madagascar, and the closeness of the lyrics to everyday life, which according to Dama (here in conversation with Gizavo and Meinhof) makes terms such as 'traditional' or 'folk' music inappropriate:

Dama: You know, traditional music is not quite as traditional as that. Why am I saying this? For example, when I'm listening to Mama Sana play in the village ... For me, this is a music of today, contemporary music. When she was alive – she lived in the twentieth century – she was playing and narrating in her songs the everyday life of the day. And how is it possible to say that this is a traditional music, folklore, you know, something outdated. On the contrary, this is a music of the present, how shall I call it, a music of the locality. And it's dynamic. And she relates everything she sees and then – because there are no definitive lyrics, you see, it's like jijy[13] – like those who do jijy, what they're doing, they narrate in the song all the events that are happening in the village. And on the following day, when they sing the same melody, other events are happening so ...

Régis: Ahhh yes, that's it, it evolves!

Dama: Yes, it is not a tradition, like a museum piece. [4] (Conversation between Meinhof, Rasolofondraosolo and Régis Gizavo, December 2005, Paris)

The polyphonic singing of the 'sarandra', the acoustic guitars and kabosys of mangaliba, or the electric guitars and drum kits of tsapiky that accompany local occasions, straddle what could be seen from a Western point of view as the most traditional of tribal rural rituals as well as modern sports arenas or discothèques. But whereas Mallet sees in tsapiky from the Toliara region foremost a regional rather than an ethnic identifier, other styles of music are often also used and marketed as typically ethnic and thus invariably exotic. Thus the music of the internationally acclaimed group Salala was identified with the Antandroy (also referred to as Tandroy) people of the extreme south – the Antandroy region – by both the musicians themselves and their Africolor label. In an attempt to create a musical and cultural identity distinctive from the dominant Hauts Plateaux and the capital city of Antananarivo, ethnic background becomes an inspiration, a reference point and a marketing strategy all at once.

This is how Mbasa (of Salala) described to us his decision *not* to follow in the footsteps of Mahaleo, then and now one of the most famous groups of Madagascar, and instead to develop his own idiom of the Tandroy people:

> I myself don't play an instrument, so every time when I tried to get hold of a guitarist, naturally I get someone who plays in the classical format, that is, folk, like Mahaleo, and that's when I told myself, oh I am from the south, I am a Tandroy, I have listened to beko, so I've become that, I am the red soil, I am the burning sun of the south, so when I sing I need a rough voice not a honey-sweet one. So that went round in my head, and that has guided my compositions, that I should not become imprisoned by my own love. Because love, that was for Mahaleo. [5] (Meinhof's interview, April 2009, Nantes)

Similarly mangaliba is claimed by its practitioners not only as the music of and around Fort Dauphin but also as the music of the Tanosy people and is performed in this spirit. Hence Hazolahy, one of the more successful bands from Fort Dauphin who made the leap into Tana and from there to the international scene, recreate local customs and rituals when they perform their music in mangaliba rhythms on stage. One of our informants of Fort Dauphin, Daday, here in answer to questions from co-interviewer Dama, even claims to have invented the term mangaliba (also spelled mangaliaba)[14] so as to create a distinctive rhythm for the music of Fort Dauphin. Even if this claim may not be entirely credible this does not matter here, since what it underlines is the desire of creating an identity for a local practice:

Dama: Because you said there was no rhythm as a benchmark, so as to distinguish, to know, to identify that this is the music of

Fort Dauphin ... So mangaliba is now the point of reference for the music of Fort Dauphin. Is that it?

Daday: Yes that's it. The rhythm of Fort Dauphin exists already, but it's not mangaliba. It was me who gave it that name, I called it mangaliba.

Dama: And the story of mangaliba?

Daday: Mangalibas? Well, every time I play in Tulear, in Beheloka, in Morombe, and there are a lot of people who are asking what is the rhythm of Fort Dauphin because in Morombe it is banaky, in Tulear it is tsapiky, pecto, in Diego it's salegy, in Fort Dauphin there is nothing! So I started to search for the rhythm of Fort Dauphin and to enhance the status of the rhythm of Fort Dauphin. I chose mangaliba to rename this rhythm of Fort Dauphin. [6] (Meinhof's and Rasolofondraosolo's interview, December 2009, Fort Dauphin)

To what extent ethnicity or locality, or a combination of the two, functions as the key identifier for the musicians themselves is not always easy to differentiate since ethnicity can also be a very useful strategic device. Hence Salala continued to perform under a Tandroy identity ticket, even when Senge left Salala, setting up his own group of that name, and was replaced by Daniel, of Antanosy/Fort Dauphin origin. Similarly the newly formed group around Senge, consisting of Senge himself and the musicians Yvon Mamisolofo (Mamiso) and Jean Ramanambintana, which in 1999 won the coveted RFI African Discovery Award, was officially marketed by RFI as Antandroy music even though Mamiso grew up in the Betsileo region much further north in a village outside Fianarantsoa. But RFI's own website calls the group Senge a 'mouthpiece for the Antandroy Community', on a website created in 2001 and still active today:

All three members of Senge are descended from the Antandroy, an ethnic group based in Madagascar's deep south. The Antandroy region is a poor, arid area where people suffer the worst living conditions. Indeed, the region is known locally as 'the land where water hides' and Madagascans know the Antandroy as 'the people from the land of thorns'. Migrating to the towns to escape the hardships of their home region, the Antandroy generally work in low-qualified, low-paid jobs, scraping a meagre living as night-watchmen and rickshaw drivers. Poor and ill educated, they have had to put up with years of social and racial prejudice – and, in the past, they were also discriminated against by the first French settlers. According to popular belief the Antandroy are a cruel, aggressive people prone to lying but, paradoxically, Madagascans also respect the tribe's courage and bravery in face of danger. (www.rfimusique.com/siteEn/biographie/biographie_ 6286.asp, accessed 8 March 2010)

What we can see here is an exoticization of ethnicity for marketing purposes irrespective of the actual background of the musicians themselves. By contrast, Mamiso himself, who lives and performs today in Lyon, describes his geographic and musical origins in very different ways:

> I started music at the age of five. My father was a primary school teacher and a peasant at the same time. In Fianarantsoa. And my mother was 100 per cent peasant. So music is for me, I was born with it. In the countryside, as you know very well, songs are part of the life of the peasants. When our parents take us to work in the field and all that ... there we sing a lot ... And we were also brought up in a Christian environment, we're Catholic and what interested me in this was that from the very beginning the fact that we sing a lot in church, and in my family everyone sings. And my father, he is a primary teacher, but he also plays the organ. He plays the organ in church.
>
> The tomb of my parents is in Ambalavao. I started music when I was five, when my father was telling us stories every night. He was telling tales before we fell asleep but, at the same time, he was playing the guitar. And then, when he finished playing, I would grab the guitar, and when he was playing, I would often watch him. I would look at what he does with his hand, and then do it and he would tell me that it sounds good what I do. So every time he does that, he passes me the guitar, I was five/six years old. [7] (Meinhof's and Rasolofondraosolo's interview, April 2009, Lyon)

The social dimension of translocal capital

If ethnic and regional background can lend cultural capital to musicians, they also translate into social capital in the form of social networks that connect the places of origin with Antananarivo. People who have migrated at different stages from the provinces to the capital city provide vital support systems for newcomers.[15] Insofar as there are practising musicians among them they add a further potential since they now also offer connections to the musical scene

Figure 1.2   District 67 Ha

of Antananarivo. Such networks have spatial, human and institutional properties. As far as spaces are concerned, social networks for 'les côtiers', the migrants from the coastal districts who have moved to Antananarivo, criss-cross four districts of the city. Together these districts have the collective name of 67 hectares, '67 Ha', named as such because of the actual size total in square kilometres. Incoming migrants from the coastal regions turn to it or are directed to it. It is here where on arrival they find other members of their extended families, former neighbours from villages or towns, and where they encounter other artists from their regions (Figure 1.2).

Ricky Olombelo, in conversation with Ulrike and Dama, describes this as follows:

Ricky: That is really very well known in Mada ... The name of the district is 67 Ha ... a district with all the different ethnic groups of Madagascar ... And almost all the different groups of Madagascar are here ... 80 per cent of the migrants are in 67 Ha. And that is the artists' network, those who come from the coastlands, you see.

Ulrike: So this is really the district of the nation's migrants. And is that true for all the ethnic groups or only a few of them?

Ricky: No, all of them ... Because there is the Antandroy, next to them the people of Mahajanga, and next to them those from the north, Diego, Nosybe and from the south-east of Madagascar, you see that's ... that's good ... 67 Ha. [8] (Meinhof's and Rasolofondraosolo's interview, December 2009, Fort Dauphin)

Hence when we were looking for Anna, the young singer whom we had first encountered in Fort Dauphin in 2007, and who by 2009 had moved to Antananarivo to try and make her career there, it was in the district 67 Ha that we found her. Mamiso, too, having been recruited by Senge into his new band once the latter had split from Salala, mentioned quite incidentally that having moved to Tana from Toliara and Fianarantsoa, it was in the district of 67 Ha that he first found a bed in his cousin's flat, even though this was far away from the place where he needed to go for the rehearsals and the recordings of the group. The extract below gives a colourful account of the distances he covered every day in pursuit of rehearsals at another part of town, while also showing the significance that other already better-known musicians can have in providing links – here through Senge, who had already achieved a measure of success with Mbasa in their previous band Salala:

No, Senge, he took these songs and went to talk at the radio station – said, 'I'll start this group,' voilà, tatitata, and then he called me. 'Can you come, 'cause I found a date, the 27th April, at the CGM?', and I said, 'Yeah.' So I went up to Tana, and I lived at a cousin's house in the 67 Ha district, but at that time Jean Ramanambintana, the guys who were with us in the Senge group, their work didn't finish before 5pm. So we'd start rehearsing around 7 or 8pm or so. Like that. So I went on foot every day from 67 to Ankatso.[16] Every day, and I set back around 10pm, 'cause I didn't have enough money for a bus ticket – every day I did that – that's what for distance? One and a half hours on foot, every day. I'd arrive around 6pm or so, we'd start rehearsing, we'd finish around 10pm, I'd eat a bite with them and I'd return to 67 hectares. [9] (Meinhof's and Rasolofondraosolo's interview, April 2009, Lyon)

Audiences for concerts by 'côtier' musicians at the Glacier and other dedicated live music venues in Tana are also recruited from 67 Ha, by word of mouth, by posters and cards pinned against the walls of the houses there. Ricky explains how Tsiliva, an artist originating from Morondava who has started to achieve some national acclaim, nevertheless largely draws his audiences from there:

> When Tsiliva started up with his band, 90 per cent of the audience who came to the concert in Tsaman came from the district I told you about ... the 67 Ha ... there are the coastal people everywhere. [10] (Meinhof's and Rasolofondraosolo's interview, Toliara, December 2009)

Tsiliva, who is mentioned in this extract, is another artist of 'côtier' origin who made his way to Antananarivo from the coastal region of Morondava. Even though the other members of his group all belong to the same family or are very old friends from the same town, he and his eponymous group of 12 artists first joined up as a group once they had moved to Tana:

Marie: And all the other musicians there, the 12, are all from Morondava?
Tsiliva: Yes.
Marie: And they all went to Tana?
Tsiliva: Yeah. They were all already there when I set up my band. And they're all cousins.
Ulrike: That is all one family?
Tsiliva: And friends, childhood friends, that's it. They're all young people. [11] (Meinhof's, Gibert's and Kiwan's interview, November 2007, Morondava)

We encountered Tsiliva and his brother Julo in Morondava in November 2007, where in spite of their having been quite successful in Tana and engaged on some international touring as well, their group had only just given their first ever concert back in their home town. The event, though successful in outcome, had caused them a great deal of trepidation since two previous bands who returned to play there had been rejected by the Morondavan public. The extract below gives some insights into the complexity of the relation between leaving and returning. First they explain how for them the move to Tana, and the joining up as a group there, was at the heart of their success, something they repeat time and again throughout the interview. But success in Tana, even if based on the social capital of belonging to the same coastal region, does not easily accrue the same value at the place left behind. Thus the relationship between the people of the region left behind and those who achieve some success in Tana can be quite fraught, even if that success incorporates the cultural and social capital of point of origin.[17]

Tsiliva: And when I got my baccalaureate I went to Tana ... we were working together.

Marie: OK! So in fact it was in Tana that you started to play in those bands.

Tsiliva: Yeah, in Tana ... After that ... But when I was here, it was my dearest wish. My aim was to become a singer and ... to be famous, and so on. That was my aim.

Ulrike: And that does not work here? If you had stayed here, it would not have worked?

Tsiliva: It would not work! One has to get out a bit.

Nadia: You have to go to Tana, right ...?

Tsiliva: You have to go to Tana. Because ... Well, the band Tsiliva is the first act that comes from here ... and who ... how can I say?

Juno: Was accepted by the audience here?

Tsiliva: That's it. Was accepted. And ... we proved it yesterday! ... Because I left Morondava in 2002. That's the reason why ... they accept us. Because you can't stay here if ... If you want to succeed in Morondava, you have to get out, to go work somewhere else. [12] (Meinhof's, Gibert's and Kiwan's interview, November 2007, Morondava)

The social component of translocal capital is often realized through important mediators at personal or institutional level who are already more established in the cultural industries of the capital city. We have already mentioned the role that Senge played for Mamiso in a previous extract. In the next chapters we will pursue this theme in much more depth to analyse the enormous significance which particular key individuals in the capital city have for the trajectory of artists – by virtue of being well-connected artists themselves, or by heading important cultural institutions or other key roles in the music industry. By giving access to infrastructures such as offering free time in recording studios, issuing invitations to shared performances, or even just by lending out instruments they often make the difference between success or failure for newcomers. It is the lack of these facilities in the provinces that constitutes a large part of the pull-factor of Tana that persuades aspiring artists to leave the relative security of their homes. For example, neither the accordionist Régis Gizavo nor the valiha player Justin Vali who today rank among the most famous internationally acclaimed Malagasy musicians originates from the capital city: Gizavo came from Toliara and Justin Vali from a small village on the Hauts Plateaux. For both, their stay in Antananarivo was pivotal for their subsequent careers. In the next chapter we will discuss in more detail the role which Tana fulfils as a hub for national and transnational networking.

But against the number of artists who make the leap to Tana and launch a professional music career there are hundreds of others who struggle on a daily basis for survival and who endure enormous hardship.

In the extract below Mamiso narrates the conditions under which he lived when he moved out of 67 Ha so as to avoid the hour-long walk from where he, Senge and Christian were rehearsing together:

Then Senge and Jean found a cellar for me. I'm telling you, you can't live in there, it's like tombs! So he said that we would improve that, they said that we would buy some wooden boards. We went to buy those boards ... To make a small dividing wall. And we also built a bed with them. And he lent me his mattress, and I also had a blanket ... That is where I lived. It was filthy right next to the rubbish bins. And I lived in there. I almost caught an infection. And the mice, they were my friends. There were also lots of rats. And I stayed there for two years. When we started in 96, 97, 98, it meant that I could work there, even though I was living in ... well, I know how hard life can be, I know it ... I knew it at the age of 11 ... But when I tell you this now, while I was living there, I never had any inferiority complex, I took my friends there, even girlfriends, if they wanted to come to my place, come, no problem ... I would rehearse with my guitar, my voice, everyone knew me, that I lived there, no problem. And with Senge, we would work in the evening and we would get up at 5.30 in the morning, and the three of us, Senge, we would do the choreography and at 6 in the morning we'd practise our voices. Because Jean was working, and he had to leave at 7. So we had to work in the evening and in the morning. [13] (Meinhof's and Rasolofondraosolo's interview, April 2009, Lyon)

Mamiso gained international recognition with the group Senge, and continued to play under the name of Senge in duo with Christian for a few years after Senge's death from cancer in 2000 until the dissolution of the group in 2004. We will return to Mamiso's story in Chapter 4, to trace the next steps of his career once he left Madagascar and settled in France in 2001.

But for many aspiring musicians Tana does not fulfil its promise and musicians give up their hopes for a career in music and make their living by other means, or return home. Often groups split at this stage, while others manage to continue to play and record even while earning their living in different parts of the country. The group Teta, named after their key singer, straddling between Toliara and Tana is an example of the latter. While Teta has moved to Tana, all the other members of his band are continuing to live in the Toliara region, moving up to the capital only for occasional concerts, whereas Teta travels down to Toliara for performances in the region. And the most famous of them all, the group Mahaleo, subject of Chapter 2, has managed to stay in the centre of the musical life of Madagascar in spite of its seven members earning their living in their different professions in Tana, Antsirabe, Morondava and Tamatave. A similar pattern exists transnationally for the group Damily, where Damily lives and performs mainly in France, whereas his brother and fellow band member Rakapo stays in Toliara. We will revisit these transnational groups in Chapter 3. Many groups, however, do not manage the difficulties of either staying on collectively in Tana or surviving a geographic split. The story of the group Sandratsy that we encountered in Fort Dauphin in 2007 illustrates the enormous difficulties that provincial musicians face in their efforts to make a professional career. Consisting then of the female vocalist Anna and three male musicians – Mauretus, Mamy and Dhimby – they had formed after a year of training paid for by the British NGO Azafady with its local Fort Dauphin director Brett Massoud. Azafady plays an important role in the stories of many of the musicians from Fort Dauphin we encountered – Fassio, members of the Hazolahy group and many others had their first opportunities through the cultural initiatives of Azafady. Originally conceived as a training programme for unemployed adults, successive stages of funded sub-projects provided instruments for rehearsals and performances, training in instrument building and playing, and administrative support in registering songs with OMDA. At the point of our first visit there in 2007, a year-long funded project, where ten selected musicians had been employed with full-time salaries to up-train to a more professional level, had just reached its completion, with the group Sandratsy one of its successful outcomes. This is how Brett explained to us his mission:

> So we put together a group; the intention is to get them up to so that they can do a cabaret,[18] a wedding, because musicians need money, so if they cannot get money from their music they need to do another job which wrecks their capacity to do music because they're busy working.

So we said for one year we'll give you ten guys a salary, we had an audition – you know Miary Lepera and Fanjy and ... Samoela ... they came down from Tana and we did an audition and we selected the ten best people and we put them together and we paid them to rehearse four times a week, and the intention was to get them to a level where they can get a salary for doing a wedding or a circumcision... because they were all musicians ... but they had no experience in playing together, doing interpretations of other people's songs, so we rehearsed them for a year and that finished in October, and they can now do a cabaret till the morning and they do. They get work here. (Meinhof's and Rasolofondraosolo's interview, November 2007, Fort Dauphin, English original)

Azafady's initiative was to counteract the complete lack of facilities in a town like Fort Dauphin. Most musicians did not own instruments other than home-made kabosys or flutes which are not amplifiable. In 2007, there were no recording facilities, no sound systems and no rehearsal spaces other than those provided by Azafady. Since it is the absence of these facilities that causes many musicians to leave for Tana before they have sufficient connections, creating hardship and – for the majority – ultimate failure, Azafady was trying to delay their departure by giving important initial help in producing demo-tapes:

The thing that they wanted was that even if we could put together just a 'maquette' [Brett uses the French word for 'demo recording'] not broadcast quality, just a maquette, because for the musicians here, if they ... have some talent, their only option now is go to Tana make a recording and then go around try and find a producer, someone, a sponsor, a job in a restaurant ... and that can take months, when you have no money in Tana, trying to get a studio to record in – ... it's a very slow process, so people have to leave their family ... leave everything they have to support them, their source of food and go to Tana to search for fame ... so if we could help people make at least a maquette level recording in town then they can send it away, it saves them a few months in Antananarivo struggling, trying to get a recording done ... so we bought a big computer with a big memory and we do basic recordings for people here. It's all for free, we don't charge people anything for anything, just depends on how much time we have, do we have the budget to buy the CD *vierge* [Brett uses the French word for 'blank recordable CD'] ... Mauretus gets a salary every month so he is on the payroll, so there is no real expense for us apart from his salary and he is in the system now ... funded by London. (Meinhof's and Rasolofondraosolo's interview, November 2007, Fort Dauphin, English original)

However, even the group Sandratsy, which showed such promise in 2007, failed once they had moved to Tana. In 2007 it was Anna's dream to go to Tana and take part in the Malagasy version of the television show *Star Academy* (*Pas à Pas*):

Anna: I'd love to go up to Tana to do the *Pas à Pas*, but I don't know when they'll start with the next casting.

Ulrike: So it's really Tana that attracts you?

Anna: Well of course. Because *Pas à Pas*, that's great, isn't it? [14] (Meinhof's interview, November 2007, Fort Dauphin)

As a follow-up to their participation in a workshop with Dama and Ricky during our stay in 2007 they were sponsored by the two famous artists and by Azafady to record a demo in Ricky's Vazimba production studio in their Centre Rarihasina in Tana. The recording of several of their own songs plus one by and with Dama himself has still not found a producer and the group has now dispersed. On our second visit to Fort Dauphin two years later, we encountered Dimbhy, who had returned from Tana and was now working in the offices of Azafady, but found no more trace of either Mauretus nor Mamy. Anna, having also returned to Fort Dauphin after the recording was finished, was eventually 'redis-covered' by the leader of the Rabaza group in 2008, who, together with the groups Hazolahy and Dadah de Fort Dauphin, are among the better-known mangaliba groups. Originally from Fort Dauphin, but now living in Tana, Rabaza was looking for a singer and dancer for their concert 'back home', and having chosen Anna for that event whisked her away back to Tana. However, the relationship with Rabaza did not work out either and Anna left the group again in July 2009. But she managed to stay on in Tana and is now on the brink of some success through the help of an important figure, a Monsieur Bivy from recording studio and record label Mars, who is also a close collaborator of another influential musician, Rajery. Monsieur Bivy supports Anna in developing her own songs and as support act for Hazolahy and Dadah de Fort Dauphin, and in addition Anna also performs with a well-known pop-musician, Billante. Hence she has diversified her style of music in the hope of a national or even international career. There is currently some prospect that she may be invited to perform at the Angaredona Festival in Tana in September 2010.

Hence out of the group of four aspiring young musicians of Sandratsy, it was only Anna who managed to develop her career further.[19] In her success, the cultural and social elements of translocal capital are very much in evidence, but it also shows that translocal capital alone does not yet translate into a successful career. In the next chapter we will engage with the different dimensions of the capital city that give it such a pivotal role in the translocal and transnational careers of musicians.

Translocality in Morocco

The picture from Morocco (Map 1.2) is significantly different from that of Madagascar, although it is undoubtedly the case that there exists a clear rural–urban divide in terms of standards of living, levels of education, general quality of life and cultural practices. Nevertheless, the focus of the Moroccan fieldwork from the outset was the relationship between provincial town and metropolitan city, and although

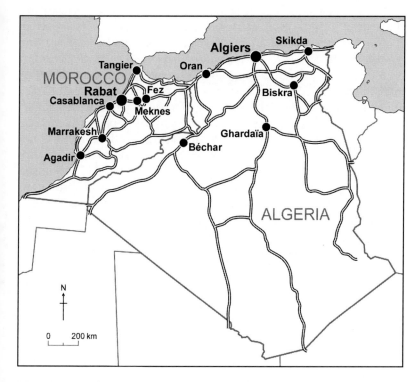

Map 1.2   Map of Morocco

Morocco boasts a rich and diverse range of music played by musicians in rural village and mountain locations (see for instance Hoffman 2002; Schuyler 1985; Lortat-Jacob 1981), the data we were able to gather about musicians in provincial rather than rural sites was more relevant to the TNMundi project's concerns with transnational networking among musicians and cultural producers.

A key theme which emerges from the Moroccan fieldwork (which encompassed Casablanca, Rabat, Meknes, Fez, Marrakesh and Agadir) was the notion that being a musician in a provincial Moroccan town poses real challenges in terms of access to rehearsal space, training, the media, recording studios and so on. This difficulty was mentioned time and time again by musicians we met from Fez and Meknes, and this despite the fact that these towns are both historically established with their own well-known cultural identity and infrastructure. The difficulty encountered by the musicians we interviewed from these locations may of course be linked to the genre of music that they represent, namely rap.

Shabka, which brings together five friends from Fez, is a rap group which draws on various influences including US gangsta rap, reggae and ragga, but the lyrics of their tracks are in Moroccan Arabic (*darija*). (Fez is Morocco's third largest city and has a population of about 1 million.) Shabka first got together in 2000 and, like many fledgling groups, faced challenges in terms of access to rehearsal space and recording space. Nevertheless they released their first album in 2003 and then won second prize in the 2006 Tremplin competition of the Boulevard des jeunes musiciens Festival in Casablanca (for more details on the Boulevard des jeunes musiciens, see Chapter 2).[20] The group members are all students and therefore part-time artists, yet they have managed to release three singles over the past six years, although there is as yet no second album, despite being announced for 2009 on the group's MySpace site. Three of them study in Casablanca, one in Fez and another member studies in Spain, coming back to Fez during the vacations (such as during spring break when I met the group). When I met with the group in March 2008, some of the members alluded to the challenges of being musicians in Fez:

> there's no decentralization in Morocco ... especially in the artistic field ... all the companies, everything's in Casa ... [...] no perfor-mance venue in Fez ... (except the youth club ...). (Otmane) [15] (Kiwan's interview with Shabka, March 2008, Fez)

Furthermore, when discussing a rap compilation which had just come out that spring in Morocco ('Memnou'aa fi radio' – 'Prohibited on the radio'), Otmane speaks about the dominance of Casablanca (and Rabat) in the cultural scene and reveals something of his frustration concerning 'provincial' rappers:

> when you see, if you see the artists who are part of this compilation, it's just rappers from Casa, from Rabat, from Salé. There are no groups from Fez, no groups from Tangier, no groups from Marrakesh, from Agadir ... that's why I am telling you all the events take place in Casa–Rabat, Casa–Rabat, that's it, all the media are based in Casa–Rabat, all the organizers, the communications agencies, everything happens in, we are here, in Fez, a little marginalized but there are good groups in Fez, there's Fez City Clan, Shabka, another one as well ... and these groups make enormous efforts [...] here in Fez, but our music's not better than Casa, but it's acceptable ... the Fassi accent is accepted in Morocco, compared to the Casaoui accent ... because Fez, spiritual capital, and here in Fez, the families are very very conservative 'mouhafith'. (Otmane) [16] (Kiwan's interview with Shabka, March 2008, Fez)

Another example of a rap group from Fez which is aware of the challenges of living on the 'peripheries' (at least in terms of the musical genre of rap is concerned; one must not forget that Fez has an established reputation as the centre of more 'high art' and musical forms such as Arab-Andalous music) can be found in the case of Fez City Clan. Fez City Clan came together as a group in 2001. Made up of five MCs and DJ Toto, the group took its first steps in the local Fez nightclub scene but it was only after winning the 2005 Tremplin competition of the Casablanca Boulevard des jeunes musiciens that things really started to take off for the group. In 2006, Fez City Clan released its first album 'Fez' and toured Morocco in a series of concerts that summer. When we met them in March 2008, the group were holed up in a Casablanca apartment, working on their new album (which was being recorded at Ali Faraoui's Plein les oreilles studio – see Chapter 4 for more details about Ali Faraoui's own story). Even though the group's founder DJ Toto has set up his own recording studio back in Fez through which the group also supports the local hip-hop scene, the group nevertheless felt it necessary to record their second album in Casablanca. Band member Simo explained that being able to spend three months in Casablanca in order to record was 'a dream ... a pleasure' [17]. He also goes on to compare Casablanca and Fez: 'Casablanca's more of a creative city than Fez' [18] (Kiwan's interview with Fez City Clan (extract Simo), March 2008, Casablanca).

The perception that certain artists have that they are somehow on the periphery is something we encountered when interviewing musicians who are based in Meknes, some 81 miles/130 km east of Rabat. While Meknes, like Fez, is clearly a historically significant centre and, indeed, one of the four imperial cities of Morocco, with a population of about 850,000, we are using the notion of periphery here both in relative terms and specifically in relation to the urban music scene. In other words, and in this specific sense, Meknes can be seen as being peripheral to Casablanca. This was the view put forward by Otmane and Hatim, two members of the rap group H-Kayne, when we interviewed them in April 2008 at home in Meknes. Despite the fact that H-Kayne are one of the most prominent rap groups in Morocco, and have been since their success at the 2003 Boulevard des jeunes musiciens Tremplin competition, it does not diminish the sense that Otmane and Hatim share that Meknes musicians are up against a highly centralized urban music scene and media infrastructure which are concentrated in Casablanca and Rabat:

Hatim: We've realized that even as H-Kayne and everything etc., it's not that we have difficulty, but there are groups here in Meknes, from Fez, but we feel that it's really mega-centralized in Casa–Rabat ... the radio stations, etc. [...] the radio station which is supposed to be ... Hit Radio, we don't have it in Meknes, we don't have in Fez ... [...] Us – they call us 'come and do some interviews'. I've done them, it never got broadcast [...] me, I'm not interested in being on the radio if the people from my town ... don't hear me, you see, if you want to come to my town, no problem I'll do an interview ... but yeah, it's, it's, there's nothing here in Meknes, there's nothing, there's nothing.

Nadia: And in terms of media, isn't there a local radio station?

Hatim: ... There is a local radio station, there is a local radio station, it starts at – it's part of the RTM group, SNRT... [...] it starts at 2pm, it finishes at 7pm I think ... they're OK, they play groups from here and everything but nobody listens to it, you see, but yeah, even if it's the communications agencies as well, you see, the communications agencies, they've got this thing, for example, say they'll have the choice between a group from Fez or Meknes and another which is from Casa or Rabat, I think that if only because of proximity and everything, it will come down in favour of the bloke from Casa, journalists are the same ... journalists, like, the bloke who works in the morning etc., they're based in Rabat, in Casa, he wants to do something on rap, he'll straight away do it in Casa, he'll go and see the rappers who are in Casa. They're not going to go down to I don't know where ... so we sense that, but we, we, as far as H-Kayne are concerned, it doesn't affect us, we, they play our tracks, whether we're from Casa or not, we get called up for the big festivals and everything. I'm talking about groups which gravitate around us – Mehdi K-Libre ... people who have been around for a long time, who have proved themselves, who have brought out their CDs ... but you realize that, there you go, the media aren't really interested, you see. [19] (Kiwan's and Gibert's interview with Hatim and Otmane, H-Kayne, April 2008, Meknes)

In the case of Shabka and Fez City Clan, it is possible to argue that the musicians think of themselves as somehow being on the periphery to Morocco's hip-hop scenes and both groups identify their participation in the Casablanca Boulevard des jeunes musiciens Festival as being crucial to their success and greater national visibility. However, both groups, and in particular Fez City Clan, tend to emphasize their translocal cultural capital in the sense that their Fassi origins are played up not only in the group's name, but in the group's first album, entitled 'Fez'. Otmane from Shabka also points out the distinctive Fez accent is something which sets them favourably apart from Casablanca groups, as indeed does the fact that they come from Morocco's spiritual capital. Of course, on the other hand, the fact that Fez *is* Morocco's spiritual capital and is thereby invested with a great deal of clout in terms of 'high cultural forms' (cf. Fez Festival etc.) may also partially explain just why hip-hop is fairly marginalized in the city.

If Meknes and Fez are perceived by some musicians to be on the periphery, what of the regions and towns much further from the Casablanca–Rabat strip? This question led us to the south-western Souss region in Morocco, and to Agadir, the capital of that region. Agadir is situated some 311 miles/500 km south of Casablanca and has a population of 300,000. While Agadir is a well-known destination on the tourist circuit, conjuring up images of sun, sand and sea for many Westerners and Moroccans alike, the town is a long way from Casablanca. One can reach Agadir by a very expensive internal flight from Casablanca or take the train to Marrakesh, followed by an overnight coach journey southwards on to Agadir. The town was entirely rebuilt after a devastating earthquake in 1960 yet, despite its modern architectural features, it retains a decidedly provincial, laid-back feel, in stark contrast, of course, to the cities of Casablanca, Rabat but also Fez and Meknes. It was in Agadir that we were able to meet up with Ali Faiq, one of the founders and lead singers of the Agadir-based group Amarg Fusion. Amarg Fusion's musical repertoire is based on the *amarg*, the sung poetry of the *rwais*, the itinerant professional musicians from the south-western Souss region, yet, as Ali points out, the *raison d'être* of the group is to fuse the music and repertoires of the *rwais* with more Westernized rhythms, melodies and instrumentation, all the while avoiding a superficial collage of musical motifs.

The story of Ali is in itself an interesting one, given that his father was an internal migrant from the rural Souss who came to Agadir in the 1960s to work in the growing tourist sector. Ali grew up in Agadir and then left in 1997, when he returned to the countryside, to his home village, where he lived for ten years, and when we met him in April 2008 he had only recently moved back to Agadir with his family six months earlier. He makes a living from his music and the group tours nationally and internationally to a range of different festivals. Musically, Agadir has started to make a name for itself on the 'world music' and 'nouvelle scène marocaine' circuit thanks to the creation of the Timitar Festival, run by former Institut français arts officer Brahim el-Mazned. El-Mazned has become a key sponsor of Amarg Fusion and has promoted the group nationally and abroad. Ali explains that before Amarg Fusion performed in high-profile international festivals such as Timitar and the Boulevard des jeunes musiciens, the main source of income for the group was the local wedding and ceremonies cycle:

Ali: Before, six years ago in Morocco, the majority of groups don't know that there's a press dossier, that there's a technical specifications sheet, how there are going to be relations with international musicians, like that, now we are managing to build on this. And before we used to only play for people from our region, from our town ... [...]

Nadia: And in terms of your musical training, well, have you always sung? How was it that you became involved in music?

Ali: Really, for me I've always sung ... it's true because we have this custom of traditional ceremonies ... weddings and all that ... it's our training school. [20] (Kiwan's and Gibert's interview with Ali Faiq, April 2008, Agadir)

Despite being a long way from Casablanca and Rabat, Amarg Fusion have managed to penetrate the national music scene and have been able to record an album in Agadir:

Nadia: And you've recorded in Agadir?

Ali: In Agadir, yes. Because we always work with our own means, because it's very difficult to go to Casablanca and, to tell you, there you go, the first, there you go, the 15th day, so you've got to finish songs like that. It's very difficult, so we chose a studio where we had already recorded our first album, so the experience has evolved and also it gives us confidence to do what we have already. [21] (Kiwan's and Gibert's interview with Ali Faiq, April 2008, Agadir)

When we met in the spring of 2008, the group were putting the finishing touches to their second album, co-produced with the Agadir Timitar association and to be distributed by a Casablanca record company (Platinum Records). What is interesting about Amarg Fusion is that they would appear to have been able to overcome the fact that they are geographically a long way from much of the cultural and musical infrastructure of Morocco, and their national and international appeal has perhaps been bolstered by the fact that they are from the faraway Moroccan south-west. The notion of translocal cultural capital certainly comes into play here since Ali repeatedly pointed out during our interview that the group's main focus was to valorize the south-western musical heritage (*patrimoine*) by working with the historic repertoires and instrumentation of the *rwais* (using the *ribab*)[21] as well as singing in Amazigh (Tachelhit Berber):

Ali: For us, we chose ... because there's also this cultural variety in Morocco, there are lots of types of heritage, it isn't just one heritage any more, there's a rich variety, we, we chose the *rwais*. The *rwais* are the Souss troubadors, they've got their own characteristics, and also the *rwais*, really, it's that, they are, the features of the music, of the songs, is disappearing, like that. So, we, we are responding to the UNESCO call ... above all to preserve this heritage, especially as it's disappearing, in terms of the modes, in terms of the metrics, in terms of the poetry, in terms of ... I mean, people, especially today's generations, they can't listen to this heritage any more, so, we, we have tried to formulate it, to reawaken it in some sense.

Nadia: OK. When you say that it's disappearing, it's ...?

Ali: I mean that the songs of the *rwais* have special features, above all the modes ... The modes are old, so now people can't sing in these modes any more ... the new *rwais*, they can't sing in these modes, they manage to create their work ... to interpret, to borrow from others, the modes, to sing like that, I'm distracted, you know. I can hear the music [music in café where interview being carried out] ... it doesn't matter, it doesn't matter ... so what's disappearing ... as I said a moment ago, there's a call, from UNESCO, the 15th October 2002, or 2001, I think, which says that it's necessary to preserve the musics from the Mediterranean, and among those musics, there is the music of the *rwais*, which is old, we're conscious that the *rwais* are no longer like they were in the years at the start of the century, in 1900 or in 1880 like that, the generation of Hajj Belaïd and Aboubakr Anchad, people aren't able to keep this heritage, we say that we mustn't keep it as it is, but that we should put creation and creativity into it ... which is what we have done with Amarg Fusion [...] We have also tried to preserve the instrument, the *ribab*, this instrument is also disappearing. [22] (Kiwan's and Gibert's interview with Ali Faiq, April 2008, Agadir)

Despite this clear atttachment to the notion of 'musical heritage', Ali points out that the group does not set out to fix or folklorize the *rwais* repertoire:

I mean it's not to preserve the modes. It's not to ... to sing songs like the *rwais* did ... in the mode ... the mode is to create ourselves ... to compose songs about that, so like that we will preserve them ... we don't want a frozen heritage ... that's to say, which runs the risk of always being folkloristic, for tourists and all that, we want a heritage which we want to share ...
[...]
And also, we haven't imitated the *rwais* ... we don't imitate the *rwais*. We play it in our own way. And we can say that that's the music of the *rwais*, but in our style. [23] (Kiwan's and Gibert's interview with Ali Faiq, April 2008, Agadir)

So the Moroccan case studies discussed above show how although these musicians have all enjoyed varying degrees of success without physically migrating (in a permanent sense) to Casablanca or Rabat, Casablanca nevertheless is important for all of them. Crucially, all groups were able to attain success by participating in the Casablanca Boulevard des jeunes musiciens. This would suggest that in the Moroccan case it is not possible for aspiring provincial musicians to bypass Casablanca in search of a national or international career. However, it is important to stress that even if all of the Moroccan musicians discussed share some form of perception that they are on the creative margins, they all tend to play up their local cultural and musical specificities, be it through the name of the group (Fez City Clan, Amarg Fusion), the repertoires, the language or the musical styles. To a certain extent we could argue that this assertion of locality as a marketing tool is a clear illustration of translocal cultural and social capital. This observation links more broadly into the question of strongly localized identities, a recurring theme in the Moroccan fieldwork. Such local identities are paradoxically reinforced by the Casablanca-based Boulevard des jeunes musiciens movement which presents up-and-coming groups as 'representatives' of their particular home town and, to a certain extent, pitches them against one another. So, in Morocco, the cultural scene is strongly centralized, with Casablanca as the jewel in the 'new music scene' crown, yet this does not preclude strong localized identifications among provincial musicians; if anything, it reinforces them. It is to the specific role played by the large metropolitan cities of Casablanca and Antananarivo that we turn in the next chapter.

2
Metropolitan Hubs in the South

In the previous chapter we investigated the translocal networks that connect musicians from rural and provincial regions in Madagascar and Morocco with their metropolitan centres. In this chapter we will turn to the metropolitan cities themselves so as to view their role as central hubs, within their countries and transnationally. The focus here will be on some of the influential artists who live in Antananarivo or Casablanca, and on the people, institutions and facilities that underpin their work. As we will see, these artists and cultural producers not only exert great influence on the musical scenes and local musicians of their own countries and cities, they also are hubs for transnational networks of artists who have migrated to Europe and elsewhere in the world, and who return to their countries of origin for inspiration, concerts and concert tours, recordings of songs and networking in general. Many musicians we interviewed, especially Erick Manana and Justin Vali, both of considerable standing in Madagascar and Europe alike, repeatedly stressed their need to return to Madagascar to resource themselves afresh.[1]

This chapter will focus specifically on the role of these metropolitan centres as hubs in their own right, radiating outwards, while Chapter 3 will add the North–South perspectives of the migrant musicians living in European centres, especially Paris.

African cities and globalization

Given that our own particular perspective is focused on the relatively new role of African cities in the directing and redirecting of artistic energy, it is worth considering some of the broader debates about the relationship between certain African cities and processes of globalization. One of the key recurring themes in the literature which looks at these dynamics is the notion that rather than being the 'losers' of economic and cultural globalization, many African urban centres and their populations are avidly embracing the opportunities that globalization brings with it. This is very much the line adopted by Sonja Hegasy in her analysis of Moroccan youth culture where she insists that Moroccan youth 'is actively and creatively involved in "bringing the North south"'. Moreover, Hegasy adds that 'This youth does not regard globalisation as the irresistible export of the Anglo-Saxon model, but as a process of modernisation that any culture ought to aspire to' (Hegasy 2007: 31).[2] Of course, as Lemanski (2007) points out, some cities of the South are already global players (Mexico City, São Paulo) and within Africa, Johannesburg, Lagos and Nairobi are key urban centres, with Johannesburg in particular displaying many of the characteristics of Global City political, economic, social and cultural infrastructure.[3] However, Lemanski usefully warns against naïve globalization enthusiasm where African cities are concerned and shows through her case study of Cape Town that it is difficult for African cities to simultaneously achieve global competitiveness and badly needed socio-economic redistribution. A similar caution is underlined by Ambe J. Njoh as regards the temporality of globalization and African cities. Indeed, Njoh (2006) shows that a number of sub-Saharan African towns were in pre-colonial times regional and international centres of trade, learning, art, craft and culture. This was the case of towns located within the pre-colonial kingdoms of Western Sudan, Ghana, Mali and Songhay. Towns such as Timbuctu, Djenné, Katsina, Kano and Bornu were able to develop through their multiple links with Europe, the Arab world, India and China (Njoh 2006: 20). The demise of such African trade centres coincided with the transatlantic slave trade and European colonization which respectively led to the diverting of attention from more rewarding activities for Africans. A useful image that emerges from Njoh's historical account of the role of African cities is how through their turning into 'clones' of European cities they became 'little more than "warehouses" for primary commodities bound for European and North American economies' (Njoh 2006: 23). Bearing in mind the dangers and temptations of such cloning, our empirical discussion of Malagasy and North African capital cities will consider ways in which cities such as Antananarivo and Casablanca are creating their own particular type of cultural infrastructure, yet nevertheless are fully participating in transnational processes of cultural globalization.

In the previous chapter we have already discussed in some detail the role which metropolitan centres in the South have as *passage obligé* for all artists who aspire towards a national or international music career. The reasons for this centrality are multiple. On the one hand there are the steadily growing facilities of the music industries – concert venues, festivals, recording studios, professional promoters and their supporting print, audio, audio-visual and internet media. Secondly, all international cultural institutions and embassies have their main, or even their only, site in these metropolitan cities. Especially in Madagascar, where cultural policy at governmental level is subsumed in a department that includes tourism and sport, agencies such as the Alliance française, the Centre culturel Albert Camus, the Cercle germano-malgache (CGM) – an affiliate of the German Goethe-Institut – and other international institutions associated with foreign embassies are the main support agencies and funders for local, national and transnational artists. We will discuss these in more detail in Chapter 5. Thirdly, and this is the main focus of this chapter, these cities house the most influential artists and cultural producers: key individuals whom we have described in the Introduction as 'human hubs'. Hence it is the multiple layering in metropolitan cities in the South as centres where spatial, institutional and human hubs overlap and interact that gives them such a vital role in cultural globalization and transnational networking.

Human hubs in Antananarivo: Mahaleo

Key individuals can have pivotal roles for different reasons. They may be in charge of significant institutions such as Eckehart Olszowski, director of the CGM in Antananarivo since 1980, of whom we will hear more in Chapter 5. They may be organizers of important festivals such as the director of the Boulevard des jeunes musiciens Festival in Casablanca, who has created a vibrant musical scene by bringing together artists from within the country with those from the outside, they may be music promoters or owners of record labels or venues. Or they may be individual artists or groups of artists who themselves act as mediators, promoters, talent scouts and teachers for others. In Antananarivo there are a few such musicians who command sufficient authority through their artistic achievement and commitment that they can continue to inspire and support the careers of others. Ricky Olombelo with his Centre Rarihasina, Rajery with his group of valiha players and other artists selected from all over the country, and Hanitra from Tarika with her cultural centre Antshow are all instances of influential musicians who continuously search out, support or direct other musicians. However, no group has had longer and more lasting influence in inspiring and supporting other musicians than the members of the group Mahaleo.

In the last chapter we briefly mentioned this most enduring and influential of bands. In spite of their continuing success in Madagascar and abroad, Mahaleo have never left Madagascar except for regular concert tours. Their significance in Malagasy cultural life and their widespread links to civil society make them the perfect example for exploring the intricate links existing between translocal, metropolitan and transnational networks. We will therefore discuss them in some detail, as a musical force but also in connection with their role in public life. The group is named Mahaleo after the first name of one of its founding members, Dama, whose full name is Zafi*mahaleo* Rasolofondraosolo. Mahaleo comprises seven musician friends who went to school together in Antsirabe in the late 1960s, and on to university in the 1970s. Their national fame as musicians began during the student revolts and general strike of 1972 in opposition to the neocolonial regime of President Tsiranana, the first president of Madagascar, after Madagascar had gained its independence from France in 1960. The year 1972 resembled in some ways the European and American student movements of 1968, with the engaged songs of Mahaleo becoming as much part of the Malagasy students' self-identification and point of reference as the American and European folk and protest singers had done for the 1968 movement. More than three decades later with a good 300 or so original songs in their repertoire, after a 35th anniversary celebrated in 2007 not only in the massive open-air stadium of Antsonjombe in Antananarivo with a 30,000-plus audience but also in two sold-out concerts in the legendary Olympia in Paris, Mahaleo command formidable audiences that cut across and unite several generations (Figures 2.1, 2.2, 2.3).

Mahaleo comprises four singer-songwriters, Dama, Raoul, Bekoto and Dadah, who all play guitar, the bass player Nono, the percussionist Charle, and Fafa who says of himself in the film *Mahaleo* 'Moi, je suis juste une voix' (*Mahaleo* 2005). The combination of the polyharmonic blending of their seven voices with contemporary and traditional instruments created a range of acoustic styles that blend the sounds of Western instruments – guitar, bass, harmonica, grand piano, keyboard, drum kit – with those of the kabosy, the flute sodina, and many home-grown drums and shakers such as jembes and korintsanas. Although mainly identified as a group from the Highlands, Mahaleo's range of rhythms, themes of lyrics and use of language with some dialectal variation are often inspired by the different regions of Madagascar that were already discussed in the previous chapter.[4] The group has never stopped developing new material and all four singer-songwriters continue to compose new songs. For their 40th anniversary already in planning for

Figure 2.1   Mahaleo concert in the Antsonjombe stadium, Tana, 2007

Figure 2.2   Mahaleo poster for the Ambatolampy concert, 2007

Figure 2.3   Mahaleo concert sign for Paris Olympia, 2007

the year 2012, each of the singer-songwriters plans to pre-release his own solo album of previously unpublished and new songs, as well as a new album of shared 'Best of Mahaleo'. Pre-releasing is very important for their audiences, since concerts by Mahaleo are as much concerts as shared performances, and unknown songs are less enthusiastically welcomed than those already known. Hence, so as not to be stuck with a repertoire of the same music year in year out, Mahaleo try to pre-release those songs that they aim to introduce (or reintroduce) in concert. As a result of this strategy, any Malagasy audience – whether they be in Madagascar or in the diasporas – comprises hundreds of people who know by heart most of their songs so that concerts become impressively sung polyphonic shared events,[5] where audiences need to be told when *not* to sing.[6] Since 2005 and 2007 respectively, their world music appeal has steadily increased, mainly as a result of the release of a full-lenth prize-winning documentary film *Mahaleo* by Paris-based independent film company Laterit and two years later of a 'long-box' from the Olympia concerts, comprising, apart from a CD, a DVD with a choice of subtitles in several languages. Since then their Malagasy public has gradually been complemented by a more international mix.

In spite of their lasting success, Mahaleo never fully professionalized their musical career but continue to work in their full-time careers. The two brothers Dadah and Nono are both surgeons in HJRA, the general hospital of Antananarivo, Raoul, the late brother of Dama, was a general practitioner in Tamatave, Bekoto and Charle, both trained as sociologists, work for NGOs, supporting peasants' rights and environmental projects respectively, Fafa, now retired, used to work as a civil servant. Dama himself after a degree in sociology and training as an agriculturalist spans multiple careers, combining the development of an agricultural training centre on his farm in Morondava with cultural consultancies. Between 1994 and 2002 he was elected for two terms as an independent non-party *député* in the Malagasy Parliament, first representing the capital city itself and subsequently the large rural district of Ambatofinandrahana in the Fianarantsoa province.[7] Mahaleo's double role as musicians and as university-trained professionals underpins the role they play in the public sphere and civil society of Madagascar.

The influence of Mahaleo

During our interviews, the group Mahaleo invariably was mentioned as a key reference point for, or direct influence on, the careers of many of the musicians we spoke to (see also the quote by Mbasa in the previous chapter, p. 30): from Erick Manana – now himself of 'Olympia' fame – who used to carry their guitars for them onto stage before being invited to join them there himself, or Mamiso who copied their songs and style of singing while busily writing his own, to the multitude of young musicians of today who continue to perform their songs all over the country and abroad, sometimes without even knowing their source. Even the young French-born singer Rachel Ratsizafy, whose career path we will revisit in Chapter 3, quotes the songs by Mahaleo as a source for her acquiring the Malagasy language, although it was only during their concert in the Olympia that she realized that the songs she'd been listening to during her childhood were Mahaleo songs:

> Rachel: But then I realized all of a sudden that I knew so many of their songs [by Mahaleo], their lyrics; in fact, that is how I learned to speak Malagasy, by listening to the lyrics and trying to understand, asking my family: 'What does it mean? And what does that mean?' I even have a Malagasy dictionary [laughing]. And that is ...
>
> Marie: And now do you speak Malagasy?

Rachel: Yes, I do. I don't speak the literary language but at least people understand me [laughing] ... And I manage really welll! Yeah!

Marie: And everything they were talking about during the concert, could you understand it completely with no trouble?

Rachel: Yeah ... Well, when it comes to specific vocabulary or really complicated words, I sometimes struggle a bit, but I understand it with the context ... For example, I understood everything they sang ... I understood the topics they were talking about, all of this. [1] (Meinhof's and Gibert's interview, June 2007, Paris)

Mahaleo in general, and Dama in particular, are among the 'human hubs' in the Malagasy music scene who never followed any temptation to migrate abroad, but whose influence stretches across many transnational networks. Apart from music-inspired links, they also interconnect with several NGOs in Europe, acting as their key mediators for various developmental projects in Madagascar. Some of these projects specifically thematize the link between music and civil society. Thus Dama, in addition to his performances with Mahaleo, also joins forces with fellow Antananarivan musicians Ricky Olombelo and Hajazz in developing and performing for the cultural and environmental project Voajanahari.[8] Other networks are purely devoted to music. In recent years Dama has co-founded a new group – the Madagascar All Stars – who apart from himself and guest member Ricky are all French-based, thus forming a vital transnational link for the group with Antananarivo and the rest of Madagascar. We will revisit this group in Chapter 4. But none of these other links and networks compare quite to the significance of the group Mahaleo itself. The popularity of their songs is formidable. They are not only heard all over the capital city, on radio, television, CD or cassette, and in innumerable cover versions by other musicians, in clubs and restaurants all over the island, they are just as likely to be heard on taxi brousse journeys as on Air Madagascar flights. So where does this lasting influence stem from and what are the reasons for their continuing strength? Since Dama is not only a committed artist but also a highly reflective thinker it is worth quoting in some length from some of the many interviews he has given us during the past decade. In a conversation in 2003 in Paris this is how he explained to us his role as artist and singer-songwriter. First of all, he explains the way in which he writes his songs and from where he draws his inspiration:

The music that I make, those are songs that invariably reflect life in Madagascar. That's how it is. I write songs that narrate life in

Madagascar. And the life of the people, and what I think about it all. I write such songs. And I think that reflects that I am not disconnected from the realities of everyday life there. That I am right in the middle of it, and that I live in the middle of it. So when I compose ... then that echoes always the way I live, what I think, what I feel. What hurts me, what gives me hope. And I sing that. Because I am among the people of Madagascar. I can't write songs just like that, songs that pop from the sky. I sing what I feel. What I live, What makes me vibrate, what hurts me ... voilà, I create in relation to all that. [2] (Meinhof's interview, June 2003, Paris)

Mahaleo songs provide a vital link for the many Malagasies who have migrated to many countries in the world, with the largest concentration in France. We mentioned before that as a result of the film *Mahaleo* and some high-profile concerts in the Olympia in 2007 and La Cigale in 2009, Mahaleo have also started to attract substantial international audiences. However, their key followers still remain the Malagasy people – at home or in the different diasporic settings worldwide. Never allowing themselves to be signed over to a record label, their concert organizers and promoters have often emerged from the diasporas themselves, some of them highly professionalized like Lova Ramisamanana from Kanto Productions or Marie-Clémence Paes from Laterit, both situated in Paris. But some Mahaleo tours across Europe or the Americas – France, Switzerland, Austria, Germany, Canada or the USA, to name but a few of the countries they have been invited to – can also attract hundreds of spectators often only by word-of-mouth and internet dissemination of local amateur organizers who do not shy away from the financial risks they are taking on as individuals or on behalf of their associations (see also Chapter 6). In the same interview of 2003 Dama explains the bonding between Mahaleo and their diasporas worldwide as follows:

It's the music that makes the connection, because I don't know if the Malagasies who live here have really much time for music, for them it's always the music from Madagascar. They find themselves back in their country through the music. And so we've made a synthesis of the different facets of life in Madagascar and of the Malagasy people – what are our hopes, what are our points of reference, our cultural values – the importance of our traditions, our cultural heritage, our cultural diversity, the significance of what we call the 'système d'entraide' [system of mutual support], the significance of what one calls solidarity. Because solidarity has become a word that one uses no matter when. Yet it is the solidarity that is the lifeblood of the village – whether it's in relation to the rice-cultivation, the work on the land, everywhere we use a system of mutual support, the villagers have their debates, there is a local democracy, the people discuss how to build a little dam, a village school, a country road. How to care for the village, how to defend it against the thieves who steal their zebus [Malagasy cattle]. All of this system is already in place. Hence this is our cultural wealth, our civic wealth, one could say. The local civil society already exists, one only needs to take it up, to reinforce. But the problem is – we always say the solution is to be found elsewhere. And yet the solution already exists in Madagascar. And the music always puts this back in saying, we must begin with what we already have. And the others need to reinforce what we already have. That's a bit how we present the issues through our music. [3] (Meinhof's interview, June 2003, Paris)

What makes Mahaleo so remarkable given the seemingly universal appetite for Western commercial music and for home-grown pop, rock, hip-hop and metal music by the young, is their lasting cross-generational appeal. Between 2003 and 2009 we visited several of their open-air concerts not only in Antananarivo but also in the provinces, and were amazed to see that the audience invariably consisted of large multi-generational families, side by side with groups of youths, male or female or mixed, old couples and young, between hundreds or tens of thousands of people, many of them turning up hours before the concerts start with blankets and picnic baskets, Mahaleo T-shirts and caps even for the tiniest toddlers, and everyone old enough singing, humming or mouthing their lyrics. The film *Mahaleo* by Laterit captures this atmosphere in exemplary fashion in the live episodes filmed during their 30th anniversary concert in 2002 in the Antanimana stadium in Antananarivo (*Mahaleo* 2005, see www.mahaleo.com). And yet there is none of the 'mobbing' behaviour of crowds associated with rock-star concerts in the North.[9] Mahaleo have retained the respect of their audiences, undoubtedly because of their refusal from the very beginning to turn themselves into 'stars'.

This is how Mbasa narrates his early encounters with Dama after the group Mahaleo had already achieved national fame:

I went up to Tana, and my dream, my really hopeful dream, was to see Mahaleo in flesh and blood on stage. And I got even more than I had expected. Mahaleo [at that time Dama was still called by his first name Mahaleo] had his room in the same corridor as me at the university. And every time we passed each other in the corridor I didn't know what to say, no didn't know what to say. I wanted to talk but didn't know whether that was OK to talk to him. And that went on for a little while, but then since Mahaleo is an unpretentious kind of guy he spots that this is going on. So every time he sees me he says, 'hello little brother', and that has taken away my inhibitions, and after that we did quite a number of things together. For example, for our debut concert as Salala we were at the Goethe-Institut, the CGM, with Olszowski, and we were on the same ticket as Dama and D'Gary, Samy and Ricky. Practically with the whole set that always appeared at the CGM. [4] (Meinhof's interview, April 2009, Nantes)

Mahaleo continue to inspire many young aspiring musicians, in spite of the many different styles of popular contemporary music that can be found in Madagascar just as anywhere else in the world. It was her performance in duo with Dama for the song 'Mimoza' during the first Olympia concert which turned the young French-born Aina Randrianaivosoa from occasional background singer to a solo artist in her own right. In Madagascar itself, as part of the celebration of their 35th anniversary, national television ran a two months' long campaign to find 'Mahaleo junior', something which some fearful members of their public interpreted quite wrongly as Mahaleo's wish to retire from the music scene and to hand over the baton to the next generation. A large number of groups were allowed to present their version of Mahaleo songs on television to be voted on by the public, until three groups were selected for the final showdown. Those three were then invited onto stage by Mahaleo as an introduction to their big anniversary concert in Antsonjombe stadium, thus creating a unique opportunity for the young musicians. The winning group itself was announced the night before the concert, in a televised show during which Mahaleo were presented with the *Chevalier de l'ordre national du mérite* by then President Ravalomanana, thus receiving national media exposure.

Mahaleo and politics

This latest public honour is one of many public recognitions that members of Mahaleo have received during their career. Accepting the *Chevalier de l'ordre national du mérite* from Ravalomanana could have easily been interpreted as the group Mahaleo allowing themselves to be co-opted to support an increasingly unpopular president. Yet in spite of their appearance on the scene during the political unrest in 1972 and Dama's eight years as an independent member of the Assemblée nationale, in spite of regular attempts by different ruling powers to co-opt them to their cause, and in spite of their strong public engagements in their personal lives and through their lyrics, Mahaleo as a group have always steered clear of directly supporting any political party. By inverse, Mahaleo's role in the political turmoils of Madagascar, where successive presidents have invariably been ousted by disappointed demonstrators in the street, has not been uncontroversial in the opposite direction either. Some of their songs, such as the bitingly satirical 'Bemolanja' – an attack on the false promises of the rulers to bring 'black gold' (petrol) to the people – were banned from public media and official distribution, only to emerge on the black market by pirated cassettes. The expectations of the public that Mahaleo would support a particular president, as for example Rossy had done to his later regret in directly supporting Ratsiraka, or Bodo had done in supporting Ratsiraka's rival Ravalomanana, is invariably high, and rumours abound about the ways their support would fall.

The latest two crises in 2001–2 and – at the time of writing – the still unresolved crisis of 2009–10 are cases in point. In 2002, the then mayor of Antananarivo, Marc Ravalomanana, forced his great rival, long-serving president and autocratic ruler Didier Ratsiraka, into exile, after a disputed election victory in December 2001 and six months of strikes and drastic blockades of the capital city had caused severe food and petrol shortages in Antananarivo and great hardship to the people countrywide. Ravalomanana, officially elected and subsequently internationally recognized by the summer of 2002, was in turn ousted in 2009 by 'a vote of the street' in favour of Andry Rajoelina who had succeeded him as mayor of Antananarivo. During both crises home audiences in Madagascar and in the diaspora in France rallied to Mahaleo concerts. During the 2002 concert in the Parisian concert venue Saint-Martin when the conflict between Ratsiraka and Ravalomanana supporters threatened to divide the diaspora, it was sufficient for Mahaleo to metaphorically invite their audiences to a shared meal with 'hors-d'œuvre, plat et dessert' for it to be understood that this appeal to the great tradition of the *fihavanana* – the Malagasy concept of eating together – symbolized an appeal to unity for the Malagasy people (Meinhof 2005). In 2009, this implicit message was no longer enough. When Mahaleo announced a concert in June 2009 in Paris in La Cigale – a concert that had been planned by Lova and Kanto Productions more than a year ahead as a follow-up to the Olympia – it caused ripples of dissent among the diaspora. After the concert in La Cigale this is how Dama explained Mahaleo's reasons for choosing a particular repertoire of old songs that appealed to solidarity among the people, but also to introduce the songs by more direct calls to the basic democratic principle of 'fokonola':

> This was in the context of the current political crisis in Madagascar. The population is divided, the Malagasy citizens are divided into two camps. Those who are for the old President Ravalomanana, and those who are for the President of the Transition. And this division also creates waves, shock waves, if one can say it like that. This division has repercussions here in Europe as well, amongst the diaspora, in the heart of the diaspora there are many divisions. And when the concert of the group Mahaleo was announced – because this was a concert already prepared a whole year before, as one of the great productions of Kanto – there were a lot of people of the diaspora who said on the internet, 'why are Mahaleo not saying anything about the current situation?' Voilà. Hence if Mahaleo give a concert here in Europe in spite of the political situation in Madagascar, that means that this is not innocent, this is not without significance, and there are even reports on the internet that say that the concert is for HAT, for the President of the Transition. Hence we Mahaleo ... we're in the middle. We're being targeted. Those in favour of TGV say we're for TGV, and those in favour of Ravalomanana say we're for Ravalomanana. That's why I explained in the concerts that we've already been talking about these things since '72, but in '72 we were actors ourselves. But we do not agree with this system of presidential rule, with presidents who can each time create their own political party [...] presidents who succeed each other in setting up their own party. Because that invariably turns into a party of opportunists. The people all want to become members of the president's party to be near power. So this is how it starts. And then there are the others who are not on that path, so every ten years there's trouble, there's a crisis. And it's against that we have to fight, against that presidential regime. [5] (Meinhof's interview, June 2009, Paris)

The strategy of directly voicing their independence from either political opponent and appealing through their songs to the solidarity between all Malagasy people resolved the tension which concert organizer Lova had perceived in the building up to the concert and turned a potentially conflictual evening into another Mahaleo triumph.

Human hubs in Casablanca: the Boulevard

In Morocco it is an emblematic example from Casablanca which best illustrates the ways in which metropolitan cities in the South house nationally and internationally significant human hubs: the Boulevard des jeunes musiciens movement. Established in 1999, this festival was the result of the aim of a number of young friends and cultural activists based in Casablanca to give a platform for 'alternative' urban music – in Morocco this encompasses hip-hop, metal and fusion/electro. In addition to organizing a professional musicians' stage with headlining acts from Morocco, Europe and the United States, the originality of the Boulevard is its Tremplin ('springboard') competition which gives new and emerging acts a chance to perform. In effect, the Boulevard has developed into much more than a three-day cultural event and has become a motor for musical and artistic creativity across the country (groups from all over Morocco aspire to take part in the Tremplin competition and winning the competition opens the gateway to hitherto elusive national and international career opportunities). However, the ultimate aim is to develop the cultural scene and infrastructure in Morocco. As such, a career abroad is not seen as the ultimate and defining objective of the Moroccan up-and-coming groups we studied – rather it is Casablanca and access to the growing cultural network there.

Here, we concentrate on the work of two people – Momo Merhari and Hicham Bahou – founders and directors of the Boulevard and its association 'EAC-L'Boulevart', in order to show how particular individuals can literally become human hubs who cultivate and direct the development of creative synergies (see Holton 2008). Momo and Hicham are two friends who are passionate about underground Moroccan music and it is this enthusiasm which led them to start organizing the annual festival. The festival was first held in 1999 at the FOL – the Fédération des œuvres laïques – a 400-seat theatre belonging to the French organization of the same name in Casablanca's Maârif district, where Momo was employed as the *régisseur* (stage manager) and youth worker. In the years running up to the launching of the Boulevard des jeunes musiciens, Momo and Hicham had encouraged numerous amateur/student rock and metal groups from Casablanca to rehearse and perform at the FOL. Hicham Bajjou, a musician (singer-songwriter and gumbri/guitar player) and member of the Boulevard team, explains below how the Boulevard founders joined the FOL federation of associations, and called their own association l'ACAL. They did this so as to be able to organize their own musical events at the venue. However, when the concerts they were organizing started to attract more and more attention from Casablanca's youth, and when 14 heavy metal musicians who were part of the Boulevard scene were arrested and accused by the government of Satanism, a schism arose between the FOL and the Boulevard directors. In 2005, the ACAL asked to leave the FOL venue, and this led to the establishment of a new association with a new status – the EAC-L'Boulevart:

> In fact, the association, I'll explain what it was, it was the artistic association which organized the events at the FOL, was composed really of a majority of French people. Whereas, normally in the statutes, it's a Moroccan association. So, it was when we became part of the FOL, and we began organizing concerts, that we realized that there was an association, that we had a framework, which we could use to organize concerts. And it was then that a director of the FOL, who suggested that we became part of it, because at that time, the association, you just had to present yourself, there was a vote and that's all [...] they weren't as motivated as us, we, we were completely involved, we really wanted to do a whole load of things. And so that's how we got involved in the association, and then how it came apart afterwards, because the FOL didn't like the way we managed it ... if you like, the FOL became a little more popular, there were lots of people who came, who took advantage of the concerts, and they, they didn't like that. [6] (Kiwan's interview with Hicham Bajjou, March 2008, Casablanca)

Hicham Bajjou explains how from 2003 onwards, the popularity of the Boulevard des jeunes musiciens Festival meant that the organizers had to move it to the open air. Today, the festival attracts about 150,000 spectators over a four-day period and it is held in the open-air COC stadium. It is thus no exaggeration to claim that a whole generation has now grown up with the Boulevard and indeed thinks of itself quite self-consciously as 'la génération Boulevard' (as indicated in the 2010 edition of *L'Kounache*, the magazine which is published during the annual festival).[10] The huge popularity of the Boulevard is due to several factors, not least the fact that at the time it emerged Moroccan public and private sources of funding or support for contemporary popular music (*musiques actuelles*) in Morocco was virtually non-existent. The fact that the event is conceived and organized by young people who are close to musicians, and indeed the fact that many of the Boulevard team are successful musicians themselves, adds to its appeal. The festival entrance ticket is also cheap (40DH for four days in 2007), which means that it is genuinely a popular event in the true sense of the word – something which I observed first-hand during the 2007 festival (Figures 2.4, 2.5). Public and private sponsors soon realized this and what started off as a virtually unfunded festival now attracts sponsorship from partners such as Coca-Cola, the Ville de Casablanca, the CCME (Conseil de la communauté marocaine à l'étranger), the Institut français and Instituto Cervantes. The Boulevard has received support from the Ministry of Culture since 2005 and indeed one informant seemed to argue that it was frustrating that the Ministry of Culture tends to organize its own events rather than 'accompanying' those that emerge bottom-up: 'Is the role [of the Ministry] to organize events or to support events?' [7] (Kiwan's and Gibert's interview, April 2008, Casablanca). In other words, the informant's comment stems from the fact that, in his view, the Ministry of Culture should be a *partner* for cultural events which develop within civil society, rather than mainly organizing its own festivals.

Figure 2.4   Boulevard crowd, 2007

Figure 2.5   Boulevard crowd, 2007

The Boulevard and politics

The relationship between the Boulevard and the Moroccan political authorities has indeed been an interesting one. One informant explains that as organizers they are often caught up between the conflict which opposes the Islamist *intégristes* and the government and that they wish to remain completely independent of political concerns:

> We don't have sleepless nights because of the sponsors, we have sleepless nights because of the authorizations, because of lots of things, but that's all, there's no, if you like, the problem with the authorities, it's that before they didn't understand at all what we were doing, for them we we were extraterrestrials and now they're scared of the Islamists, that means, if the Islamists attack us, they attacked us last year in the parliament ... so as a result, it's a new order, that's to say, if they authorize us they're scared about the reaction of the Islamists and everything, and us, we're in the middle. [8] (Kiwan's and Gibert's interview, April 2008, Casablanca)

Nevertheless, in 2003 the Boulevard team were drawn into an overtly political affair, when 14 metal musicians were arrested and detained on suspicion of Satanism. The musicians who were arrested were part of the Boulevard scene and although they were all released after many weeks of mobilization, this affair ('l'affaire des 14' as it is known), which was shortly followed by the 16 May terrorist attacks in Casablanca, led the Moroccan government to alter its stance on the Boulevard. From then on, it is arguable that the 'nouvelle scène musicale' was regarded in a more benevolent manner, since the movement was seen by some as a potentially useful counter to mounting Islamic home-grown fundamentalism, rather than representing an attack on the moral fabric of Moroccan society. Even more compelling, in 2009, the 11th Boulevard Festival was cancelled due to severe financial strain (500,000 dirhams of debt were incurred after the 10th Festival in 2008) and King Mohammed VI stepped in and made a royal donation of 2 million dirhams. This donation served to pay off the Boulevard's debts and, beyond that, it has also been put towards the financing of the Boultek, a centre for contemporary music set up by the Boulevard team in November 2010. Nevertheless, despite this royal donation, the Boulevard does not come under the royal patronage of King Mohammed VI and remains an independent movement for cultural innovation.

Indeed, the political significance of the Boulevard cannot be overstated in a context where the country's youth (demographically the majority of the population – 55 per cent of Morocco's 30 million population is under the age of 25) feel that they do not have a voice in Moroccan public life, where their liberties are constantly under threat and where there is a cultural and political gulf between the generations in power and young people.[11] By offering musicians and artists a space for self-expression, the Boulevard organizers and many of the musicians from the 'nouvelle scène' claim that they have somehow reconnected with the 1970s music protest tradition associated with legendary bands such as Nass El Ghiwane or Jil Jilala or that they can be seen as the twenty-first-century version of this sort of cultural and political spirit of engagement and resistance. This vision of the political significance of the Boulevard movement is nicely summed up by Momo in an interview featured on ARTE's *Metropolis* programme in 2007 where he also discusses the position of the Boulevard vis-à-vis the fundamentalist Islamist movement:

The youth of this country had been waiting for 40 years to express itself, you see they've been waiting, they wanted to express themselves, they wanted to have young people representing them. These artists have done that. The young people of this country identify with these groups now, instead of identifying with Americans, or with French or English groups, well no, they identify with Moroccan groups and, as a result, there's such a, a return, a certain pride in being Moroccan already [...] these musics are, if you like, part of a Morocco which is resisting the obscurantists, they are part of those, we do the same work as the police, I mean, in relation to that, except that they pick up the pieces afterwards, we block them before. We reach the target group which interests them because [the Islamists] try to recruit young people and all these young people which we have at the festival, I mean, there are about 150,000 spectators at ours, over the four days, and these are young people who they can't reach, we constitute a sort of barrier to their fascist ideology if you like. [9] (Momo Merhari interviewed for *Metropolis*, ARTE, 2007)[12]

The Boulevard and the fostering of musical creativity

The Boulevard des jeunes musiciens is not just the largest urban music festival in Africa, it is largely responsible for the fostering of musical and creative talents across Morocco. Through the organization of the Tremplin competition for unknown groups, which is held each year before the main festival, successive musicians have been able to gain national (and often international) visibility for themselves since the winners of the Tremplin categories (metal, rock/fusion and hip-hop) all get the chance to perform at the main event and then often go on to perform at a whole host of other festivals around the country and abroad. There is a partnership between the Boulevard and the Festival d'Essaouira, and several other festivals that the Ministry of Culture organizes in locations such as El Jadida and Safi. In that sense, the Boulevard and the Tremplin competition in particular is quite literally a springboard for aspiring musicians from around Morocco. Many of the groups who make up part of the effervescent 'nouvelle scène marocaine' were 'discovered' through the Tremplin and the Boulevard, including H-Kayne, Darga, Fez City Clan, Barry, Haoussa and Moby-Dick. Other groups came together thanks to the concerts organized at the FOL before the actual festival was launched (Hoba Hoba Spirit, Immortal Spirit, Total Eclypse, Reborn). When speaking to young urban musicians in Morocco, the vast majority of them, if not all of them, cite the Boulevard in general and Momo and Hicham in particular as playing a key role in the development of the group. This comes through very clearly in Hatim's comments about the Boulevard as a *passage obligé* for aspiring Moroccan artists:

In 2003, Fouzi, the DJ who we started with at the beginning, he's a guy who has a shop here, it was the only place where we could rehearse, there was a microphone and everything ... 'guys, there's this thing, the Boulevard des jeunes musiciens, it's people I know, they're doing this thing, it's a springboard [talent contest], bla bla bla', yeah but, we take it, we don't give a damn, us, what we want, is, you know, we want to get our stuff out ... 'but no go on, it can do it, it can do it' and we went, just like that, I mean, he told us 'give me the application form, I'll send it, you never know'. He sent it, Momo, listening to it, he said to me, he said 'yeah, why not?', we came ... [phone interruption] by pure coincidence ... Momo liked it, he phoned Fouzi ... he told them 'OK, no problem ... you can take part in the Boulevard', we went ... um ... the atmosphere was a little electric at the start you know, lots of groups staring each other out and everything, 'they're from Meknes, they're from Casa' ... you know ... and so we performed, there were 11 groups, but I can say, in 2003, it's really, Momo says it, it was then that there was the best potential, the best groups, there were 11 groups selected, we performed, the public loved it ... it was the first time that the five of us had got up on stage, I mean with Khalid and with his new songs ... we had never performed them on stage ... it worked, we got down, they said 'it's you, you're going to win', we won, we were really happy, that was really the trigger because, well, there were lots of journalists there, lots of foreign media as well, so we started to have our first articles ... and from then onwards, also with Hoba Hoba who won the same year ... it was the start, we started to hear about the new wave of young musicians, it's really from then onwards, before 2003, I don't think that there was such a craze around this movement ... it started, there were film-makers in 2003 ... good films ... it was a good year, 2003, that was really the springboard, the launching pad, that was it and through the Boulevard we were able to do other festivals ... those which they are more or less affiliated with, that is, Essaouira Festival, popular arts I think. [Nadia: That's in Marrakesh isn't it?] Yeah, Marrakesh and the twinning which they did with Garorock and there, Garorock as well, the same, unforgettable, you know, we did two years in a row ... same thing, good atmosphere, it was good, well, in any case, the Boulevard, I think that in any case, all the groups, the Boulevard is part of their past, I don't know of any group today that we know which hasn't gone through the Boulevard, I don't know of any. (Hatim, H-Kayne) [10] (Kiwan's and Gibert's interview with Hatim and Othmane, H-Kayne, April 2008, Meknes)

Hatim's perspective is corroborated by Hicham Bajjou, who was part of the Boulevard movement in its early FOL days. In the extracts below, Hicham Bajjou explains how Momo and Hicham Bahou played a sort of 'promoter' role for many unknown musicians from the late 1990s onwards. In particular, here Hicham Bajjou is speaking about how his own former rock band, Total Eclypse, was asked by the Moroccan Ministry of Culture to perform in a series of summertime festivals around the country:

Hicham: There was a contact I think through the Boulevard, because I think that I must have talked about the Boulevard. I talk about it as a platform which is very important. It's the platform which sort of plays the intermediary at all the festivals in general, especially state festivals or private festivals as well, which are organized by communications agencies, which means that every time there is a festival which wants to invite a young contemporary music group it calls the Boulevard so that, and then it asks them to suggest a group, or two groups or three groups, it depends on the style they want. So the Boulevard played the role of a sort of agency, you see, for the groups, but in an indirect manner, not regularly, especially during the summer, especially on occasions.

Nadia: So who was the interlocutor, or who is it, if it still exists, this intermediary work?

Hicham: It is a little less the case because now the groups, they're a bit more well known, now they contact them directly. Before it was groups who weren't known at all, people, well, who were known to a few fans here, you know people who followed the concerts a bit, but otherwise the institutions and private firms. Well, what they did was to contact Momo and Hicham, it was over there, that's why I have brought you here. The FOL, you see, the FOL is just opposite. So over there it was a theatre and it's over there that we organized the festival a little bit. You see the gate, the big one, the blue one? So over there there's a theatre inside, a little space, a courtyard, where there are music, also dance and art rooms as well, and so over there, it was a little bit like the HQ. So people called, because Momo was working there as stage manager of the theatre, and Hicham and Momo were a team, well an association, in fact a cultural association which is federated by that federation, which for a while has no longer existed by the way, for some years now, since 2003, but here I am really talking about the Total Eclypse period, 1999–2002, 2003, it was still working, you see that was a little bit like the HQ – we would all meet up here, people would phone to get some groups, to get ... and then they specified their requirements – whether they needed a rock or metal band, or I don't know, it depended on the occasion. So afterwards they would put them in contact with the band itself and that was it. [11] (Kiwan's interview with Hicham Bajjou, March 2008, Casablanca)

Ten years after the first edition of the Boulevard, and when asked to reflect on the forthcoming programme for the 2008 10th anniversary festival, Momo pointed out that he and his co-organizers no longer need to invite foreign headlining acts to bring in the crowds but that the majority of headlining acts are from within Morocco:

if you like, the programme, we're starting from a sort of retrospective if you like on the ten years, that's to say, that we're going to have lots of Moroccan groups ... who have performed for us ... all the headlining acts now ... we can allow ourselves to have Moroccan headliners ... that means groups which can bring people in whereas before we couldn't do that, so it will be the occasion to valorize that ... and then that's it so there'll be a lot less foreign bands, lots more Moroccan headliners with two stages which are practically the same. [12] (Kiwan's and Gibert's interview with Momo Merhari, April 2008, Casablanca)

The Boulevard and the fostering of artistic creativity

Aside from the evident centrality of Momo, Hicham and the Boulevard in terms of cultivating musical talent and careers in Morocco, the movement has also encouraged and enabled the emergence of a whole range of artistic creativity surrounding the festival. The Boulevard 'community' includes not only festival organizers in all their forms, but also includes young journalists, photographers, graphic designers, illustrators and film-makers. The EAC-L'Boulevart association thus has

Figure 2.6   Boulevard Guide, 2007

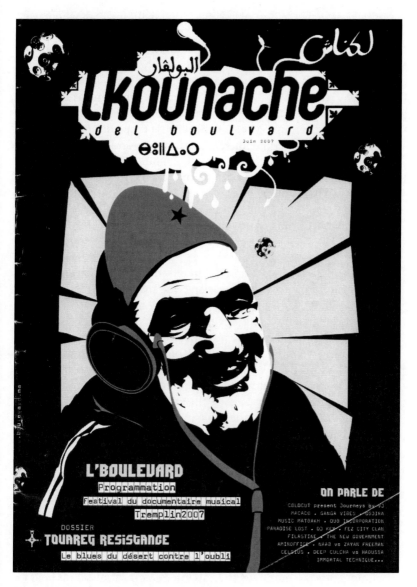

Figure 2.7 L'Kounache *magazine cover, 2007*

at its disposal a whole host of creative individuals, many of whom work for the festival on a voluntary (unpaid basis) but who hold paid jobs with communications or graphic design agencies elsewhere. Out of this has emerged a distinctive visual identity for the Boulevard movement. For example, the festival has spawned its very own glossy magazine *L'Kounache*, which comes out each year at the same time as the event. *L'Kounache* includes witty and engaging articles in French and *darija* on the programme's groups. More broadly, it adopts an editorial line which celebrates Morocco's contemporary urban music and visual arts scenes as well as their translocal and transnational links (Figures 2.6, 2.7).

The notion of a Boulevard artistic 'community' whereby mutual support has been available to musicians, illustrators, photographers, filmmakers and graphic designers from Morocco is expressed clearly in the following extract from an interview with Hicham Bahou (co-founder of the Boulevard):

> a lot of musicians work and are involved in the Boulevard, in fact it is organized in part by musicians, the magazine which we bring out as well, it's lots of musicians who write and illustrate it, who do graphic design and ... and we function, how can I put it?, like a tribe, like a family, that means we give the priority to the people from our community when we're looking for something, or when we want to delegate, someone to help us for these tasks ... we first go and see the people around us ... and so there's a sort of circle which means that it gets bigger at the same time, it's the same people so there's the same discourse ... there's the same spirit and you can see that. [13] (Kiwan's and Gibert's interview with Hicham Bahou, April 2008, Casablanca)

The fact that the Boulevard has become such a pole of creativity is reflected in the existence of a whole host of cultural events which take place in parallel to the music concerts, such as the 2007 exhibition of the Boulevard photographer Jif's photos of the 2006 Boulevard or the 2010 exhibition which celebrated Moroccan urban creation, 'Downside up and outside in', at the Casablanca Villa des Arts. In addition, the Boulevard is associated with an annual Music Documentary Festival which also takes place alongside the music events. This international festival was held for the fourth successive year in February 2010 and is an EAC-L'Boulevart production which receives support from a variety of sources including the Institut français de Casablanca, the Instituto Cervantes and the University of Casablanca (Faculté des sciences juridiques, économiques et sociales, Ain Sebâa).

The remarkable vibrancy of the Boulevard movement is thus testament to the many ways in which human hubs such as this one can generate such diverse forms of artistic creativity. Furthermore, the Boulevard has also had a clear impact on the cultural 'infrastructure' in Casablanca. The Boulevard team have set out to work towards the professionalization of the music scene within Morocco and they have done this in a number of ways. Firstly, they have set up Morocco's first Centre de musiques actuelles, the 'Boultek', at Casablanca's Technopark, a major site for innovative technology and communications. Boultek offers musicians rehearsal space (three rehearsal studios), a recording studio and a web-radio as well as housing the EAC-L'Boulevart association. It will also house a multi-functional theatre for different musical and cultural events and two training rooms.

The establishment of the Boultek is a major achievement in a context where most of the musicians argue that one of the main challenges they face is access to rehearsal space and appropriate recording studios (see Chapter 5 on the role played by foreign cultural institutes in filling this gap). Momo and Hicham have been working on the professionalization agenda for some time now and in 2008 the Boulevard also hosted a 'Salon professionnel' in order to raise awareness and stimulate debate about issues such as copyright, piracy, etc. In June of the same year the Boulevard also organized a conference on the theme of copyright in association with the private youth radio station, Hit Radio, and the BMDA (Bureau marocain des droits d'auteurs). In addition, the 2010 edition of *L'Kounache* magazine includes practical guidelines on how to obtain the 'carte d'artiste' (available since 2008), which entitles artists to specific provisions concerning healthcare insurance, etc. Other ways in which the Boulevard works towards professionalization is in the promotion of certain artists. Momo has 'mentored' and encouraged the development of the Casablanca punk band Haoussa, for example, giving them access to the Garorock Festival in Marmande (France) in 2008, after which they were approached by a Paris-based record label called Besaata for the recording of their first album.

The link with the Garorock Festival is a case in point; it is has been twinned with the Boulevard des jeunes musiciens since 2007. Garorock takes place in the village of Marmande, near Toulouse, in south-west France. This twinning between the Boulevard and Garorock, which began in 2007, involves a North–South/South–North exchange of technical and artistic expertise. Beyond a general shared outlook in terms of the artistic direction of the festivals, the twinning means that each summer Garorock sends over a number of technicians and sound engineers to Casablanca and each spring a number of Moroccan musicians and cultural promoters are invited to the Marmande Festival, some of whom undergo professional training during their stay. The twinning of the two festivals arose out of transnational personal connections between Momo and Ludovic Larbodie, the founder of Garorock, and director of a music events company in Toulouse (Première Pression). In fact, Momo and Ludovic met through Marlène – a French woman based in Casablanca, and who is part of the Boulevard organizing committee. Marlène, who is from Toulouse herself, is a childhood friend of Daniel – one of the sound technicians who works at Première Pression.

The twinning of the Boulevard and Garorock has allowed a number of Moroccan-based acts to gain international exposure and professionalize. This has been the case for the hip-hop group H-Kayne who, as a result of being programmed twice at Garorock, were signed to one of France's largest tour management groups – À gauche de la lune. Despite this apparently more familiar South to North element of the festival twinning, the main thrust of the link is to develop broader projects related to the enhancement of cultural infrastructure and artistic opportunities for Moroccan musicians *within* Morocco. For example, plans are afoot to link Garorock with the Timitar music festival in Agadir by capitalizing on the regional twinning of the Aquitaine and Agadir regions. Larbodie also has further plans to draw on the regional links between Midi-Pyrénées and Marrakesh in order to develop a *musiques actuelles* festival in Marrakesh. At the time of interview (June 2007) it was clear that apart from the Boulevard–Garorock link, these other provincial/regional ties were at 'drawing board' stage. Nevertheless, these ideas which are taking shape do reflect a significant degree of sincerity and indeed result from multiple personal and family connections and interests in the Maghreb. Larbodie is himself half-French/half-Algerian and a number of his collaborators have family ties in Morocco. The 2010 Boulevard had a partnership with the Spanish Pirineos Sur Festival (Aragón) in the form of a residency between Moroccan and Aragón-based musicians with a focus on flamenco, Arab-Andalous, Berber and gnawa musical influences.

Beyond festival twinning, Momo and Hicham are involved in developing North–South and South–South networks of music professionals so as to be able to promote Moroccan musicians transnationally. The first of these professional networks is known as 'Time of Morocco' and, as Momo explains, it is mainly a diasporic network:

> It's a network of cultural operators, above all Moroccans, who live abroad, that means guys who have performance venues, there are guys

who have labels ... guys who are tour managers, guys who have got cultural associations ... it's like that, you see. Who are a little bit all over Europe, and the goal is to, that's it, is the promotion of Moroccan groups. [14] (Kiwan's and Gibert's interview with Momo Merhari, April 2008, Casablanca)

The South–South network is in its early stages but in the spring of 2008 Momo and Hicham had just returned from an important meeting of music professionals and festival organizers in Nouakchott (Mauritania) where discussions had focused on developing links and opportunities for African artists in the South.

Antananarivo as spatial hub

Previously in this chapter we have discussed at some length the role of Mahaleo in Antananarivo so as to show in an exemplary fashion the way in which key individuals can act as human hubs in metropolitan cities in the South. Other artists, too, have vital roles in this respect, though we lack the space to discuss them here in more detail. Ricky Olombelo, for example, provides a significant link between musicians from Antananarivo and those from outside the capital city through his cultural centre Rarihasina, that is affiliated to and centrally housed in a building owned by the University of Antananarivo. Like Mahaleo, Ricky also fulfils multiple roles as singer-songwriter, performer, teacher and music promoter, and is for many musicians the first point of call (see also Fuhr 2006). Antananarivo's role as a spatial hub is underpinned by a lively music industry with many indoor and outdoor venues for concert performances, cabarets and festivals. Increasingly some of its recording studios are used not only by local and national artists but by migrant artists, too, often taking up its cheaper facilities to record their initial takes before producing and mastering the CDs in the more sophisticated studios of the North.

Similarly, a communication specialist and music promoter such as Jaobarison, with his Antananarivan firm Media Consulting, not only promotes concerts in the city and nationwide but also invites migrant artists from the northern hemisphere to Antananarivo and in turn sends artists from Madagascar abroad. It is these developments which nationally and internationally underpin the centrality of Antananarivo in the professional networks of musicians. In an interview in 2007, Jaobarison described his progression from journalist to director of a communication and promotion firm in competition with mainly foreign businesses. He sketches a competitive environment with many mainly foreign businesses and only two or three local ones. His previous contacts as a journalist now come to his aid in developing his own communication business. However, in order to put Media Consulting on the map and to make it distinctive from all the other competitors, he decides to organize events, not necessarily to make money but mainly as a publicity venture. He explains how this immediately captures the attention of the public:

> In the past, the organizers of shows would go for simple posters and spots. But when I took care of communication, I organized documentaries and TV shows about the artists: interviews, stories about their lives ... And I also took care of the settings and everything that revolves around the event. That really created a sensation with the public, they developed a real passion. Hence the first show was a genuine success. So I carried on in the same vein and it worked again. After that I realized that I could start a career in this field. Because I think that it does offer something to society. So I set to work and went on to professionalize this job more and more, because at the time it was not professional at all. That is to say, all the people involved in the organization of an event were working in an informal way. To give you an example: I'm a concert organizer, but in the past the organizer would also have been the director of a bank or a manager in this or that company. That means, there were no professional organizers. That is why I decided to professionalize this career. Because when I saw people who organized a big concert, for example a youth association or a workers' club, they'd meet over the weekend, and they'd decide, 'Hey, let's organize a concert,' and then they'd ask around: 'You, are you available tomorrow, Monday?' 'No I'm working, sorry ...' That is how it would work back then. But as soon as we started working, it began to change, bit by bit. That is how it started and we've continued ever since ... Since 2004 we've done roughly 30 concerts per year. And we don't only organize concerts in Madagascar but also in France and in La Réunion. We take the artists there, and we try to organize something there, in France and in La Réunion, soon in Mayotte as well. But administratively speaking, it all starts from here. Our contacts in Paris, La Réunion or Marseille, they only do the ... let's say 'material' preparation, for example the booking of venues. But even when they book venues we're the ones who pay for that. So they only do the most basic administration. They can take care of the tickets selling and ticket reservations and all things related

to the logistics of the artists. For example, with Mahaleo, when we arrive somewhere, it is those people who will have booked the hotel rooms, organized the transport, the food, etc. But everything to do with the budgeting that's always done from here, from Madagascar, that means it's Media Consulting that organizes everything. The other people are there to help us to realize the project. That's how it works. [15] (Meinhof's and Rasolofondraosolo's interview, November 2007, Antananarivo)

Organizations such as Media Consulting are part of an emergent professionalized music industry in Antananarivo itself through which Malagasy artists can tour in France and worldwide. Yet whereas Paris-based firms such as Kanto Productions attempt to broaden the audience through a 'world music' appeal, placing artists in the jazz venue New Morning or even the most famous concert halls such as La Cigale or even Olympia, Media Consulting is specifically targeting the global networks of the diaspora, using venues in Paris such as Tana Orly, a venue and community centre, named as such because of its vicinity to the Parisian airport Orly, and Tana, the French abbreviation of Antananarivo, or the Espace Chevreuil in Nanterre. In the extract below he explains that this can cause some misunderstandings for artists whose expectations are formed by entering an international rather than a diasporic music market.

Jaobarison: The problem is that ... Well, some of artists don't understand the situation. They think that by playing abroad, they will have a magnificent show, something grandiose. For example, some artists came to my office yesterday. I'm going to send them to France. And when we were discussing the fees and when I told him how much it was, they missed the point. And we needed to have some discussion. I had to explain how it works. Because they thought that when they play in France, for example, there'd be lots of foreigners, three, four thousand people in the audience. But that is not how it works at all. Mostly the audience is made up from ...

Dama: The Malagasy community.

Jaobarison: The Malagasy community.

Ulrike: It's the Malagasy themselves?

Jaobarison: Yes, the Malagasy. So for an evening you get 1200, maximum 1500 persons for each event. Sometimes only 300, 200 people. Hence it is just so that the Malagasy

> community, the Malagasy diaspora can enjoy concerts by Malagasy artists ... And there's also the United States, there's Canada. Because there, too, is a strong Malagasy community, especially in Montréal. When we play there, as we did in 2006, there were circa 400, 500 Malagasies. And yet there were plenty of Malagasies who weren't able to come to Montréal, because the promotion wasn't very good. Hence for the next time – when we go in May – we're already starting the promotion to prepare the people. Because it didn't work out with the first concert. But this time we hope to get a big crowd. [16] (Meinhof's and Rasolofondraosolo's interview, November 2007, Antananarivo)

Casablanca as spatial hub

As we saw above, the Boulevard des jeunes musiciens movement can be seen as an example of a human hub with Momo and Hicham at the centre of this dense network of musicians, visual artists and journalists. It is, of course, no coincidence that such a multi-layered and vibrant artistic community has developed in the metropolitan city of Casablanca. Casablanca is not only Morocco's economic powerhouse, it has also been the main site for a whole host of cultural and artistic facilities, including the few recording studios which are geared towards the new musical scene (Plein les oreilles, D-cibel), record labels (Clic, Platinum), journalists and significant print media such as *Tel Quel* magazine, *L'Espoir citoyen* or *Nichan*, faithful partners of the Boulevard, and the spirit of urban cultural creation that it espouses. Given such cultural critical mass, it is no wonder that commentators have been tempted to compare Casablanca's cultural scene with the Spanish *Movida*. The term *Nayda* (renaissance) is often used to describe the new music scene and is one which is readily adopted by the actors themselves.[13]

Gateways for migration: Antananarivo as *passage obligé*

Capital cities in the South are also gateways for artists who wish to leave their countries. In the lives of many Malagasy artists who eventually migrated to France and other countries it is again Antananarivo that provided the gateway. In this way, the capital cities in the South act as *passage obligé* at par with the post-imperial cities of the northern hemisphere, and allow connections that go beyond the networkings of the diasporas described by Jaobarison. Two of the most famous Malagasy muscians in Europe, Régis Gizavo and Justin Vali, have early careers which illustrate this alternative pathway in very different ways.

Justin – real name Justin Rakotondrasoa – is internationally known by his artistic name Justin Vali, after the valiha, the most iconic string instrument of Madagascar which his family has been building for generations and used for purely ceremonial purposes in their village.[14] It was only because of Justin's visit to Antananarivo[15] as a trader rather than a player of the valiha that he encountered a tour operator who auditioned for valiha players to join a folk music ensemble for a French tour. Justin put himself forward and was one of four players that were selected. Below he tells us about this fateful visit to the capital city:

> First and foremost I am a musician of the sacred temple, because like all my family that is where I learned to play. So from there, we did small concerts in the village: weddings, school fairs and such like. But in Tana, in the city, I was not famous in any way, not at all, not at all! Except of course as a valiha retailer, like all my brothers … And it was there [in Tana] that I met a tour manager who was trying to form a traditional band to tour in France. So we entered the selection and I was chosen to play the valiha by the other valiha players, there were four of us in the band … And so the adventure started! [17] (Meinhof's and Rasolofondraosolo's interview, May 2006, following the concert by the Madagascar All Stars at the Traumzeit Festival in Germany)

Once arrived in Paris it took several years for Justin to establish himself, not so much through the Malagasy diaspora, although their social networks enabled him to survive in the early years, but through connections with Paddy Bush, brother of British singer Kate Bush, and subsequent links with world music star and director of the British world music festival WOMAD, Peter Gabriel. We will revisit Justin's world music career in later chapters when from his home in Lille and subsequently Paris he becomes one of the most influential valiha and marovany players from Madagascar.

Similarly to Justin, the accordionist Régis Gizavo's career also bypassed the diasporic networks. In his case the entry into the international world music scene came through winning the coveted 'best newcomer' prize from the annual Radio France International (RFI) competition. But in order to fulfil his wish to leave Madagascar for a more promising musical career in Europe he had to first leave his home in Toliara and make use of the facilities and social networks offered by Antananarivo – to find a recording studio, record his own songs, to enter a competition and simply to be one of the best. This is how he explained to us the 'start of his adventure':

> Two years before (it all started), I told myself: I'm gonna try this. I wanted to come here [to Paris], leave Madagascar, to see something else. I thought, well, I have a few songs, I was already in Tana, so I tried to find a recording studio and it was far from being easy ...
>
> And there I met Kiki, Rageorges' uncle, I went to their place and asked: 'I'd like to record my music, I'd like to enter a contest but I have nothing ... Could you lend me your studio just for an afternoon or for a day?' and they agreed.
>
> Rageorges said, 'No problem but I have to talk about it with Kiki,' and Kiki was still really young, so very young. So we tried to do this, and I managed to do a song, then we did two, three others and we sent the recording from Madagascar but I was not expecting anything ...
>
> And one night, I was in front of a TV shop and I saw my video clip appear on the second channel – that was in 1990. On Antenne 2 at 8 o'clock in the evening! I saw it and I was like 'What am I doing there?' ... there were all the artists who'd won the contest with RFI [Radio France International]. I was in!
>
> Then the radio RTM called saying I'd won a prize and that's how it all started ... They gave me a ticket for the award ceremony the following year and so I left Madagascar ... The beginning of the adventure! [18] (Meinhof's and Rasolofondraosolo's interview, June 2006, Paris)

For Régis, whose career we will also revisit later, it was the encounter with European-based musicians during the award-winning ceremonies in Guinea-Biseau that kick-started his career. From his home in Paris Régis has become one of the most renowned Malagasy musicians in the world, not only as a solo artist in his own right at many festivals, or in accompanying world music stars such as Cesaria Evora on tour, but together with Dama, Justin Vali, Erick Manana, Marius (Fenoamby) and Ricky Olombelo as fellow member of the transnational group Madagascar All Stars.

Casablanca as gateway to international migration?

As we saw in Chapter 1, Casablanca is generally regarded by musicians from provincial towns and cities as the *passage obligé* if they are to get ahead in their careers as artists. The *passage obligé* is generally the Boulevard Festival itself which as we have seen brings multiple opportunities for those fortunate enough to participate and perhaps win the Tremplin competition (see the stories of H-Kayne, Haoussa, Darga, mentioned above, and Fez City Clan, Shabka and Amarg Fusion in Chapter 1). But what is so compelling about Casablanca is that it seems that many musicians are not aspiring to leave Morocco via Casablanca. In other words, Casablanca is not just a springboard to 'greater things' across the Mediterranean/Atlantic. Clearly, one should not exaggerate matters – the cultural industry in terms of new music is still a fledgling one with artists facing huge challenges in terms of copyright, piracy, recording and distribution of their material. Nevertheless one cannot afford to ignore the growing cultural dynamism of Casablanca's urban music scenes (setting it apart from many of its Arab/North African neighbours) in any broader consideration of cultural globalization and music since the prime academic interest in these two themes tends to focus solely on cities in the northern hemisphere. It is only after having considered some of the cultural dynamics within the context of globalization in the South, that we now proceed to an examination in Part 2 of the musical networks and diasporic creativity in the North.

Part 2
The View from the North

3
Capital Cities as Global Hubs

This chapter will trace the dynamics between African and European capital cities, taking as its theoretical backdrop recent and current thinking about global cities and cultural globalization. As such, the first part of the chapter will focus on these theoretical considerations and then move onto the main empirical discussion where we will first explore the more predictable role of Paris as a hub or *passage obligé* for North African and Malagasy migrants and their descendants, and then consider the lesser-known role of other major European cities such as London, Amsterdam and Vienna for North African and Malagasy musicians. We will show how Paris and these other cities in the North offer multi-layered opportunities for migrant and migrant-origin artists based there and furthermore how the presence of such artists has come, over time, to transform the cultural fabric of the cities they reside and work in.

Theoretical considerations – global cities and cultural globalization from below

Many scholars have claimed that the city is a fruitful prism through which to study a vast array of social and cultural processes (for example the Chicago School and early accounts of the integration of newly arrived immigrant populations). In the context of globalization, the city is seen as a particularly useful space since it is considered to embody and facilitate localized forms of the global (see Dirlik 1996, cited in Robertson and White 2003: vol. 1, 13 or Durrschmidt 2000 on 'microglobalization' of everyday lives in the global city). Furthermore, the city is regarded as a significant object of study because it allows us to move beyond a national framing of social and cultural processes and practices (see Meinhof and Triandafyllidou 2006 and Aksoy 2006). Nevertheless, much of the literature on global cities tends to privilege a financial, corporate and economic perspective on the concentration of flows and networks which one finds therein.[1] It is in this context that Michael Peter Smith (1999) is critical of Saskia Sassen's work on global cities. Smith argues that Sassen's discussion (Sassen 1991) of the global city has focused too much on processes of globalization which emanate from 'above' – which has meant that corporate and financial indices are some of the main features of the account. Smith's critique is accurate up to a point, although Sassen's later work (see Sassen 2007) does tackle the question of the global city being a site for the emergence of agency among migrant workers, especially migrant women. Nevertheless, it is significant that in order to counter the risk that analyses of global cities may become blind to questions of individual agency, Smith instead argues for an approach which foregrounds the notion of the *transnational* rather than the *global* city. This point resonates with pleas that scholars do not ignore key globalization processes from 'below' which emanate from individuals or small organizations based within cities.[2] Such pleas are not far removed from arguments that certain researchers, including ourselves, make for the importance of empirically grounded work on urban and *cultural* processes of globalization. (See, for example, Appadurai 1996 and McNeill 1999.) Indeed, Appadurai's reference to postnational 'diasporic public spheres' is of particular relevance to our own work in capital cities where there is a large concentration of diasporic artists whose creative activities are mediated through a transnational imaginary (Appadurai 1996: 22). But whereas scholars such as Sassen have argued that the emergence of global cities has led to a 'new geography of centrality and marginality' (Sassen 2007: 111), we wish to go beyond such paradigms, arguing that diasporic musicians and cultural operators come to occupy extremely significant cultural roles in Europe's major cities, yet without the economic power normally associated with the class of transnational elites. These artists' 'extensive connectivity' to their countries of origin and their 'extensive global consciousness' (Robertson and White 2003: vol. 1, 6) mean that their presence in major European cities can be read as localized, concrete manifestations of cultural globalization and its associated networks and flows.

Paris as *passage obligé*

It is undeniable that throughout the twentieth century Paris has been a key site of cultural production and encounter for artists in general and post-colonial artists in particular, especially Francophone musicians of

North African and sub-Saharan or Indian Ocean origin. More specifically in relation to music production, historian James Winders (2006) has shown that during the 1980s and 1990s, Paris could be considered the 'capital of afro-pop'. Winders's research focuses mainly on sub-Saharan and central African musicians. However, it is also the case that musicians and cultural actors from the Maghreb and Madagascar have sought to pursue their careers in the city, either migrating for work or to study and falling into music 'by accident', or as artists escaping the economic hardship and lack of opportunities of their poverty-stricken and musically under-resourced countries, or indeed in the case of North Africans by being forced to flee their country of origin because of political repression or violence. While migration from Madagascar is by and large a post-independence phenomenon, with a strong influx from the 1980s onwards, the presence of North African musicians in Paris dates back to the early twentieth century. Daoudi and Miliani (2002) show that the first recordings of kabyle music in France took place in 1910. By the mid- to late 1930s, North African musicians were starting to create and perform on a regular basis in Paris's growing number of *cafés maghrébins* (mainly in the Latin Quarter) (Daoudi and Miliani 2002).

With the advent of independence in Algeria, Morocco and Tunisia, many musicians returned to their countries of origin, reflecting a widespread sense of optimism in these newly independent states. This did not, however, lead to a flourishing of record labels and cultural infrastructure south of the Mediterranean, which meant that Paris still continued to occupy a central role for North African artists, even if the channels of production and distribution became more community-oriented. Indeed, it is from this period onwards that the Barbès district in north-east Paris became a key site for the recording, editing and marketing of North African music (the 'souk business'). Malagasy musicians, too, started to record with Paris-based labels such as Label bleu and Cinq planètes.

Other socio-cultural and political circumstances, both within and beyond France, meant that by the mid-1990s Paris clearly occupied a *passage obligé* role. The year 1981 saw the arrival of the socialist-led Mitterrand government which introduced two significant pieces of legislation affecting African immigrants in general, and thereby also North African and Malagasy artists. In October 1981, the right of foreign nationals to form associations was granted, leading to the establishment of numerous civil society organizations of a cultural and artistic nature. The same year also saw the liberalization of the airwaves and a whole host of *radios libres* were set up as a result: Radio Beur and Radio Soleil in Paris. Other media outfits such as Radio Nova were key in promoting world music during this period. Community radios directed at specific diasporas followed in the wake and included music broadcasts. The year 1992 saw the foundation of Fréquence Paris plurielle, catering for dozens of different language communities, among them from 1998 onwards the Malagasy programme 'Echos du capricorne', produced in principle from the living room of two sisters, Claudia Solofolandy and Claudie Benoît, and their respective husbands.

North African musicians in Paris

In contrast to the opening up of Paris as 'world music capital', the political, social and cultural climate in the Maghreb, and in Algeria and Morocco in particular, was one of closure. In Morocco, the period from 1958 to 1990 is known as 'les années de plomb', whereby the regime systematically cracked down on social and political critique or dissent – explicit or suspected – through mass arrests and imprisonments (see, for example, Daoud 2007; Vermeren 2006). In Algeria, Islamism was gaining ground and the cultural ambiance was generally not favourable to musicians. The situation worsened following the disqualified victory of the FIS (*Front Islamique de Salut*) in the elections of 1991 and the ensuing civil war which consumed the country for the rest of the decade. Nowhere was artistic flight so apparent than in Algeria from the late 1980s onwards and during the civil war from 1991. Artists such as Khaled, Chaba Zahouania and Souad Massi felt obliged to leave and settle in Paris. The assassination of singers such as Cheb Hasni in 1994 and Matoub Lounès in 1998 only served to further reinforce Paris's role of *passage obligé* or, rather, safe haven.

One key manifestation of the migration of artists to Paris against the backdrop of political repression and violence in Algeria was the development of the artists' collective known as Louzine. This collective of musicians and visual artists was until recently based in a disused factory in Arcueil, a suburb on the south-eastern outskirts of Paris. One of the main founders of the Louzine collective is a guitarist-singer-songwriter called Hocine Boukella, an Algerian who has been based in France since 1985. Boukella came to France to undertake doctoral study in the field of genetics but suspended his studies in 1988 in order to develop his artistic career (music and illustration). He was already singing and playing guitar in a student group in Algiers and, once in France, created various bands, among which was the group Cheikh Sidi Bémol in 1992, and subsequently Thalweg, which plays 'Berber-celtic' music. In 1998 he took a leading part in the creation of the artists' collective Louzine with musicians of the Orchestre national de Barbès (ONB). It is clear that the

Louzine collective and the creative synergies which emerged out of it were facilitated due to the fact that significant numbers of Algerian musicians found themselves in Paris at the same time and for similar reasons, namely escaping the political context and civil violence in Algeria:

> well I have the impression that everyone left ... all my generation ... [...] there are loads of musicians who came during the 90s, practically all the musicians from Algiers ... came here. So at the time, everyone, lots of people were leaving Algeria. And so, we all effectively found ourselves in Paris with the same residence permit problems ... and all that ... and it's a gregarious reflex when one leaves for elsewhere, I think, everyone, we all inevitably find ourselves in the same place ... That's it, that is to say, really naturally, people were making music together ... at the time, there was Karim Ziad, Aziz Samaoui, Moustafa Moutawi and everything, all those people lived for example in the same apartment ... with, I remember, for example, on the same landing in Clichy, there were two flats which were rented out and there were only Algerian musicians, there were six or seven musicians ... because at the time, they had just arrived, so 'has someone got a plan for a flat?' because at the time we had just arrived, it's like that. [1] (Kiwan's and Gibert's interview with Hocine Boukella, February 2008, Ivry, France)

The Louzine collective was established in 1998. The building had originally housed the record label Samarkand which produced Hocine's brother, Youssef Boukella, the founder of the group Orchestre national de Barbès, and Hocine had a workshop on site as well. When the lease ran out, the musicians who had gravitated around Youssef and Hocine (including members of Gaâda Diwane de Béchar) decided to take over the lease and create the association called Louzine. In order to pay the rent, the musicians organized jam sessions (*diwane*) and concerts at other venues in and around Paris (including the Cabaret Sauvage, Maison des Jeunes de Fresnes and La Clé) and then were able to finance the setting up of their own recording studio on site and eventually their own production and distribution company (Cheikh Sidi Bemol Productions and Undergroone respectively). The principle of 'auto-gestion' was thus very much at the heart of Louzine's *modus operandi*, and, according to Hocine, stemmed from the fact that they were a collective, concentrating a certain amount of 'critical mass':

> basically, being, like that ... um a collective, you see, in a sense, that really obliged us to look at all the aspects of our work, you see, well

since there aren't so many production companies which are interested in our work, well we decided to create a company, a production label. [2] (Kiwan's and Gibert's interview with Hocine Boukella, February 2008, Ivry, France)

After ten years of existence, the collective officially disbanded when the lease came to an end in 2008. Nevertheless, by 2008, a significant number of diasporic Algerian musicians and visual artists emerged as professionals, in part thanks to the collective, including acts such as Orchestre national de Barbès, Gaâda Diwane de Béchar, Zerda, Samira Brahmia, El-Gafla and Fatima Groove as well as illustrators such as Gyps or photographers such as Halim Zenati. The building may no longer physically 'house' the collective but the network still exists online at www.louzine.net, where up-to-date news and links about concerts, albums and exhibitions are readily available. Furthermore, the impact of the collective has been felt far beyond Paris in Algiers – firstly, in terms of the emergence of a public 'back home' the Louzine musicians' music has become well known and appreciated there, despite the absence of formal distribution networks until fairly recently and, secondly, the Louzine has become well known to aspiring musicians wanting to leave Algiers and make a living from their art in France:

and it's true that it was … really … from '98 until 2008, it was a very very good experience … because there were quite a lot of encounters, and you wouldn't think it but it's in this place that we all … um … moved forward in our work if you like, be it Orchestre national de Barbès, or Gaâda or Sidi Bémol … there were loads of bands which were set up there as well. Young bands and um … and as well as that … we have a very very good aura, if you like, in Algeria, in the musical milieu, and all that, in Algiers all the musicians know the Louzine … they think that it's a big thing as well … I don't know if you have come to the space? […] It's a space … you'll see in the documentary, it's very old … so there are musicians who came from Algeria and well, who had the address and as they arrived were astonished to see … it's a sort of hovel! And um, there you go so … actually … Louzine allowed us to make contacts with Algeria … we made contact with Belda Diffusion for example … who is a young producer in Algiers […] it allowed us to make contacts with people like that, with Algerian bands more than anything … like Index, a young band called Djmawi Africa. [3] (Kiwan's and Gibert's interview with Hocine Boukella, February 2008, Ivry, France)

So the trajectory of Hocine Boukella and his entourage within the Louzine collective is a significant example of the ways in which Paris is a cultural magnet for Algerian diasporic artists who are able to professionalize and then diversify once they are established in the city's diasporic networks. Moreover, the Louzine experience also demonstrates how transnational cultural dynamics are expressed locally and then refract back 'home' again. Of course, due to the colonial history, the relationship between Algeria's musicians and the city is a long-standing one, with much of the music which is known as 'Algerian' actually having been recorded and/or mastered in Paris. This phenomenon certainly resonates with Hocine Boukella's own experiences as both musician and music fan:

> And I think that the ... well, personally, arriving here in France, I know that it's easier to find, for example, records by Algerian singers, while I, I like a singer called Cheikh Hammada, he's a bedouin singer, in Algeria I had one of his records and I looked, but there I didn't find anything ... here, I discovered him! Slimane Azem's the same. He's a kabyle singer who was banned in Algeria, you see ... It's here that you're going to discover him, you know. Because in Algeria, there's nothing ... all the music groups who are in Algiers, it means that as soon as they start to become a little famous, they go elsewhere ... they don't stay in Algeria, because there are no concerts. [4] (Kiwan's and Gibert's interview with Hocine Boukella, February 2008, Ivry, France)

Closely entwined with Hocine Boukella's story is that of the group known as the Orchestre national de Barbès (ONB). The group was founded by Hocine's brother, Youssef Boukella, a bass player and songwriter, in 1995 and was initially set up as a 'live' group made up of 12 musicians from Algeria, Morocco and France. The hub status of Paris was key in the formation of the group and its eclectic fusion of musical styles – rock, jazz, gnawa, chaâbi and Arab-Andalous sounds. Moroccan songwriter and keyboard player Taoufik explains how the idea of mixing musical genres is at the heart of the ONB project – something which became possible through the Paris 'circuit'. The importance of Paris as a diverse city of immigration and transnational cultural flows is captured in the name of the band – Barbès being a neighbourhood in the 18th *arrondissement* which has been a transit and settlement site for generations of immigrants of North African origin. Its numerous cafés and music shops selling cassettes of all types of North African and Middle Eastern music, but particularly rai music, has made Barbès the centre of a well-known 'souk business'. Taoufik explains the choice of the name of the band further:

> Because Barbès is an immigrant neighbourhood, it's a neighbour-hood of encounters especially for the North Africans, well, it's starting to change. We and above all those who came before us, there were lots of immigrants [...] It's the neighbourhood that before coming to Paris, I didn't know about the 15th, nor Chinatown, the 13th, the most famous neighbourhood among novices like I was before, it's the first neighbourhood. After the Eiffel Tower, we know about Barbès [...] and it's an obligatory passage of transition. [5] (Kiwan's interview with Taoufik, February 2004, Paris)[3]

ONB rehearsed at the Louzine and also recorded their third album *Alik* (2008) there, and some of the musicians who play with the ONB also session with other Louzine musicians. For example, this is the case of bass player Khliff Mizialaoua who plays with the groups Gaâda Diwane de Béchar and Cheikh Sidi Bémol and singer-songwriter Samira Brahmia. So clearly Paris should be seen as a key hub for these North African (mainly Algerian) artists, with Hocine and Youssef Boukella dou-bling up as key human hubs (see the Introduction for more on human hubs) since it is they who were instrumental in the establishment of such a vibrant and influential network of artists and musicians. The fact that the Louzine collective has gained such notoriety in the Maghreb (and in particular in Algeria) also shows how a diasporic movement can influence creative processes back in the country of origin, effec-tively facilitating the emergence of a 'transnational public sphere' (see Robertson and White 2003: vol. 1, 29).

A further example of the way in which the Parisian context favours the emergence of creative musical encounters can be found in the group known as El-Gafla (meaning 'caravan of the desert' in Arabic). El-Gafla would not have formed if it had not been for the variety and range of musicians present and active in the capital's cafés and small concert venues. El-Gafla is a group which has some difficulty describing itself but is often advertised on flyers and posters as being *rock algéro-alternatif* (alternative Algerian rock). In actual fact, as Karim Chaya, the founder and singer of this eight-man group, points out, the aim was to create an eclectic mix of musicians and musical styles – Karim, who was born and brought up in Algiers and who came to Paris in 1993, sings mainly in Arabic, kabyle (Tamazight) and French but also has texts in Spanish. The French violinist of the group had classical Western training, the

Auvergnat accordion player brings a touch of musette to the group, the Italian guitar player is mainly a blues, funk artist and the derbouka player is of kabyle-Polish origin. The music is a mix of Algérois, gypsy, East European, funk and musette sounds. This degree of *métissage* (mixing) was made possible by being in Paris and in particular by frequenting the cafés and bars of the highly diverse Ménilmontant area of the city (11th and 20th *arrondissements*). Karim explains:

> The objective, in fact, I didn't want to do something which was 100 per cent North African, Algerian. I wanted instead to have a mix in my music [...] when I stumbled across musicians who were completely different to me, with a completely different musical culture to my own, the objective was that, to set up a group, [...] each one added his own distinct musical touch [...] A Celtic side – that's my Berber culture which comes out. Gnawa, popular Algerian – it's also my culture. [6] (Kiwan's interview with Karim, El-Gafla, October 2003, Paris)[4]

In fact, the group El-Gafla is very closely linked to the neighbourhood Ménilmontant, as explained on their webpage hosted on the Louzine website:

> From Algeria to Paris, via Cameroon or Poland, the seven members of El-Gafla form a sort of International Orchestra of Ménilmontant, a corner of Paris as diverse and as popular as their music. From bars to squats and from concert venues to festivals, the noise rings out and the caravan passes by, followed by a broad and faithful public, bringing together all those who appreciate the energy of Gnawa Diffusion, the sweet melancholy of Souad Massi and the straight talk of Zebda. [7] (www.louzine.net, accessed 1 December 2009)

Indeed, Karim argues that Paris was key to the formation of the group and will remain key because of the encounters that the city, and Ménilmontant in particular, provide:

> I like this city a lot. I don't think I could leave this city [...] and I've had some amazing encounters in Paris [...] in musical terms. France is the mix of all its cultures [...] I feel really really good in Paris. [8] (Kiwan's interview with Karim, El-Gafla, October 2003, Paris)[5]

Whereas the musicians mentioned above came to Paris for non-musical reasons, generally to undertake university studies or to travel, and then became musicians once they were settled in the capital, other artists explicitly make the decision to leave their country of origin in order to pursue their musical career in the city. This was the case of Karim Ziad, a drummer and singer-songwriter from Algiers, who has collaborated with many North African, European and American artists. Ziad became interested in percussion from a very young age (four–five years old) and as a young man was part of a hard rock group in Algiers. But it was the Algiers wedding circuit which meant that he could earn his living alongside his biology studies at university. Determined to make a living out of his own art rather than through wedding music, Ziad emigrated to France in 1989 and enrolled in classes at the Emmanuelle Boursault music school in Paris, before going on to become the drummer for rai musicians Cheb Mami and Khaled and kabyle musician Idir (he has also worked with musicians who are part of the Louzine collective – in particular Mehdi Askeur of the Orchestre national de Barbès and Khliff Miziallaoua who plays with the Orchestre national de Barbès, Cheikh Sidi Bémol, Gaâda Diwane de Béchar and Samira Brahmia among others). He was Cheb Mami's drummer for 12 years but he has also collaborated with several well-known jazz musicians such as Nguyên Lê, Bojan Z, Louis Winsberg and Jeff Gardner, and worked for two years with the world-famous Austrian jazz musician Joe Zawinul. After having toured the USA with Zawinul's band, Ziad decided to set up his own group – Ifrikya (Africa in Arabic). Ziad's original plan had been to come to Paris to study music and return to Algeria to teach what he had learnt. As he puts it: 'we had our feet there [Algeria] and our head in Paris' [9] (excerpt from interview with Karim Ziad on www.algeriades.com, accessed 2 December 2009). But a combination of the political context in Algeria and the multiple opportunities he was offered once in Paris meant that Ziad decided to stay on:

> Oh yes, I left, it was horrible. There was that as well ... which gave me a kick in the backside ... [...] there was, actually, this movement, this, this, lots of musicians left Algeria, because, actually, in Algeria we were finding it difficult to make music. To live from our music, in any case. [10] (Kiwan's interview with Karim Ziad, July 2008, Paris)

Ziad's networks and career have been highly eclectic and he manages to straddle multiple music scenes – world, North African, jazz. While he initially was obliged to work the wedding circuit in order to finance his music studies in Paris, his collaboration with Cheb Mami opened the door to numerous other opportunities and today his own group Ifrikya has released three albums (the first and third signed and produced in Germany and the second produced in France).

In parallel to his professional activity as a musician, Ziad has taught for the past five years at the Didier Lockwood music school in Dammarie-lès-Lys in the Île-de-France region. In self-assured fashion, Ziad argues that his influence can now be felt among European jazz percussionists in Paris, who are able, better than in other European cities, to understand and play North African rhythms effectively:

> now in jazz groups, that we now hear, I recognize the touch that I brought to France. That is, now all the drummers, all of them without exception, use my part. It's part of the schools [....] and there are very good drummers who are in Paris and who play it and it's the only country where there are Europeans who manage to play music from the Maghreb effectively, for example you can't find that neither in England nor in the United States, nor elsewhere. It's just in France. Why is that the case also? Because, actually, I've been teaching in this school for four or five years. [11] (Kiwan's interview with Karim Ziad, July 2008, Paris)

Despite such apparently bold self-assurance, Ziad admits that his music has not met with widespread popular appeal in France and he cites a number of possible reasons for this: the fact that he is labelled as a jazz musician, with all the attendant elitist assumptions which go with such labelling, the fact that he sings exclusively in Arabic and Berber, and the effects of media coverage. Nevertheless, Ziad has a clear popular following in Algeria, Morocco and Tunisia – his records sell very well there, and his second album *Chabiba* (2004) was particularly successful in Morocco. Ziad is also popular and respected among gnawa musicians in the Maghreb and it is for that reason that he was appointed artistic director of the international gnawa music festival in Essaouira in 2000. He continues to invite European musicians to play with local *maâlems* (masters) and maintains that the development of gnawa music in the 'world music' scene – that is, beyond its original sacred and ritualistic *lila* context – should be welcomed since it has allowed the gnawa to keep their musical practices and repertoires alive. Ziad's connection with the gnawa in North Africa seems to have emerged due to his activities in Paris – namely the recording of an album (*Maghreb and Friends*) with Paris-based French-Vietnamese guitarist Nguyên Lê in 1998, during which they invited gnawa musicians such as Bnet Houriat to collaborate and perform with them on stage.

The Parisian North African music scene which has gravitated around the Louzine artists since the late 1990s does not just involve migrants who emigrated to France as adults. It has also come to attract post-migrant musicians, or so-called 'second-generation' artists, who were born or brought up in France. This is the case of Hichem Takaoute, bass player, drummer and percussionist, who was born in Casablanca but who came to France at the age of three with his parents. After a childhood spent in Corsica, Hichem moved to Marseille at the age of 18 to be able to make a living out of his music and, after a decade, moved on to Paris, motivated once again by his musical career. Once in Paris, he began to work as a session musician with various groups and musicians such as Raikoum, Karim Ziad and Cheikh Sidi Bémol, and then in 2000 he set up his own group, Zalamite, with two other musicians. (Zalamite's compositions and repertoire draw on flamenco, salsa, rock, gnawa and chaâbi rhythms and melodies.) Hichem underlines the importance of the Louzine as a site for encountering other artists: 'In fact, the first place where I rehearsed in Paris was the Louzine, and given that the ONB was rehearsing there, lots of groups, you inevitably know everyone, you see' [12] (Gibert's interview with Hichem Takaoute, February 2009).

Another significant network in Paris is the New Bled collective which was founded by music producer Mohand Haddar. Haddar, who is of Algerian Berber origin, came to France from Algeria at the age of four.[6] New Bled is a record label but is also involved in artist booking, artist management and cultural events' organization. While New Bled draws on North African influences and themes, it is also a broadly defined electronic music outfit which works with artists and cultural promoters from non-North African backgrounds (India and South-East Asia, Cameroon, Turkey, Spain, France, Italy, Senegal). The majority of artists and music producers who are part of the New Bled collective label are based in Paris but some artists are based in Rome or London. At the heart of the New Bled project is a desire to create an innovative platform for 'musiques urbaines métissées' (urban fusion music) in Paris. This objective takes various forms, including the signing of musicians and DJs to the New Bled label, the organization of cultural events in the city's main concert venues and nightclubs, the establishment of the annual New Bled Festival (which has been held six times now) and, most recently, the opening of a new concert venue and North African restaurant – the French K-Wa. We can read the experience of the New Bled collective as one which is concerned with the *process* of constructing and consolidating a Parisian hub for what Mohand refers to as electro-world music. New Bled's creative project is anchored in an explicit acknowledgement of cultural and musical duality (multiplicity?) which characterizes young people of post-migrant French-North African origin. For Mohand, an acknowledgement of his own 'double culture' as he puts it was the starting point for the New Bled project:

> the reason for all these club nights, all these events, it ... stems from an attitude, from a conclusion about a number of facts, that is, I am of Algerian origin, the idea is that as an individual, I have a double culture which is inevitably Algerian and French, because I was practically born here, I came to France, I was four years old, and the idea is that as an artist, you can express this double culture, I express it as an individual on a daily basis in terms of my lifestyle, but as an artist, you have to express it, I was going to say through a music which is inevitably a little bit new, through a musical movement which integrates, I'd say, the influences of both sides of the Mediterranean. [13] (Kiwan's interview with Mohand Haddar, December 2003, Paris)

So the starting point for Mohand and his associates was to organize club nights known as 'les soirées du nouveau son maghrebin à Paris' ('new North African sounds in Paris nights'), 'les Grooves du Ramadan' ('Ramadan Grooves') or 'Oriental Grooves' at the Divan du monde and Cabaret Sauvage, targeting young people of North African origin and their own mixed musical tastes (rai, hip-hop, soul, electro). After a number of years organizing club nights, New Bled then moved into the production of records and the organization of an urban music festival known as the New Bled Festival which brings together musicians from the Maghreb with the French-North African 'made in France' scene. More recently, New Bled has also moved into artist management, and in 2008 Mohand Haddar opened an innovative venue called the French K-Wa which is at once a restaurant, bar and concert venue in the 20th *arrondissement*. Mohand refers to New Bled's activities as a 'musical movement' whose objective is to carve out a space for world-beat, electr'oriental and electroworld artists within the French music landscape. And on one level it is clear that the challenge has been met since Paris can now be regarded as being a key node in a transnational 'electroworld' network which is defined by the fact that it is neither world 'roots' music nor world 'pop' music (for example Faudel, Mami, Khaled ...). Other nodes include Barcelona, Istanbul and London.

Beyond the musical dimension of New Bled's activities, the visual aspect of the collective's work also merits some attention since, from the outset, New Bled has consistently worked with graphic designers and video artists in order to produce a complex visual identity for the label, whether this be in the form of flyers advertising their club nights, posters for the New Bled Festival or through the use of certain visuals during live DJ sets. The recurring theme of these visuals has to do with a humorous engagement with the history of North African immigration to France – humorous because the visuals play on a certain number of well-known images or clichés surrounding the Maghrebi immigration experience in France (the overloaded Peugeot 504 travelling back to the 'bled' for the holidays; the corner grocery shop run by the North African migrant; check-in desks at Charles de Gaulle airport) but they do not fall into the 'folklore'/exoticization/babouche trap. Rather, they point to a sort of post-migrant imaginary which is part and parcel of New Bled's translation of global processes (mass migration) into localized cultural forms, or what Appadurai refers to as when 'global facts take local form' (Appadurai 1996: 18) (Figures 3.1, 3.2).

The playfulness of New Bled's engagement with North African immigrant and post-migrant experience in France as expressed in the visual dimension of their project is not unique, of course, and we find similar motifs and tropes among other artists such as the Paris-based group Binobin. Binobin, which in Arabic literally means 'in-between', is a

Figure 3.1　New Bled club night flyer

Figure 3.2   New Bled club night flyer

group made up of seven musicians from North Africa and France, but at the core of the group are the two founding members – brothers Badr and Adlane Defouad. The brothers were born and brought up in Agadir in the south of Morocco and came to Paris as adults in order to study. Badr, the older of the two, came to Paris in order to undertake doctoral study in mathematics but, before that, moved from Agadir to Marrakesh and then to Rabat before making the leap to the French capital. The motivations underlying his internal, then international, migration were linked to his studies – he went to Marrakesh then Rabat and finally Paris to pursue his university education, but in parallel to that Badr studied the violin and guitar at the conservatoires of Agadir and Rabat. Once he was in Paris (he arrived in 1990) he played music with fellow students in several groups at Nanterre, Orsay and the École normale supérieure and it was only later that he decided to make a living out of music, by first playing with multiple groups and mainly Algerian artists (some of whom were part of the Louzine collective) and then in 2000 by founding Binobin with Adlane. Adlane also emigrated to Paris in 1990 and pursued undergraduate and postgraduate study in pharmacy, biochemistry and management. Like Badr, he also studied music in parallel, by attending a private music school in Paris. Despite playing with some of the Louzine musicians, Badr and Adlane explain that they were not formally part of this scene since their music is mainly acoustic as opposed to rock/amplified and also they focus on compositions rather than adapting and interpreting pre-existing repertoires which characterize some, but by no means all, of the musical projects which come under the Louzine umbrella. They are, however, part of the New Bled network (see above) and Mohand Haddar organizes bookings and concerts for them (non-exclusively).

Both brothers adopt an intellectualized approach to music and this is reflected in their attempts to document and classify a vast range of Moroccan 'traditional' music. They undertook this musicological research in the municipal and Sorbonne libraries in order to develop their knowledge of Moroccan music and to refine and advance their own musical project. This interest for Moroccan music developed once they were settled in France. Up until then they had been mainly interested in 'Western' pop music (such as the Beatles, Paul Simon and the Eurythmics) and rap, and Badr points out that they would not have been able to develop a credible expertise on Moroccan rhythms and instruments had they not been in Paris since the resources only became available to them once they had moved to the city (this is similar to Hocine Boukella's sense that he 'discovered' Algerian music in Paris – see above).

Similarly, Badr argues that the musical fusion which defines Binobin's mixture of gnawa, aïta (chaâbi) rhythms and instrumentation with pop, latino and jazz has been facilitated precisely because in Paris there are significant numbers of musicians who can play Moroccan music although they may not necessarily be of Moroccan origin themselves:

> that's also the advantage of Paris, it's that ... we can ... if we want to play music of Moroccan origin, we don't have to play with Moroccans only ... Because the others have also listened to stuff, so already they have ... there is openness. In that sense, Paris is a little bit the ideal for fusions. And as a result, we've had the oppor-tunity to play with French people of course, French-French already, Moroccans, Algerians, but also Reunionese musicians, so we were saying a moment ago, [...] Ivoirians, Senegalese, Polish ... so ... and each one brings his own sensitivity of course, I mean, in terms of interpretation. [14] (Badr Defouad – Kiwan's interview with Badr and Adlane Defouad, July 2008, Paris)

Binobin's understanding of fusion or *métissage* (they use both terms) is self-reflexive and complex. Badr and Adlane are keen to point out that it is not just a case of mixing influences, rhythms, instruments and languages in a superficial manner but rather the notion of fusion underpins the central dimension of the Binobin project because it reflects how they see their own subjective selves as 'world citizens' or 'citoyens du monde':

> I had in mind, this idea that fusion could be musically fluid ... and that it could create something else, it's not just collage, [...] I mean, when I say that, that is a new musical culture which is not sterile [...] it's, it provides a new departure point, as if we were talking about new musics, of a new world etc. which was neither somewhere nor rooted in one country or another and the idea that we have behind this is that we see in the end [...] like a lot of my friends at the time ... we feel more and more like citizens of the world. [15] (Badr Defouad – Kiwan's interview with Badr and Adlane Defouad, July 2008, Paris)

The expression 'citoyen du monde' ('citizen of the world') is frequently employed by both Badr and Adlane and it seems to point to the fact that they see themselves as part of a wider transnational or global imaginary, which is not diasporic in the nostalgic – long-distance nationalism – sense, but rather which embraces a cosmopolitan world-view. Such cosmopolitanism manifests itself in the brothers' use of *frarabe* in their songs, for instance. *Frarabe* is a mixture of French and Maghrebi Arabic and in actual fact many Moroccans speak a mixture of both these languages in addition to Berber (Amazigh) and Spanish.

Malagasy musicians in Paris

It is undeniable that Paris is a global hub for many Francophone African musicians and the discussion of the Louzine and New Bled networks and their associated human hubs reveals that the city functions as a cultural magnet for artists who are active outside the mainstream 'pop' scenes (for the Maghreb this scene would include mainly rai artists such as Khaled, Cheb Mami and Faudel). For Malagasy artists and cultural operators, Paris fulfils a similar cultural hub function. However, there are important differences between the Malagasy and the North African contexts.

To start with, Malagasy out-migration to France is much more recent than that for the Maghreb, with hardly any artists as yet belonging to a second generation, though there are a few notable exceptions such as Rachel Ratsizafy. Secondly, as was already discussed in Chapter 2, although successive political crises and repressive regimes in Madagascar created a cycle of instabilities with presidents being removed from office by the vote of the street, actual repression of artists, though existent in some ways, did not endanger their lives. Artists were neither imprisoned nor killed as a result of support for oppositional politicians or presidents forced into exile. What motivates the majority of Malagasy people to leave their country of origin then and now is the poverty, lack of infrastructure and scarcity of educational and professional opportunities at home. Most Malagasies in Europe today come or came as students or budding professionals and not as refugees, and musicians are no exception. Erick Manana, Edgar Ravahatra, HAJAMadagascar and many others came as students and stayed on. Others like Régis Gizavo or Mamiso (real name Yvon Mamisolofo) from the now dissolved group Senge who were already struggling artists in Madagascar came to escape a situation in Madagascar where a full-time career in music was not a feasible option, and managed the leap abroad often as a result of winning a competition or linking up with other already migrated artists during touring or festivals. Thirdly, for most artists the connection to their country of origin remains invariably strong. Connections are sustained either directly through return visits to home regions and families, through occasional concert engagements in Madagascar and through visits from Malagasy-based artists touring in France, or indirectly through the networking of the diaspora in France and worldwide. Although there are notable exceptions that we will return to later, most lyrics by Malagasy artists are created in the Malagasy language, expressing themes relating to Madagascar (Meinhof and Rasolofondraosolo 2005).

Fourthly, there is less evidence of specifically urban styles or 'experimental fusion' music as we have seen in the Louzine or New Bled networks, with more emphasis on acoustic, albeit amplified, instruments than on electric guitars or bass. Hip-hop or rap, while existing, is less significant than in the North African scene. Musical innovation is rarely bent towards the electronic but is more often seen in the bridging of intricate Malagasy rhythms with gospel, blues or jazz elements, with different world music and classical music styles. And finally, there is no spatial concentration of a large Malagasy diaspora in a particular part of Paris comparable to the Algerian- and Moroccan-dominated *arrondissements* and *banlieues*. Malagasies, and Malagasy artists, are spread across the city and its outskirts, with many connections held to individuals – friends, family members from and in Madagascar – and linking with individuals in other areas of France and other countries. Networking – if not neighbouring in the physical sense – is strong, with Paris and Parisian events for and by the diaspora with European-based or incoming Malagasy artists creating many opportunities for identity performances (see also Rasolofondraosolo and Meinhof 2003). It is these interconnections between the cultural capital of the artists, the social capital of the networks, and the resulting financial opportunities for artists to make their living and fully professionalize which underpin what we theorized as 'transcultural capital' – an opportunity, often strategic, of making use of all the resources that a Malagasy origin and artistic inspiration offer. However, many Malagasy artists in Paris are not exclusively defined by their diasporic connections but straddle different scenes at different times, or cross over from one to the other. The rewards of being able to strategically exploit both the diasporic/neo-communitarian and the cosmopolitan potential of the capital city are substantial, and both artists and artist promoters are fully aware of these opportunities.

A young Malagasy-born music promoter and entrepreneur, Lova Ramisamanana, is a primary example of someone who is keenly aware of the necessity of keeping the support of the diaspora while branching out to the Parisian, French and international music scenes but he is also conscious of the nostalgia of the diaspora which makes them prefer the stars from home to those who have left and developed in the new *métissage* of Paris. Lova developed in the past decade from a DJ and small-scale tour organizer for the Malagasy diaspora and their artists to a major promoter with his own communication, marketing and event-promotion business, Kanto, a name which according to their website means 'perfection' in the Malagasy language:

> One meaning of the Malagasy word 'Kanto' is perfection, an essential quality that we wish to develop for all our activities. The company consists of a creative, dynamic and rigorous team, enabling it to perform in marketing and event communication. [16] (www.kanto.fr/, accessed 25 April 2010)

We charted Lova's trajectory in a series of interviews with him in the wake of his increasingly diversifying concert ventures – starting with the neo-communitarian locations in Tana Orly and the Espace Chevreuil in Nanterre, and gradually moving to more mixed settings, with the centrally located jazz and world music venue New Morning up to the internationally renowned concert halls of La Cigale and especially the Olympia in Paris. Extracts from three interviews – 2003, 2006 and 2009 – give an interesting insight into these processes of mixing the diasporic with the global *imaginaire*.

In 2003, he told us how he arrived at the age of ten in Paris, went to business school, and in 1999 set up an association called 'Nouvelles Générations Malgaches' with the aim of promoting Malagasy culture and supporting schools in Madagascar. Gaining his first experience with concerts and exhibitions by and for the Malagasy community in Tana Orly and Nanterre, but also in organizing tours across the different Malagasy associations in provincial cities in France and in Switzerland, he set up Kanto in 2003 as a professional concert-promotion agency, aiming to create a broader more mixed public for Malagasy music:

> Talking about the New Morning, where I organized concerts, I always try to sell tickets in Fnac [Parisian music chain stores] and concerts are listed in Parisian newspapers such as *Nova Magazine*. In fact I always try to open up but the community is necessary as a basis to make the shows viable, especially in financial terms. So we also promote the concerts on Croissance and Sobiky,[7] but also via mailings ... Sobiky. com is quite open, younger, it's really interesting. [17] (Kiwan's interview, April 2003, Paris)

At the same time, he acknowledges in 2003 that some of the more cosmopolitan Malagasy artists resident in France such as Régis Gizavo or Edgar Ravahatra, or at the time even Justin Vali, who play at international or national festivals rather than for Malagasy community events, are far less well known to the diaspora than the artists from back home, such as Dama and Mahaleo, Rajery or Jaojaoby, so that the Malagasy diaspora too cannot be taken for granted as supporters of lesser-known artists in France.

> The concept behind what I'm doing is to try and share something [...] I'm not saying that I will organize a concert specifically for the community. In fact I'm doing it because I love the artist. But there is always a worry about how popular they are and I don't want that. I already organized one or two concerts where I loved the artists, like the concert with Edgar Ravahatra that no one knew so there were between 5 or 60 people in the New Morning, while Erick Manana attracts more like 500–600 people. But what prompts me is my love for the music, the love for the artist, it's about love, love. [18] (Kiwan's interview, April 2003, Paris)

Since 2003, Lova's concert productions have managed to move out from the purely communitarian settings to a gradually more mixed public by introducing the big stars of Malagasy music to major international concert venues, such as the first ever Malagasy concert in the Parisian Olympia in 2007 by Mahaleo, followed in 2009 by Erick Manana and Jaojaoby also in the Olympia, and by Mahaleo and Lolo sy ny Tariny in La Cigale.[8] Crossing over from the communitarian to mainstream venues is however a gradual and complicated process, and mainly restricted to already established famous artists rather than opening a window of opportunity for new arrivals or lesser-known musicians

Ulrike: I'd like you to tell me what has happened since the Mahaleo concert in the Olympia. How did you carry on ...

Lova: Working?

Ulrike: Making all these connections?

Lova: In fact, Mahaleo was the starting point as I told you during our last interview. We were already working with the diaspora, in small venues in the suburbs but then we wanted to work in bigger venues to promote the music properly and as I said, Mahaleo was the real starting point. And ever since then we carried on, a year ago in La Cigale with Lolo then in September we got Jaojaoby to play here in the Olympia. So now, two years later, we're coming back with Mahaleo to La Cigale. So for about two and a half years we've been running four concerts in the Olympia, because we're also coming here in November with Erick Manana. We did four concerts in the Olympia and two in La Cigale. So we're really working, you can't believe it! And it's starting to take off. We haven't yet reached our absolute goals – we've given ourselves five years for that. We're halfway there. We're halfway and at the minute, I think we're in a good position to get what we want! ...

In terms of promotion we've created a network pretty much everywhere where there's a diaspora link, that's sorted. And we started having partners such as RFI, France Outre-Mer, France Inter so we're getting some more international links. But that is, well it is a long-term ambition. We have a five-year plan and we're now halfway there ... We're also getting asked to produce artists but unfortunately we're not well equipped yet to launch new artists.

So at the minute, we're staying with Jaojaoby, with bands, people whose success is assured, so we know we will fill up the venues, whether it is the Olympia or La Cigale.

In the New Morning, we can still take some risks; do some things that are slightly more conceptual, like listening to Lolo who is really a composer and songwriter, but people still come and tell us about upcoming artists and ask: 'Could you do something for them? ...' But at the minute we always say no, we just can't launch someone just like that in La Cigale, expecially knowing that today we still have a big, well 70 per cent of the audience comes from the diaspora. So that's 30 per cent of foreigners who're not from the diaspora. The diaspora still makes up 70 per cent. But we're working on it, because we know that ... Well, Mahaleo won't always be here. So it is a turning point for us in the two, two and a half years to come. We'll be looking for new artists, Malagasy bands that are slightly less famous but with whom we will still try to fill up La Cigale, with people like Ricky for example, that generation, and maybe the Madagascar All Stars as well. We'll be working on this for the next two and a half, three years, to find other artists besides Mahaleo, Lolo sy ny Tariny and Jaojaoby. [19] (Meinhof's and Gibert's interview, June 2009, Paris)

However, Lova not only promotes Malagasy artists in Paris and other venues in France, but he also organizes one concert per year in Madagascar itself. Thus he works from the opposite direction of Media Consulting (see Chapter 1), which, from its base in Tana, exports artists from Tana to France but in an equally entrepreneurial spirit. Although Lova is not averse to using the communication channels of the foreign cultural institutions that we identified in Tana, such as the CGM, the Alliance française and the Centre culturel Albert Camus (CCAC),[9] so far his events remain largely independent from these more established support structures. Instead Kanto Productions engages for the required period with a local private production team to set up the concerts.

Lova: We're doing one big concert in Madagascar each year. So the year is completely full.
Ulrike: You also do a concert in Madagascar?
Lova: Yeah, last year it was Yannick Noah, we did that in April. And this year ...
Ulrike: Where in Madagascar did you do that?
Lova: Just in Tana, we organized one concert in the Palais des Sports. And normally we should have Francis Cabrel on the

30th October, but with the recent events, it's still on stand-by. At the same time, we do a big event there and it really fills us up.

Ulrike: That's really interesting. How do you organize that? Do you have someone?

Lova: I have a team.

Ulrike: You have a team there? But it's not Media Consulting?

Lova: No, no, it's Kitana Production.

Ulrike: So you're competing with them. Is your team working especially for you?

Lova: They are, but not all year long. For example, we worked more or less three months for Noah ... I have four core people but then it can go up to 50 people when the event is getting closer. But I have a team there with whom I'm working. [20] (Meinhof's and Gibert's interview, June 2009, Paris)

Beyond the Malagasy diaspora

Not all Malagasy artists in Paris are embedded in and nurtured by the diaspora. Internationally renowned artists such as Régis Gizavo or Justin Vali[10] have from the beginning used Paris as a hub for their activities across the national and international festival scene, and for links with incoming international artists from Madagascar as well as from other parts of the world. We have already introduced Régis Gizavo in Chapter 1 when we followed his progress from Toliara via Tana to Europe. This is how he described to us his eventual settling down in Paris itself after having won the RFI prize in 1990:

Régis: When I arrived in France, it was for the award ceremony of this particular contest, so I went to Guinea-Conakry with everyone from RFI, and journalists filling nearly half of the plane, and it was the same even in Madagascar when we had the RFI award ceremony. I think that you've seen the cars in Tana, Mafy, RFI and so on. Well it was the same. So this was a real opportunity because it's not always that one ... can travel with journalists, and have some critics from the press ... It was a pretty serious affair. So I arrived there and I was accompanied by a Guinean group. That was the start, because at every RFI event, they always invite the African stars. So there were Ray Lema, Manu Dibango and some others.

And these guys there, ... most of them live here in Paris. And they're usually accompanied by French musicians, the core of the Parisian scene. And there was this guy whose name was Francis Lassus and he saw me play and that's how it started. It was love at first sight for him. He was walking outside my room and heard me play and then he said: 'Yes! You're the one I want. I must invite you to Paris, I'll find you a place to stay.' And so it all started.

So I went back to Madagascar afterward and left again for the 'Francopholies' in La Rochelle, together with a band of Malagasy musicians, only Malagasies. They returned home but I stayed because the guy insisted I should go to his place ...

Ulrike: Francis Lassus?

Régis: Francis Lassus. And he put me up at his place. He did everything so I could ...

Dama: Stay?

Régis: Yes, stay, voilà. Then we formed a band called 'Bohe Combo'.

Dama: How?

Régis: Bohe Combo ... It had a Parisian sound, because there was Charles Bonnard from Cameroon, a guitarist called Pascal Danaé from the Antilles and Jean-Michel Pile, a French Jew, and also Salut Lolo, the singer who has her own group now ... And me, Francis Lassus and David Mirandon who accompanies me these days. [21] (Meinhof's and Rasolofondraosolo's interview, December 2005, Paris)

From the very start of his arriving in France, Régis struggled to be part of the international world music scene, and the harshness of his initial years is registered in one of his best-known songs, 'Mafy', which means 'hard', and which tells the story of his first attempts to come to terms with a cold and 'rice-less' Paris (for an essay focusing on Régis's lyrics see also Meinhof and Rasolofondraosolo 2005). However, engaging with musicians as diverse as Manu Dibango, Ray Lema and Les Têtes Brûlées, the Cape Verdean star Cesaria Evora and the Corsican group I Muvrini, to give just some examples, but also serving as a contact point for touring Malagasy artists such as D'Gary and Rajery, Régis's career is a prime example of an artist who has made good use of the urban networking potential of the French capital. From his home in Paris he departs on tours worldwide, including festivals such as the renowned world music festival WOMAD in the UK. Having started his musical career with the best newcomer prize of RFI in 1990, his recent solo album *Stories*, recorded with Louis Mhlanga and percussionist David Mirandon, received the Spin the Globe award from the Washington State independent college-community radio FM in 2006. And yet in spite of his international world music appeal Régis dreams of crossing over to the very scene which other Malagasy artists are trying to expand from, namely that of the Malagasy diaspora.

Régis: The difference between the Mahaleo band and the others is ... Well Lolo as well ... He was really famous ... they're different, because Malagasies are really attached to their past and these bands were there, that's it. While when I sing my songs, it is something really different. And on top of this they need to understand me ... People who see Erick when he plays, they're singing along, because these are lyrics that people really understand. While with me, people struggle, except with two or three songs that they manage to understand. It is because I only played for one year in Madagascar and then I came here directly ... I played there but I was not really famous there, I was on the telly a bit, that's all. But I focus on my own music and all of these new things, very new ... While Malagasies are attached to music, that's really nostalgic, voilà, that's how it is. With my music, well you can dance to it, but at the same time people are trying to find themselves in the music, they want to listen to the accordion, they want to sing ... And it takes time ... That's why I said earlier that I wanted to go towards the Malagasy community and I want to play ... even for Malagasy community events in order to try to ...

Ulrike: A-ha, a-ha ...

Régis: Just to play for them, really. [22] (Meinhof's and Rasolofondraosolo's interview, December 2005, Paris)

Régis's appeal to the diaspora has recently improved with the formation of a new group, the Madagascar All Stars, which comprises, apart from him, Justin Vali and Marius Fontaine (Fenoamby), who both live in the Parisian area, Erick Manana from Bordeaux and Dama (Mahaleo) from Antananarivo, with fellow Antananarivan Ricky Olombelo as regular guest. Their appeal ranges across purely diasporic events such as the 2009 RNS in Nantes[11] as well as international events such as in the UK the Brighton Festival (2005) and the African Festival in London (2006), and in Germany the Traumzeit Festival (Duisburg 2006) and the folk and world music festival in Rudolstadt (2008), to name but a few. Following an initiative by Josielle, director of the Parisian branch of the French–Malagasy travel agency Jacaranda, the emergence of that group is another instance of the way in which Paris focalizes translocal and transnational movements. We will return to them in the next chapter where we specifically focus on multi-sited, transnational ventures.

Paris thus creates opportunities for meetings between artists and different musical styles from all over the world which enhances for many Malagasy musicians the already substantial musical diversity of their Malagasy roots. We have just referred to the wide range of different music covered by Régis and there are many other examples of artists that one could introduce here who blend their Malagasy roots with new musical influences encountered in Paris. Paris-based guitarist and music teacher Mira Carson, a musician originating from the Androy region in Madagascar, for example, lists classical Western music set for guitar, including Bach, Berlioz and Villa-Lobos, among his musical influences, whereas French-born Rachel Ratsizafy, having evolved as a gospel and jazz singer, ironically re-encountered her Malagasy roots via a Spanish guitarist, Olivier-Roman Garcia, who had developed a passion for Malagasy rhythms and harmonies:

> Rachel: I came to Paris to do jazz among other things. And so I've been part of a jazz band – Jazzpel – for three, or even four years … I arrived in Paris two years ago. Two years. I was following this jazz band and we were touring here and there in Paris. And then Mr Olivier-Roman Garcia appeared. [23] (Meinhof's and Gibert's interview, June 2007, Paris)

Olivier himself describes his introduction to Malagasy music as follows:

> It so happened that I'd been working for quite some time in the Indian Ocean region, especially in Madagascar and La Réunion. So I met Leila Negro, a singer from La Réunion who also organizes tours around the Indian Ocean. And one day this proposal came up that I should go on tour and accompany a Malagasy singer who is called Tiana and is really well known there … So I said yes without really knowing Malagasy music, but when I received the CD, I had such a shock, like a cold shower. Because there is an entire culture behind it, a culture of guitar playing that is extremely strong. I'm Spanish

and I know what I'm talking about from the guitar culture in Spain. But I did not know this country where the guitar culture was equally strong. There is a specific way of playing, harmonies, special types of tuning and so on. So I said yes but when I got the CD, well I had to work hard ... I don't know, it took me something like two or three months to manage [laughing]. I called all the Malagasy pals I knew. Voilà, so it went. And from then on, I became passionate about the country and all, and then I went on tour. And once I arrived back in Paris I called Rachel to see whether she would like us to work together and that's how this album was born. [24] (Meinhof's and Gibert's interview, June 2007, Paris)

Their album, entitled *Natural Born Stranger*, and released in January 2008, draws on gospel and jazz influences but for the first time in Rachel's musical career comprises songs that mix the Malagasy language with English and French. It also includes one song with a valiha accompaniment by Justin Vali, who had just met up with both in a Parisian studio two weeks before we met them for our first interview.

Our last example for illustrating the musical crossroad that Paris represents is a young female singer, Seheno, who heads a transnational band of that name. She developed her distinctive musical style in collaboration with an Indian percussionist, Prabhu Edouard. Having grown up in a family in Madagascar that was already well known on the musical scene of Antananarivo as the group Ny Railovy, Seheno specifically chose Paris as her new home to build on the 'métissage' which she already recognizes within the Malagasy music itself:

And then I left to come here. Because I had connections and friends here, who were in the music industry, and who told me that I should come, that it would be great ... And gradually I met other musicians as well – after all Paris is a crossroad where one can meet a lot of musicians with many different nationalities, so I met Brazilians, I played Brazilian percussions, then I met Indians, so I did some Indian music as well and it went on like that in France. [25] (Meinhof's and Rasolofondraosolo's interview, April 2009, Paris)

Apart from her Indian percussionist, Seheno's group also comprises two French artists, the Malagasy artist Mamiso from Lyon, whom we've already encountered in Chapter 1, and an Indian-German musician from Cologne. Among the Malagasy musicians we encountered, her musical style is arguably the most experimental, though she, too, insists on her Malagasy roots and on her need to sing in the Malagasy language:

> This experimentation is what interests me. In fact, it's always about going to the roots and then again, nowadays I'm living in a world that is urban I would say. And even if I'm inspired by the land, I'm also living in the city so I'm trying to get the best out of both to do something personal. I don't pretend that I represent *the* Malagasy music or *the* Malagasy spirit but, on the other hand, I represent one contemporary side of Malagasy music, contemporary in the sense of current, in the world of today. Even if my roots are from Madagascar. [26] (Meinhof's and Rasolofondraosolo's interview, April 2009, Paris)

As we have seen, Paris is a major hub for artists, allowing them to professionalize, record and perform, link up with different kinds of artists, be they from the same country, albeit different regions and backgrounds, or other parts of the world. Paris is also a major hub for artists who do not live there but who use its facilities. This phenomenon is one of the factors we will discuss in the next chapter, to show additional facets of the migration story: one where Paris is a hub for migrant artists who live in the provinces or other smaller towns and cities in France, or who join up with artists from other countries altogether, and secondly a situation where Paris is bypassed altogether. However, our research project also set out to trace and understand the ways in which such North–South relationships are diversified and diversifying. For example, there are a significant number of Algerian musicians in London and there are key music scenes which revolve around Moroccan-origin musicians in Amsterdam as well. It is to these other global hubs that we now turn our attention.

London

The UK is of course not historically linked to Francophone North Africa or Madagascar in the same way as France so the presence of North Africans and Malagasies in London is not part of a broader post-colonial dynamic. However, a significant number of Algerians settled in the city from the 1990s onwards, the majority of them fleeing the violence that besieged the country during that decade; indeed many Algerians left and settled all over the world throughout that period. Before the 1990s, the Algerian population stood at around 3000 and today it numbers

30,000 (Collyer 2004). Moroccans have been present in the UK since the nineteenth century but the majority of Moroccans in Britain today arrived as students or migrant workers after the Second World War (see Moroccan Memories project, www.moroccanmemories.org.uk, Cherti 2007 and Meinhof and Armbruster 2008). Much has been written about London's 'world openness' (see, for example, Aksoy 2006), the highly diverse and fluid nature of its population, and the resulting cultural dynamism of the city. However, most studies about migrant and post-migrant social and cultural networks have, for obvious historical reasons, focused on South-East Asian and Caribbean experiences. So much less is known about the trajectories of North Africans in London in general and even less is known about the lives of North African musicians in particular. The next section will therefore sketch out some key features of significant North African musicians in London. Our research on the North African music scene there reinforces our broader understanding of networks as being the outcome of overlaps between what we have called human and spatial hubs (see the Introduction and Gibert 2008b).[12]

A key figure in the London scene is Seddik Zebiri, an Algerian musician (singer and drummer/percussionist) who came to London in 1975 with his British wife, after having spent ten years in Paris. Seddik became interested in making a living from music after arriving in the UK (congas, djembe, derbouka, then later the oud). He started out by playing and accompanying groups in cafés and then formed his own fusion-reggae-latino band, Seeds of Creation, which, following a trip to Egypt in 1992, adopted a more North African-orientated repertoire. The human hub metaphor is useful in Seddik's case because in the 1990s he initiated a weekly 'international jam session' at the Samuel Pepys pub in Hackney which lasted for eight years.[13] Many North African musicians who now play together in various groups (Fantazia, El-Andaluz and MoMo being three examples) met at these jam sessions. This human hub which gravitated around Seddik was also reinforced by the wider spatial context because Hackney is an affordable neighbourhood where many musicians from all over the world happen to live and socialize.

Two of the groups which emerged out of the Samuel Pepys jam sessions are Fantazia and El-Andaluz. In the early stages, Fantazia was jointly launched in the late 1990s by Yazid Fentazi and Karim Dellali, soon after joined by Hamid Bouri. Later, Rachel Bartlett, Frank Biddulph, Sean Randle, Fawzi, Andy Mellon and Najma joined the group. In the early days, the group's original repertoire (mainly composed by Yazid) was 'Arab-jazz'-oriented and more recently it has been described as

'21st century roots music from Algeria, via Hackney, East London' (www.my space.com/fantaziahackney, accessed 16 December 2009) and it is built around gnawa, chaâbi and dance rhythms. The band's eight musicians come from Algeria and the UK. Born in Algeria in the 1960s, Yazid was a professional musician in Algiers, accompanying well-known musicians such as Cheb Mami, Chaba Fadela, Cheb Sahraoui and Fateh Ben Lala (the Orchestre national de Barbès) and touring with the Turqui Brothers in Morocco, Russia and Europe. Then, because of the political violence in Algeria, he left in 1992 to work as a musician, playing pop music covers in the tourist-related scene in Agadir, Morocco. In 1994, Yazid travelled to London as a tourist, accompanying a North African musician friend who had met a British woman. Yazid has lived and worked in the city ever since. In musical terms, Yazid's move from North Africa to the UK marked a shift from an essentially pop-rock (guitar) repertoire to a growing interest in North African instruments and rhythms (oud). The group Fantazia started out in 1994 as a duo involving Yazid and fellow Algerian and derbouka player Karim Dellali. It has toured extensively in the UK and Europe, mainly on the 'world music' and jazz festival circuit. Karim, who in 1987 arrived in London in his early twenties to study computer engineering and escape the political upheavals in Algeria, played with Yazid in Seddik's international jam sessions at the Samuel Pepys pub in Hackney. Then the duo started working with another Algerian – Hamid Bouri – whom they met in a music shop, before bringing in saxophonist Rachel Bartlett and Duncan Noble as manager. Like Karim, Rachel and Duncan were involved in the the weekly jam sessions organized by Seddik Zebiri. So Fantazia can be seen as an example of the ways in which London (and more specifically, the diverse borough of Hackney) can serve as a space for encounter and creative experimentation. Although the group draws heavily on North African influences, it acknowledges the fact that it is firmly embedded in the broader live music scene of East London and four out of the current line-up of eight musicians are non-Arab. Some of the Fantazia musicians are also involved in a smaller group, El-Andaluz, which includes Yazid Fentazi, Frank Biddulph, Karim Dellali and Hamid Bouri. As its name suggests, the El-Andaluz project is more closely related to classical Arab-Andalous music, taking the nouba repertoire as its starting point, but more broadly drawing on music from around the Mediterranean.[14]

Another group which emerged one way or another thanks to the Samuel Pepys jam sessions is MoMo (Music of Moroccan Origin), which is a musical trio involving three Moroccan musicians, Farid Nainia, Lahcen Lahbibi and Tahar El Edrissi. The group mixes electronic sampling and Western percussion with Moroccan rhythms such as gnawa, a mixture which is reflected in how the group refer to their own music – DAR – digital and roots.

So, whereas in Paris the Louzine network was instrumental in forming new creative synergies and bands among the North African musical diaspora during the 1990s, in London it appears that one key factor which facilitated the formation of a number of groups and networks can be located in the Samuel Pepys jam sessions in Hackney, orchestrated by Seddik Zebiri. The location, that is, north-east London with its mix of nationalities, was also a major factor in the formation of such networks and groups.[15]

There is no equivalence to this lively scene for Malagasy music. The UK population of Malagasies is very small and there are hardly any permanently resident artists among them. One exception of an artist who has gained some renown in both the tiny Malagasy diaspora and their associations in the UK, as well as on the club scene of London and some international festivals, including WOMAD, is Hughes Modeste. Originally from the Betroka region in the south-east of Madagascar, Hughes settled in London with his Greek wife after their encounter as fellow students in Bulgaria. A virtuoso guitarist with his own compositions of songs in Malagasy and Greek, he usually performs in a trio with an occasional fourth player. The trio typically reflects the diversity of the London scene – the percussionist and singer is of Zimbabwean origin and the bass player is of Brazilian origin. They met up in the now defunct Kashmir Club in London.[16] Hughes is a welcome support for the tiny London-based Malagasy music scene, especially since the return to Antananarivo of Hanitra, the best-known formerly London-based musician from Madagascar; at the time of meeting her, Hanitra was married to influential *fRoots* magazine editor Ian Anderson.[17] Hanitra's first group was set up in 1983 by Antananarivan Samoela Andriamalalaharijaona (Sammy) and gained international recognition as Tarika Sammy in the early 1990s, while she herself was still resident in London, though fellow group members Sammy, Noro and Solo never left Madagascar. Their music was frequently heard on the world music programmes of the BBC, such as the now discontinued influential Andy Kershaw programme on BBC1 and later BBC3, and they released several albums and toured worldwide to critical acclaim. In 1993 the group split and Hanitra and her sister Noro together with Donné, Ny Ony and Solo reformed under the name of Tarika, releasing further well-received albums and again gaining international recognition. According to the website of her Cultural Centre Antshow, Hanitra has now released a new album with a different group of musicians under the name of Tarikabe.

Another Malagasy musician, Fassio, originally from Fort Dauphin, stayed in London for a few years with his Italian wife who studied there, but left again when her work took her away to sub-Saharan Africa. In the absence of a highly developed world music interest in the hugely diversified musics from Madagascar and a corresponding lack of media presence for their work, especially in the UK's radio and television broadcasting, the possibility to work as a Malagasy artist in other cosmopolitan centres in Europe outside Paris is thus heavily restricted, and far less pronounced than for the much larger North African scene. Hence examples of known Malagasy musicians working from other capital cities in Europe are very rare. One of the more established groups consisting of two brothers, two sisters and a cousin, all Malagasy, is the group Njava who work from their home in Brussels; and in Berlin Malagasy-born Mfa Kera fronts a gospel and jazz group called Black Heritage. Having been absent from her country of birth and her Malagasy mother since the age of six she never relinquished her spiritual connection with Madagascar, and in 2007 joined the TNMundi concert in Antananarivo, re-establishing links especially in collaboration with Ricky Olombelo and Dama from Mahaleo. From his base in Vienna as well as Marseille, HAJAMadagascar with his group the Groovy People performs in various settings across Europe, while also occasionally collaborating with August Schmidhofer (Schmidhofer 1994), a renowned professor of ethnomusicology at the University of Vienna who is an expert on Malagasy music (HAJAMadagascar and Schmidhofer 2003), and who compiles a website with invaluable information links to Malagasy music (www.avmm.org/links). We will revisit HAJAMadagascar in the next chapter when we explore the mobile lives of multi-sited artists.

Amsterdam

Our research on urban music scenes in Morocco led us to follow up networks which took us to the Netherlands (Amsterdam and Boxtel), and while it cannot be argued that these sites rival the hub status of cities like Paris and London, what they do show us is that there are a number of significant cultural flows linking Morocco to Europe outside the habitual Francophone pathway. Such cultural flows are of course part of a wider context of cultural globalization but are also rooted in the recent history of Moroccan labour migration to the Netherlands, dating back to the 1970s (Gazzah 2008). We will consider two Dutch case studies here because they seem to represent two opposite ends of the post-migrant music scene.

The first case study concerns the group Kasba – whose members are from Morocco and the Netherlands. The Moroccan members are first-generation migrants and are based in Amsterdam, Boxtel and Utrecht. Kasba may be compared to groups such as the Orchestre national de Barbès in Paris or Fantazia in London in the sense that they position themselves as a 'multicultural' group which mixes Moroccan (North African) rhythms and Western music in a strongly festive repertoire which is pitched largely but not exclusively at an ethnically mixed audience. As such, the group were invited to play at the wedding of the Dutch royal family in 2002, to open the exhibition '400 years Morocco – the Netherlands', in the presence of Prince Willem-Alexander of the Netherlands and Prince Moulay Rachid of Morocco, and to participate in a special concert following the murder of film-maker and screenwriter Theo van Gogh. In 2005 Kasba recorded the leader song for the Dutch Liberation Day that was written by Thé Lau (see www.myspace.com/kasbamusic, accessed 18 December 2009). In short, Kasba seem to play the role of the 'good immigrants' in a broader Dutch context which has become increasingly hostile to Moroccan and Muslim-origin groups. This 'ambassadorial' aspect of their work may also have something to do with the fact that they have been invited to perform in government-sponsored festivals in Morocco such as the Rawafid and Rabat Festivals and have attracted the attention of Moroccan state television channel 2M.[18]

The second Dutch case study concerns the Amsterdam-based rapper Salah Edin. Salah Edin was born in the Netherlands to Moroccan parents who had emigrated from Tangier in the north of Morocco. Whereas Kasba incarnate the friendly face of the Netherlands' diversity, Salah Edin deliberately develops a provocative image which plays on fears and stereotypes held about young second-generation Muslims in the Netherlands (and Europe today). It is for this reason that Salah Edin's Dutch album entitled *Holland's Worst Nightmare* featured a cover photo-graph of the rapper resembling Mohammed B., the murderer of Theo van Gogh. His second album, *Horr* (Pure), is entirely in Arabic and reflects Salah Edin's wider ambitions vis-à-vis the Arab world. Like Kasba, Salah Edin maintains professional links with Morocco, collaborating with Marrakesh-based hip-hop group Fnaire and working with his manager Cilvaringz, a fellow Dutch-Moroccan rapper who is based there after returning from the Netherlands. Salah Edin's networks also link him to the USA (he has worked with Focus and the Wu-Tang Clan) and to other parts of the Arab world (Lebanon, Palestine). While Salah Edin's network appears to be more genuinely transnational and multi-directional than Kasba's, what links both acts is the fact that their networks do not involve France in any major way. And yet, both acts are well known in their countries of 'origin' and indeed Salah Edin was something of a reference for some of the hip-hop groups in Morocco that we interviewed.[19]

So by tracing some of the networks of musicians in Morocco itself, we are not necessarily led back to France. The cultural flows and connections which link North Africa and, in this case, Morocco to Europe are complex and multiple and while, clearly, established hubs like Paris remain central to understanding these flows, our research shows that if one starts off in Paris simply because it is a key diasporic centre for North Africans, and moves back out to the country(ies) of origin rather than starting in the country(ies) of origin and going outwards, one may miss some vitally important dimensions of North African musicians' transnational networks.

4
Beyond the Capitals: Translocality/Transnationality in Europe and the South

This chapter goes one step further than the previous one in showing the ways in which artists' networks across Europe and the 'South' are often inscribed in multiple locations beyond the highly visible concentration of diasporic musicians in capital cities such as Paris or London (see Chapter 3). Here, then, we explore two issues: firstly, the phenomenon of multi-sited individuals and groups who are simultaneously located in a capital and provincial towns and cities across Europe or countries of origin, and secondly, the resettlement of diasporic artists and cultural producers in their countries of origin. Both of these trends are inter-related in that they both highlight the spatial complexity of diasporic and transnational ties. Migrant and post-migrant musicians are not only located in 'minority ethnic neighbourhoods' of Europe's capital cities but rather live and are part of networks which straddle two or more locales. So the fractal metaphor used by Arjun Appadurai (1996) in his reflections on cultural globalization as 'cultural chaos' resonate with the trajectories of these multi-sited artists who are part of a fairly complicated network of cultural flows and translocal or transnational ties.

Translocality and multi-sitedness

Robert J. Holton (2008) sees global networks as sets of linkages between individuals which enable 'multi-centered forms of social inter-connection' (Holton 2008: 1). It is the multi-centredness of diasporic/ migrant musicians and cultural producers which concerns us in this chapter. Indeed, the fact that many of the artists and cultural producers we have worked with are active in a number of locations which go beyond the more obvious metropolitan cities, underlines the need to acknowledge what Holton calls 'multi-scalar complexity' (Holton 2008: 45), when referring to the intertwined nature of the local, regional, national and transnational dimensions of globalization. By explicitly engaging with such spatial complexities associated with globalization, one avoids the pitfalls of overstating cultural de-territorialization and simplistic global versus local dualisms (see Hopper 2007: 47). In other words by empirically describing the finer details of multi-scalar complexity, one escapes the temptation of seeing post-modern free-floating cultures at every turn. This way one can more easily adopt an approach which focuses on how the local and the global are closely linked rather than being in opposition to one another. It is for this reason that our work also closely resonates with that of Roland Robertson's on glocalization (1992, 1995 and cited in Holton 2008). Like Robertson, we also take issue with Manuel Castells's notion that there exists a polarization between an elite sphere or space of globalized flows (of information, people, objects, symbols) and a space of place which is non-elite: an ordinary grounded space of place or localism (Castells 1996). A glocal lens, or rather as we prefer to call it a translocal and transnational lens, is useful for our purposes since it allows us to move away from both methodological nationalism (Beck 2000; Wimmer and Glick Schiller 2002), which overstates a priori the ethnic clustering of migrants, and methodological globalism, which overstates global social processes. Instead we focus on the micro processes of cultural globalization, whereby migrant and diasporic musicians and cultural producers are active in complex networks, linking them to multiple locations that include both capital cities and provincial towns. As such, we are using what Holton (2005, 2008) has called 'methodological glocalism' as a conceptual frame for this chapter. In short, methodological glocalism acknowledges that 'the global and the national are co-present, and intersect and interact in a range of ways' (Holton 2008: 46). Where our work differs from that of Holton is in his view of globalization as a polarizing process which will lead either to 'greater cultural conflict or greater cosmopolitanism' (Holton 2008: 166). In our view, such a reading of globalization is rather too macro in character, which may explain the binary nature of his prediction. However, Holton is not alone in his analysis. Indeed, much of the main thrust of scholarly writing on globalization and culture takes as its frame the notion of cultural conflict and/or intercultural engagement (cosmopolitanism). Castells, for instance, argues that exclusion from the cosmopolitan space of flows would explain the rise of the conflict-ridden politics of identity (cited in Holton 2008: 20). Such dialectical analysis is not the main purpose of our work, nor do we share such deterministic predictions. Rather, what underpins our own research is a concern for the micro processes of globalization as expressed through transnational ties and circuits of musicians and cultural operators. We wish to move away from a conflict versus cosmopolitanism dualism towards a more fluid and nuanced approach to the question of cultural globalization. Artists' translocal and transnational networks and the ways in which they are made visible through life stories and everyday life engagements are prime examples of this fluidity.[1] As we shall see below, artists' networks are both spatially and symbolically complex. That is, they are spread across multiple locations, including capital and metropolitan cities, as well as provincial towns and regions in Europe and Africa. They all reflect complex identity patterns and affiliations. In this sense Castells's separation of the space of flows from identity politics appears problematic since our research reveals that migrants and diasporic individuals are engaged in a space of flows while simultaneously articulating diasporic and transnational identities.

We now turn to our case studies. We will first consider some significant examples of multi-sited individuals and groups in Europe and between Europe and country of origin, as well as those individuals who straddle both 'home and away'. This will lead us to the final section of this chapter where we will consider those artists and cultural producers who have returned 'home' after a length of time spent in Europe.

In the previous chapter we have already given some examples of groups, such as Seheno's, who have a translocal as well as a transnational dimension but whose main centre of activity is Paris. Here we want to introduce translocal and transnational groups and individuals whose centre of activity is outside Paris altogether or only includes Paris among other affiliations.

Translocality in France

An excellent example of an artist who is based outside Paris, and only uses the capital city for connections with other artists and performances, is the Malagasy singer-songwriter Edgar Ravahatra. Having arrived in France in 1975, he studied and then taught law in Saint-Étienne and Lyon without ever thinking of turning his hobby – playing guitar and singing – into a professional career. Having become disaffected from teaching law he decided to move to Paris to make his way as a musician, but Paris overwhelmed him – he told us he did nothing except listen to everyone else's music – and so he left and returned to Saint-Étienne. There in 1986–87 he formed his first group, Topaka, with his two sisters and other musicians from the Antilles, from France and from Italy.

Ulrike: What does Topaka mean?
Edgar: Topaka? Well, 'topa' is ... the water's babbling.
Ulrike: Ahhh, that's it.
Edgar: Topa, topa ... And 'ka' is the noise of the Indian percussion ... The flat hand on the instrument is the ka. And
since the Malagasies are a bit Indo-European I mixed the
two – topa-ka. [1] (Meinhof's interview, November 2007,
during the TNMundi concert in Tana)

From that moment on he composed his own songs, mixing from the
very start French with Malagasy lyrics often within the same songs.
Musically, his compositions also draw on many genres – rock, pop
and jazz, classical music and the French chanson tradition, especially
François Béranger and Georges Brassens. Hence in his repertoire we find
side by side his own compositions next to Franco-Malagasy adaptations
of songs such as Brassens's famous 'Le parapluie' and – pace the Sex
Pistols and their mischievous version of 'God Save the Queen' – a not
quite so irreverent rendering of the Malagasy national anthem. As with
many other Malagasy musicians, winning musical competitions paves
the way from amateur to professional, only that in his case the first of
his many prizes at competitions and the precondition for recording his
first album did not fall within the world music category at all:

I lived in Saint-Étienne at the time and ... I entered a contest to represent the Rhône-Alpes region for the Printemps de Bourges, a big
music festival. And I came first. So I represented my region, which
was a huge honour for me as a Malagasy to represent my region at
the Printemps de Bourges ... After Bourges, I had the opportunity to
record a single. Then I entered a few contests and went to the final
stage at the Olympia. And I won that as well. It was a national contest
and I won. And then I did some others ... One is always searching for
one's direction through life! Because we're so far away! So we always
keep the memory. And culture, culture is what is left when everything else has been forgotten. [2] (Meinhof's interview, November
2007, during the TNMundi concert in Tana)

After the success with Bourges in 1987–88 he still thought of himself
as only semi-professional, so in 1991 he entered a school of jazz in Lyon
to study musical arrangements. While enrolled as a student he became
selected as the one whose music the school wanted to sponsor for the
production of an album. This led to another competition, again as

representative for the region Rhône-Alpes, and again he entered the final at the Olympia in Paris and won first prize.

Edgar: I went to Paris for the final in the Olympia venue. And I won, I won the first prize and produced a 45 vinyl record. But it was with a song called 'Sovay'. If that isn't a name, 'vay', what's the word again?

Dama: Vay ... that's, oh, you know it's ... when you scratch it and it gets swollen and infected and you need to get rid of it.

Edgar: And I wrote a song called 'Sovay'. That is what gets infected, you see ... And this song won ... But it was already a mix and I was wondering ... But how do they do it, how do people understand a song with two languages overlapping and not necessarily understanding all of it? Well, it's just ... either they like it or they don't. But I entered the contest in competition with people who came from all over France with proper French songs [laughing].

Dama: It's the difference, the difference.

Edgar: And I arrive ... la-la-la-la with my stuff and I won ... and I recorded a song ... that was already some form of pro-fessional recognition, something starting to happen ... In fact, my development is the result of all the people that I met and who helped me. So afterwards this school pro-duced me, they told me that for three years they would take care of me and they gave me money ... I became a professional for three years ... thanks to the school. And these three years went quickly. Then I had to ... I did something on TV with a singer ... There's this big con-test organized ... right across Europe and the entire Francophone region. It takes place in Périgueux ... And my wife saw it and said 'oh la la' ... you should go ... so I went for the first time and I ... I won ... I performed 'Je me suis fait tout petit' by Georges Brassens and I won. So I went again, I did all the different elimination stages of the contest ... I was with the kids because of their holiday ... The kids were all there ... watching their daddy sing ... [laughing]. Then we went on holiday, we returned, I did the final contest, I won the money, hop! [3] (Meinhof's and Rasolofondraosolo's interview, April 2009, at Edgar's home in Roanne)

Although Edgar's musical development happens during his life in France and in collaboration with musicians of different backgrounds, the connection to Madagascar stays strong. After a concert tour with a French singer, Nilda Fernandez of Spanish origin, who in turn mixes Spanish and French in his songs, the tour organizer who is also the producer of Edgar's earlier album, suggests further collaboration on a new project. At that point Edgar suggests a focus on Madagascar:

> He told me that he was looking for a project and I said: Madagascar. He said: Go for it! This is what led to this album. So I went to Madagascar, toing and froing, voilà. So I hope that this album will get a bit more attention. And my relationship with other people, with the people of my ... community also developed. It is not restrictive; my community is really big. But at the same time, with all the Malagasy I meet ... I think that I'm meeting more Malagasy than before ... many more ... It's a good balance and it links well with my songs. I think that it is a good thing, now, I can speak and sing in French and in Malagasy ... So now I'm waiting for this release ... I still have a little bit ... well even in the difficult world economy of today ... I'm grateful to be allowed to sing and to share with others. I know how fragile this is, that life is fragile, and my career is fragile too ... You see, it's fragile ... But well, everything I have, I'm taking it and I'm grateful ... At least I'm living life to the full. Voilà. [4] (Meinhof's and Rasolofondraosolo's interview, April 2009, at Edgar's home in Roanne)

The last two extracts stem from an interview 16 months after the TNMundi concert in Antananarivo. By that time Edgar had moved away from Saint-Étienne to a remote region near to Roanne, into an old farmhouse that he wants to develop into a music and performance centre for young people, building on existing connections to a local music school where he is already engaged as a teacher. The house also functions as a meeting point for his Malagasy musician friends such as Ricky Olombelo from Antananarivo, Erick Manana from Bordeaux, and others from all over France and Madagascar, giving them the space and the time to practise and play together and to embark on occasional shared concert tours in France.

There are several other Malagasy artists who manage to develop their careers from towns and regions outside Paris, making use of both, the opportunities of their regions as well as the links with translocal and transnational networks. Mamiso, whom we have already encountered in Chapter 1, works in Lyon where he performs with a new French musical partner, Julie, while simultaneously joining forces with Seheno in Paris.

Erick Manana works with a large group of highly diverse musicians in Bordeaux, while also being a member of the transnational group, the Madagascar All Stars, to be fully discussed later in this chapter. In his 2009 concert at the Olympia Erick introduced many of his musical partners from all over the world in a series of duets, including the French chansonnier Graeme Allright, the Irish harp player Anna Tanvir, and Jenny Fuhr, a young German doctoral student of ethnomusicology who plays the flute and the violin. In March 2010, Erick and Dama embarked on a tour of Canada, performing for the sizeable Malagasy diaspora there, and a new joint album with songs by Erick and Dama is in process. Similarly, Justin Vali for many years worked from a home in Lille before resettling in Paris, and the group Mavana – four women from the same musical family – have their home base in Chartres, but also work with salegy star Marius Fontaine from the group Fenoamby, who in turn is also a member of the Madagascar All Stars. What this shows is that while Paris and other capital cities have a central role to play in the life of the majority of migrant musicians, there are considerable activities in other more provincial regions of France. For the Malagasy musicians, towns such as Lille, Bordeaux, Marseille, Toulouse and Lyon combine the advantage of local cultural support structures for artists in general with the networking potential of cultural associations arising from quite a sizeable Malagasy population resident there (see Chapter 6). Similar points can be made for the North African musicians.

Watcha Clan or diaspora hi-fi

Watcha Clan is the name of a Marseille-based group which brings together musicians from French and Algerian backgrounds around a musical project which the group has called 'diaspora hi-fi'. Watcha Clan's musical and spatial identities are complex. Musically, the repertoire includes electro, dub, jungle and reggae influences and marries these with lyrics in French, Arabic and Hebrew. Spatially, the group members are based in Marseille and Paris. The translocal dimension of Watcha Clan arose out of the group's transnational networking with musicians in Algeria (Oran), one of whom is guitarist Nassim Kouti. Nassim met the members of Watcha Clan during a residency at Oran's Centre culturel français in 2003, where the group was invited to mark the reopening of the network of Centres following the end of the Algerian civil war. The musicians remained in contact by email until Nassim moved to Paris to undertake a degree in musicology at the University of Paris 8 in 2005. Nassim's move to France coincided with an invitation from the group to work on a further residency project to take place in Oran in 2006.

Nassim was enlisted to help locate Oran-based musicians to participate
in the second residency and to suggest material for the repertoire which
evolved into the group's 2008 album *Diaspora Hi-Fi*. Nassim recorded
the album in Marseille with the group and has toured extensively with
them since its release. The involvement of Nassim has been of great
significance for the group members and particularly the lead singer
Karine, who describes Nassim as 'l'élément déclencheur' (the catalyst)
that facilitated the conceptualization of the 'diaspora hi-fi project',
and, according to Karine and Elsa (partner of group member Clément),
defines their broader *raison d'être*.[2]

> Elsa: The first time that they left, in fact, they were invited by the
>   CCF Algiers [French cultural centre] for the reopening in
>   fact of the cultural centres in Algeria and so when they left,
>   they met, among others, Nassim who we were talking about
>   a moment ago, so they jammed a little, they realized that
>   there really are things to be done and, as a result, the idea is
>   that we really have to take the time to return there to take
>   the time to really work with the musicians from there but
>   I think it's also a progressive realization that, at a specific
>   moment because it was already there, I mean, I don't know,
>   the melodies, but afterwards to tell yourself, at a specific
>   point in time, yes, well, that's it, that's what we want to do
>   as a project, it took a while nevertheless ... and yes, actually
>   the first trip to Algeria, it's a little like a realization.
> Karine: Yeah, exactly.
> Elsa: That it's, that's what we really want to do.
> Karine: Because in fact there are two things, when we went to
>   Algeria we realized that we ... it was really superficial to
>   arrive in a country, to do a concert and then to leave, we
>   wanted to get to know the groups that were there, that
>   on the one hand, and for me, it was 'back to the roots'.
>   I understood that I was Algerian whereas before I wasn't
>   aware of it at all [...] in fact it was part of all our life stories
>   in fact, this diaspora project. [5] (Kiwan's interview with
>   Elsa and Karine, Watcha Clan, June 2007, Marseille)

Karine, who was born and brought up in the notorious *quartier nord*
of Marseille, has both an Algerian and a Polish family background: her
father is of Algerian Jewish Berber origin and her mother of Polish Jewish
origin. The other group members, brothers Julien and Clément, are from

the rural Hautes-Alpes region and are of French background. What is significant about this group is its teaming of a strong local Marseillais identity with a much more transnational agenda or imaginary, as incarnated in its diaspora hi-fi project. It would seem then, that in the stories of individuals or groups such as Watcha Clan, one finds a meeting of what Castells referred to as a space of place (localism) and a space of flows (here, a non-elite cosmopolitan transnational perspective and engagement), two poles which Castells argued did not meet. Furthermore, this articulation of two seemingly distinct registers of engagement has been enabled and reinforced by a transnational, then a translocal, dimension of the group.

Gaâda Diwane de Béchar

The intersection of transnational and translocal registers is also present in the trajectory of multi-sited group Gaâda Diwane de Béchar. Gaâda is a formation of seven musicians, led by lead singer and percussionist Abdelati Laoufi, and the group members are based in Paris and Nantes. The group, which is made up of four Algerians from the south of Algeria (Béchar and Timimoun) and three French musicians, one of whom is of Malagasy origin, has been active on the Paris North African and 'world music' circuit for over ten years and is also part of the Louzine network (see Chapter 3 for more on Louzine). Gaâda's repertoire is mainly derived from traditional, ancestral songs of the southern Algerian diwane genre. Diwane music is often referred to as the Algerian equivalent of the Moroccan gnawa musical style and, like gnawa, it has a strong link with neighbouring sub-Saharan African countries such as Mali, Niger and Mauritania. The other main lead singer of the group, Aïcha Lebga, is based in Nantes, in western France. She moved there in 1995 (to La Chapelle-Basse-Mer) to live with her husband who first saw her on stage in Timimoun.[3] Aïcha met the group in Marseille and has been performing with them for several years now, commuting to Paris for rehearsals once a week. Besides performing with Gaâda, Aïcha also performs in another Nantais group known as TikiAïcha. This French translocal dimension of Gaâda is, however, of less significance than the transnational dimension since it is the strong emotional and family connection to the southern Algerian towns of Béchar and Timimoun that characterizes the group. So, it is fair to say that a diasporic or transnational imaginary lies at the heart of the Gaâda project, as summed up in the following extract from an interview with Abdelati:

> In fact the Diwane had a much more social role originally, but above all therapeutic in the beginning, really when I remember when I was

young, it's essentially social, because people meet and coopt one another and then, but above all therapeutic, but in fact it's spread, when it developed especially over the last few years by the fact that there are groups which have made it well known – it has become cultural let's say ... but in Béchar there are other things and that's it ... you have to get inside ... it's a melting pot because it's a frontier zone in all senses ... Natural frontiers ... Morocco is very close by ... so we're a little Moroccan ... it's a land of immigration [...] so there are also populations who come from everywhere but, above all, you've got, for a very long time now, the local population which we call the Eksouria, the Eksouria – they're Arab-Berbers who practise four or five styles which are very different ... so you've got Morocco, the Eksouria – the basis – but, above all, you've got the influence of the North, the high plateaux are not very far away. The North, where we are, it's not Oran, it's not Algiers, it's straightaway the mountains called the Atlas, and there are sounds from these Atlas [mountains] which are very very powerful, which have also blown in on Béchar. That's why these turbulences in the melting pot sense but the most important, the texture, the rhythm and sound come from Adrar and Timimoun via Mali, in fact the Eksouria from the south have enormously inspired ... and you've got a gnawa tradition, diwane but there's also an Issawa tradition which is very very strong in a neighbouring oasis ... by the way, Ferda add a little bit of Issawa influence ... we're more gnawa ... because I lived with Taieb ... in a neighbourhood where there's the gnawa, the wall separating me from the diwane is my neighbour's so we heard the diwane all the time. The diwane, without being there, you're there ... it gets under your skin ... Aïcha, you see, she symbolizes Timimoun-Adrar, Mali ... she's from Timimoun-Adrar. [6] (Kiwan's interview with Abdelati Laoufi, June 2007, Paris)

The Madagascar All Stars

Multi-sitedness on a truly long-distance transnational and translocal scale is not only the condition for existence but the whole *raison d'être* of the Madagascar All Stars (MAS). The group consists of five musicians, or six if one includes Ricky Olombelo, who performs with them whenever feasible (Figure 4.1).

What makes the group special is that they are indeed an 'all stars' group, comprising some of the most renowned singer-songwriters of Malagasy origin. We have already introduced most of them as individual artists in their own right in previous chapters. Thus the

Figure 4.1   Madagascar All Stars

guitar, kabosy and harmonica player Dama from the group Mahaleo
and the percussionist Ricky Olombelo both live in the capital city of
Antananarivo, though on the maternal side Ricky's family originates
from the deep south-east of Madagascar. Guitar player Erick Manana,
who grew up in Fianarantsoa, roughly halfway between Antananarivo
and Tulear, has been living in Bordeaux for more than two decades.
Marius Fontaine, the multi-instrumentalist, grew up in the far north
of Madagascar, near Diego, famous for its salegy dance and trance
music. He arrived in Paris, where he lives today, after several years
first as a sound engineer and then as a musician in La Réunion.
Régis, the accordionist of the group, comes from the region of Tulear
in the south-west, and like Marius lives in Paris. And finally Justin
Vali, who comes from a small village tucked away in the hills of the
Hauts Plateaux east of Antananarivo, plays different types of the
valiha – the original bamboo-stringed version and the metal-stringed
version – as well as the wooden-box version of the marovany. He has
only recently moved from Lille to Paris. All of the artists based in
France also perform in Madagascar in their own right, while those
from Madagascar regularly tour Europe. However, it is in their formation as Madagascar All Stars that they exemplify best of all the
working together of local, translocal and transnational affiliations –
geographically as well as artistically. Their coming together was a
deliberate attempt to demonstrate at one and the same time the

extraordinary diversity of Malagasy music *and* the possibility of transcending these differences in a shared project.

In the previous chapter we mentioned that their first performance was at the invitation of the travel agency Jacaranda's Parisian director Josielle, who wanted a group of musicians from different regions of Madagascar to musically accompany a multimedia promotional show in the Pyramides venue in Pont Marly on the outskirts of Paris in 2004 where Jacaranda presented images, film clips, travel journals and anecdotes from their clients' journeys in Madagascar. At Josielle's instigation Dama set out to bring together musicians from Madagascar or of Malagasy origin who were to express through their music what the travellers' experiences indicated, namely the extraordinary diversity of Madagascar. Their initial performance was still under the individual names of the five musicians, and while the concert had all five play together, it was clear that each musican led with songs of their creation with the others in a supporting role. Since then and many rehearsals, concerts and a first CD later, the Madagascar All Stars have emerged as a fully grown band in their own right. In an interview with Justin after one of the group's first international performances at the Duisburg Traumzeit Festival in May 2006, Ulrike asked Justin to explain how he understood the group's project:

> What's really good is that everyone of us has his own musical personality that is already truly interesting. The roots of each one of us five are very different. Even the way in which we compose our songs, how we sing, all that is all so interesting, musically it is so very interesting. Because for us to manage to play together, with five musical personalities, even if we're all Malagasy, means that we must align each other to the composition. Dama has spotted this really well. And that's why I didn't hesitate for a second when he phoned me to announce the project. And I think it will bear great fruit, because we're about to build one big tree, with many branches and many fruit. Of course it's also true that the fruit are not completely ripe, that will take a while longer I think, but I think we'll be getting a great deal of juice – the juice of our fruit, orange and all that, that's for sure! [7] (Meinhof's and Rasolofondraosolo's interview, May 2006 after the Traumzeit Festival in Duisburg)

Since 2006 the group has gone from strength to strength, with an ambitious programme of international engagements, in particular in France, Germany, the UK, Austria and Switzerland, and recently the release of their first album. One of the great strengths of the group lies not just in the range of the musical instruments they play with such virtuosity but also in the range of their voices, which allows them to sing in the complex harmonies typical for many Malagasy songs and is the trademark of non-instrumental groups such as Salala, Senge and Mavana. Again, Justin explains this in his tongue-in-cheek fashion:

Justin: And what's more, what is really interesting, really and truly, that's the vocal timbre of the five of us.

Dama: It's different.

Justin: It's different and that is wow.

Ulrike: Can you explain to me how you see that? Because if it's different how would you describe it?

Justin: Oh yes! For example, there's our boss Dama, that's a voice that really catches you, a seductive voice. No, no, one has to say that ... I would say it's even a sexy voice, yeah yeah, I have to tell the truth. And a voice that carries hope as well, and the joy of life, all that. And if one hears the voice of Erick, sometimes one gets transported into a tropical forest, or in the middle of the sugar cane fields. And there's also the nostalgia. And with the voice of Fenoamby – with Marius – that's a voice that pierces you, with its vibration, it makes the public vibrate, and there's Régis, full of spirituality, there's something that grows that, that radiates. And if one hears my voice, it's a bit a little bit like a car's engine starting up.

Dama: That's Erick, you really caught Erick there.

Justin: No, it's really amazing. And it's really important that we find two or three songs, even if we compose them together a cappella, that show the richness of our voices and the harmonies that we can create, we need to make use of that, voilà. [8] (Meinhof's and Rasolofondraosolo's interview, May 2006 after the Traumzeit Festival in Duisburg)

In 2010, the Madagascar All Stars not only embarked on a whole range of festivals and concert tours, but these were interspersed with the on-going performances of each individual artist with their other groups. To take just a few months out of their calendar: in February 2010, the Madagascar All Stars played in the Parisian Alhambra, in March Erick and Dama gave duo concerts in France, in Canada and in Rome. In May Dama returned to Madagascar for two Palais du Sport concerts with Mahaleo and in June the Madagascar All Stars performed at festivals and concerts in France. Meanwhile, Justin was performing with his Malagasy Orkestra in Paris – a large group of musicians from all over Madagascar that he brought together as an initiative of the Alliance française (see Chapter 5) – Régis, Fenoamby (Marius) and Ricky were equally busy with their own separate engagements.

What unites the musicians in a common project beyond their friendship and their love for music is also their commitment to Madagascar. Time and time again most of the Malagasy musicians we interviewed return to this objective of making a difference – outside Madagascar to influence the ways in which the country and its diverse culture are perceived by the outside world – and within Madagascar to support that diversity while appealing to their shared Malagasy roots. Indeed, we often heard the phrase which is frequently used in debates about the European Union, but here applied to the Malagasy context: 'unity in diversity'. There is thus little evidence of a free-floating post-modern identity even in the most cosmopolitan of scenarios that we have just explored. Most Malagasy artists remain deeply committed to the 'land of their ancestors', and negotiate their multiple and complex transnational ties in relation to this important link. At the same time they share this agenda with their public, thus enabling strategically what we have defined as 'transcultural capital'. In our conversation with Seheno, Dama explains how he understands the spirit behind the musicians he is engaged with:

I am already challenged ... All five of us also want to present our image of Madagascar. By touring everywhere. We're getting more and more aware of this. We did not meet just like that; we had our objective, to show a good image of Madagascar, a different image. A multiple image, that's the way we want to show it, each of us in his own way ... In five years, we would like all Malagasy artists who think alike to be on the same path. In order to ... Well, it's already quite a step, what the five of us achieved. I am in Madagascar, Erick is in Bordeaux, Justin Vali in Lille and Régis is everywhere in the world! But we did it, because we thought that Madagascar is really important. So we reduced the distances, we reduced the distances to achieve this objective. And that is a good thing. Because after all it is not that easy to create a band. We already have enough problems on our plates to deal with our own bands. So we're looking for some more problems to be together. So you could say that we were able to overcome these problems for a noble cause. Yes, one can call it that, a noble cause. [9] (Meinhof and Rasolofondraosolo in conversation with Seheno in Paris, April 2009)

Multi-sited individuals

HAJAMadagascar

An individual artist with a highly mobile trajectory across Europe and Madagascar is the singer-songwriter, dancer and occasional costume designer and make-up artist HAJAMadagascar. Although registered as resident in Marseille, where he lives for a few months of the year, Haja spends most of his time either travelling across Europe or at his second home in Vienna. Haja comes from a family of science teachers from Madirovalo and Marovoay in the Mahajanga province in the north-west of Madagascar. His life story again challenges some of the received wisdoms of globalization as a one-way street to post-modern cosmopolitanism. As was the case with the Madagascar All Stars, Haja remains firmly grounded in his Malagasy roots while simultaneously living the most mobile and cosmopolitan of existences. Let us briefly engage with some of the stepping stones in his career. As a boy and young man, Haja divided his time between Mahajanga for school and Marovoay for weekends, between a town life and one in the country-side, where he could dress only in a pair of shorts and some sandals, with feet dyed red from walking on the red soil and consuming his 30 mangoes per day, season permitting. After gaining a series of scholar-ships he finished an undergraduate degree in business studies at the University of Antananarivo, and a postgraduate management degree at the Sorbonne in Paris, while also supporting himself with a small business for trading handicrafts from Madagascar. Yet from the age of seven onwards, and having observed his uncle's guitar playing, he longed to play music:

Haja: But me, ever since my childhood, I liked to be creative. With cooking, with the instruments and all that. With music, I started when I was about seven years old. I mean, apart from singing all the traditional things, I started at the age of seven. I watched how my uncle played the guitar. I really loved that, but we did not have a guitar at home, it was not possible, it was too expensive. There was not even … Because I don't know if you remember but it was a really tough time …

Dama: Phew, yes it was!

Haja: Wasn't it? In the eighties, end of the seventies, beginning of the eighties; there was nothing in the stores, nothing at all! We were queuing to buy soap and we had to get up at 4 o'clock in the morning.

Dama: For the rice.

Haja: For the rice ... For oil, for soap, for everything! And we were playing a lot, we were singing a lot because there was nothing to do. From 4 to 8 o'clock, when the shop was open, we would put some ...

Dama: ... Stones!

Haja: ... Some stones to replace people!

Dama: Oh yeah, in the queue!

Haja: In the queue. And us, at the same time, we would play and sing, we would do anything. And that is when we built small guitars ... to kill time ... But at the same time we were always dreaming of a proper guitar. But we were playing like that, with our hands [laughing] and six strings. [10] (Meinhof's and Rasolofondraosolo's interview, September 2007, Vienna)

The first guitar, shared between him and his younger brother, finally arrives one Christmas when a guitar promotion in Antananarivo made the instrument more affordable and as a reward for having come out first in class – a precondition set by his mother:

My little brother, he loved the guitar, just like me. And my oldest brother he was always good at school, so it was not for him! [Laughing] He was always a top student so it was especially for us. So with my little brother, we were saying to ourselves: 'Ah, we're going to do something about it, because maybe we could have a guitar.' And of course it worked and on Christmas Day we got the guitar ... And I remember how we touched the strings one by one. We didn't even dare to hold it properly. We would just touch the strings and listened to the sound. So my brother and I learned how to play the guitar together. Just like that, at the bottom of our stairs, we would play all the time ... And we would always play on that staircase. Just there because it sounded good. It sounded just like in a shower. [11] (Meinhof's and Rasolofondraosolo's interview, September 2007, Vienna)

Having achieved a postgraduate place to study at the Sorbonne, Haja leaves the guitar with his young brother and arrives in Paris once more without his beloved instrument. Now it is a member of 'Le carrefour étudiant', an international association of well-to-do retired people who support students, who comes to his rescue. Having this guitar and having successfully completed his studies he now begins his travelling across Europe. His reflections below give an intriguing insight into the ways in which Europeans observe migrant musicians:

And there were some people who spotted that I was forming a band, but without a guitar [laughing]. We were singing a cappella, with some percussions. I said 'I can play instruments but I have no instruments here.' And there was this woman who gave me a guitar. She said: 'Till you get your own, you can keep this one. Or if you like you can keep it anyway.' So I got this guitar and I travelled with this guitar. Naturally I had brought a kabosy from Madagascar. I always kept it with me. And so I travelled, with my backpack, on the train, across several European countries. And it was real fun, because when I had my guitar on my back while travelling, lots of people would smile at me for no reason. So I saw that music was some kind of a door, an introduction to communicating with strangers. And I heard lots of stories about immigrants, people from Africa. But I told myself: 'What I am experiencing at the moment, that's a bit different.' But I did not understand straightaway that I got a different perspective because of the guitar. Because there, even the cops, when they see you with a guitar, they search you, of course, because they always suspect you of having drugs ... 'This guy comes from Africa, a musician, hmm' ... But when they finished searching me, they started to get more interested. They'd ask what kind of music I was playing, from which country, was I OK? And then I saw that this was not happening to my mates who were not musicians. For them it would end straightaway. With me, the talk would be more global and more interesting. So for example when I was on the train with families, some people would ask: 'Where are you going? What are you going to do there?' All of this encouraged me to do the two things I like the most: to play music and to travel [laughing]. So I said to myself: 'After all it might be possible to combine the two!' And because I had taken some management courses as well, I thought I might even be able to combine the three! So that's what got me to where I am today ... At first it was the love of music, and love for travel. But at the same time, being able to do things by myself, managing my own life in a way. [12] (Meinhof's and Rasolofondraosolo's interview, September 2007, Vienna)

Once his decision is made to pursue a career in music, and fluent not only in his mother tongue Malagasy but also in French, German and English, he develops in different directions, combining music and dance performances in concerts and at festivals with workshops and illustrated talks for organizations, institutions, businesses and expositions, such as for Amnesty International, Austrian schools, business associations and the Hannover Expo 2000, while also acting as the administrative head for his own ventures and those of other musicians. Here is how he narrates his experiences with schoolchildren:

> When I met them, they told me: 'We really ... I remembered what you told us about the taxi brousse ...' Because personally I always avoided giving a false image of Madagascar. I told them all the time that it was one of the poorest countries in the world, economically speaking. I always added *economically* speaking. On the other hand, if you want to see something rewarding, try to travel there. Because if you leave France or Austria and you go to Greece somewhere, it is going to be the same, isn't it? But if you go to Madagascar, it is a completely different world. And once you're there, don't take the plane, take the taxi brousse instead, to see what is happening. So, for example, during the workshops, I created dances where the kids are with me in a car and we're driving on bad roads [laughing]. Ahh ... So the kids understand the reality of the country, but at the same time they're having fun. And most of time, that is what is best for them. So I give them the reality of my country and at the same time they're learning something and having fun. Having diversified like that allowed me to travel even more. Voilà. And in fact, I even ... Well because I like to cook, I do that as well. For example, I organized a whole event to listen, taste, look, touch instruments and feel the scents of Madagascar. All of the five senses. This is an extremely intense experience, this is something that no one will ever forget because it is so rare to go to ... a concert or a concert with a dinner and to get everything at the same time. So I have concepts like that. I call companies and I make them an offer: If you want something special, not only versions of the Beatles songs and all the classics, here is some adventure! But you don't even have to travel, you will be there already! It is an adventure! I like this diversification a lot because I can use most of my talents, I can create a lot and it is always ... it always gives me a very strong link with my country. [13] (Meinhof's and Rasolofondraosolo's interview, September 2007, Vienna)

What this extract illustrates is the importance of embedding globalization in a transnational and translocal frame that acknowledges the significance of 'transcultural capital' in migrants' lives while not reducing the strong links to the country of origin to a myopic nationalist gaze. Like so many of the other artists we have introduced here, HAJAMadagascar thinks of himself as a modern musician playing in a contemporary mode, as someone who bridges many worlds between his country of origin and Europe. It is perceptions such as the one below which made us argue in the Introduction that 'social remittances' (Levitt 1998) are not only a form of newly acquired cultural capital that migrants bring 'home', but are part of a dynamic and on-going exchange of transcultural capital.

I cannot say that I belong 100 per cent to the countryside. But at the same time, I know that when I am in the countryside, I feel like myself. I cannot say either that I am 100 per cent a city guy, because there are those moments when I really love the countryside. So I am going on stage with this mixture: ... For example I wear no shirt and paint my body ... I was bare-chested for half of my life: at home in the countryside, it was impossible to wear anything. And I always bring these roots with me everywhere I go. And bit by bit as I went on my travels, I realized that the music I am doing now allows me to stay close to Madagascar, to have one foot there and one foot abroad. In a way, I am sharing my Malagasy values with the people abroad. But at the same time, that's not all either, because when I go home and talk with my cousins, my uncles and my friends, I also bring something from here. I tell them what is happening here. [14] (Meinhof's and Rasolofondraosolo's interview, September 2007, Vienna)

'On fait tous le ping-pong' ('We're all toing and froing'): Skander and transmediterranean multi-sitedness

The quotation in the heading from an interview with Franco-Tunisian musician Skander encapsulates his toing and froing between Paris and Lyon in France and La Marsa and Tunis in Tunisia. Skander Besbes, whose mother is French and whose father is Tunisian, was brought up in La Marsa, a well-off seaside suburb of Tunis, and since his late twenties (2005 onwards) he has lived between Lyon, Paris and the town of his childhood. Skander, who classifies himself as an electronica musician, is involved in a variety of creative audio-visual projects which range from his monthly 'set' at a nightclub in Tunis, to creative music residencies (such as Pitchworks in Aubenas, and Music Matbakh in London notably) and contemporary visual and sound art exhibitions (Design Biennale in

Saint-Étienne). What clearly stands out from Skander's experience is the significance of social and professional networking for his multiple creative projects. For instance, his involvement and conception of a residency project known as Pitchworks came about in part thanks to a brief, chance meeting in Tunis with Yann Crespel, the cultural attaché of Romans, a town near Lyon, which is twinned with El Jem in Tunisia. Crespel coordinates the Découvertes Tunisie 21 Festival which takes place in El Jem each summer and was introduced to Skander by a fellow electronica musician. The extract below highlights how the creative consequences of chance meetings and professional networks can be very significant:

> So this guy, Yann Crespel, was leaving Tunisia. I think on the 2nd or 3rd or 1st of September he was going back to France or to Morocco, I don't know, and it just so happens that I was in Tunis that day redoing my identity card so as to be able to take off and go back to Paris and I met this bloke via Khais Ben Mabrouk who phoned me so I had 40 minutes to talk with this Yann Crespel and basically, what we did, is that we put together our networks to ask ourselves 'what can we do with this?' and basically, after those those 40 minutes, two weeks later I received an email from Yann Crespel who said 'very good, we'll start someting', given that he is attached to the town of Romans, which is 40 minutes from Lyon, and I had my entry points which he saw as *the the* associative label which could be the major aid in France, that is, Jarring Effects in Lyon, he said to himself, 'let's try to do something' and we came up with the Pitchworks project which is a project in three stages at the moment [...] so Pitchworks is a creative residency project in three stages at the moment, the first stage happened in Aubenas from the 4th to the 10th February in the Ardèche as part of Tunisia week ... so present all week were Mounir Trudi and his flutist who's called Houcine ... Perhaps one of the best Tunisian musicians I've ever seen ... an incredible encounter with those musicians ... [...] the idea at the outset was to do a pan-Arab residency [...] this project, there'll be another stage in the town of Romans, from the 4th to the 10th May, as part of the BIS, Biennial of International Solidarity [...] And then the last episode will be in El Jem for the festival, the 21st August, and so afterwards, we're in the process of discussing what the outputs will be, will we make a record? ... There are partners already ... what's definite, what's come out of this already, is the contact ... there are other people who are going to join this residency. [15] (Kiwan's and Gibert's interview with Skander Besbes, February 2008, Paris)

While a chance meeting between Skander and Yann Crespel gave rise to the Pitchworks project which in itself led to broader creative partnerships, Skander's trajectory is simultaneously characterized by planned or calculated professional moves. This explains his move from Tunis to Lyon in the spring of 2006, after resigning from his job with an audiovisual company in Tunis in August 2005. So in March 2006, Skander decided to go and stay with his childhood friend (also from Tunisia), Khais (a graphic designer). Khais proved to be a particularly key person who allowed Skander to meet a variety of gate-keepers in the Lyonnais electronica scene. Indeed, the pivotal role played by Khais in allowing Skander to extend his professional network resonates to a significant extent with Holton's description of the importance of particular persons in arts-related networks (Holton 2008). Skander was able to stay with Khais for three months, during which time he was able to meet the main electronica music label in France, Jarring Effects, which is based in Lyon. Furthermore, thanks to Khais, Skander met Paralel – the group who are behind the electronica record label Bee Records. Skander is now signed to the Bee Records label and he released his album *Rituals* with that label in October 2008. Skander argues that his position as a semi-outsider (that is, as someone who is regarded as being 'de passage') helped him to meet the 'right' people in the scene:

> It's true that in Lyon it actually has put me in a strong position ... because the fact that I do not live there but at the same time to be introduced to the best platforms means that, well, I am not part of the everyday [...] for them I'm on the outside, I come back [...] ... people take time, because I'm there for just a week. [16] (Kiwan's and Gibert's interview with Skander Besbes, February 2008, Paris)

Once Skander gained access to the main gate-keepers in Lyon he himself became a mediator, introducing his friend and fellow electronica musician Mohsen (Collectif E, based in La Marsa, Tunisia) to the very same groups of people (Jarring Effects record label, Bee Records, etc.). The outcome of such encounters has a strong transnational dimension since, as Skander points out, the main future objective is to 'consolidate the Lyon–La Marsa–Tunis bridge' [17] (Kiwan's and Gibert's interview with Skander Besbes, February 2008, Paris).

It is significant that Paris does not feature in this bridging exercise. Indeed, Lyon and to a lesser extent Lille are described by Skander as the 'bastions de résistance' (bastions of resistance) of alternative electronic music, thus showing how certain genres of music and their associated human networks/hubs invite us to look beyond the capital cities. The metaphor of the human hub is highly appropriate for Skander's experiences within the electronic music scene and, indeed, the notion of the human hub can perhaps even be extended further to incorporate the idea of community. This is a term that Skander adopts himself, although it is not imbued with any ethnic characteristics. Rather, his understanding of community is very much couched in terms of musical taste and know-how: 'I've got this utopian idea of community, people who do things together, who put their know-how and material together' [18] (Kiwan's and Gibert's interview with Skander Besbes, February 2008, Paris).

If one were to try to sum up the nature of Skander's trajectory, one would have to underline the fact that his is very clearly a multi-sited and multi-scalar existence – he is at once living between Paris and Lyon (translocality) and also toing and froing between France and Tunisia. His professional and social networks are also closely bound to his Tunisian background, yet he cannot be described as 'diasporic' in the classic 'nostalgic' sense:

> In Paris, most of the people that I see are childhood friends [...] we're all toing and froing, in the summer we're all there [in Tunisia] ... There's no real need to choose when you're straddled between France and Tunisia ... the dreams of all the Franco-Tunisians, I'm Franco-Tunisian so I've got a foot, I'm at a crossroads, people often think of me as a Tunisian artist, they forget that my mother is French and that I did actually grow up speaking French at home and all that but I've never wanted to choose between the two ... we're happy with a foot on each side of the Mediterranean especially in two countries which are so close to each other. [19] (Kiwan's and Gibert's interview with Skander Besbes, February 2008, Paris)

So Skander's story at once articulates the space of flows and the space of place which Castells (1996) argues are dislocated in a broader context of globalization. In other words, Skander is a highly mobile musician who is wired into a range of cultural flows and ideas surrounding the electronic music scene. Yet he is also quite grounded in various locales which hold particular personal and professional significance for him, namely Lyon, Paris and La Marsa in Tunisia.

Resettlers

Another key dimension of the multi-sited and multi-scalar lives of migrant musicians and cultural producers relates to the phenomenon of return migration. Indeed, this was a fairly common trend among the musicians and cultural producers from North Africa whom we met during our research, though for Malagasy artists toing and froing is much more prevalent than a full return. Since we have already introduced several examples of musicians who regularly move between Europe and Madagascar we will now only concentrate on the North African examples. Some had returned to Morocco or Algeria after a lengthy period of residence in Europe, while others had spent relatively shorter but nevertheless significant periods abroad or were still toing and froing between Europe and North Africa. The decision to return is often presented by these artists and cultural producers as being bound up with a desire to participate in and contribute to the home country's cultural (artistic) development. This narrative/motivation is particularly striking in the Moroccan case where the recent 'effervescence culturelle' (cultural effervescence) characterized by the multiplication of high-profile music festivals, the liberalization of the media and the emergence of a dynamic urban music scene ('la nouvelle scène marocaine') has fed into a broader sense of cultural renewal or renaissance which in turn has motivated Moroccans based abroad to return and 'do their bit'.[4] This mix of identitarian (or what we have coined alternative nationalism) and professional (artistic/aesthetic) motivations driving individuals to return to the Maghreb once again points to one of the ways in which the transnational cosmopolitanism of diasporic artists/cultural producers often intersects with a more grounded (local or national) agenda. This certainly characterizes the experiences of Casablanca-based singer-songwriters Oum and Khansa Batma, whose stories we shall consider below.

Oum

Oum is a soul and nu-jazz singer-songwriter who was born in Casablanca but brought up in Marrakesh. In 1997 she moved to Rabat to pursue a degree in architecture at the École nationale d'architecture, but in 2003 she decided to focus on a musical career and moved back to Casablanca in order to pursue this objective. In 2004 she was approached by Philippe Delmasse, a French music producer and head of the organization Ardistique sud, who invited her to Paris and introduced her to various other music producers and executives. With hindsight, Oum reflects on her Parisian experience with mixed feelings:

> so Philippe introduced me to people in Paris, in Avignon, I worked on some songs which were suggested for me, which he chose ... I wrote some lyrics, because there were certain songs which were

just instrumental ... it was my first experience of writing a little bit, um ... it lasted for two years, during that time, well, every time that I came back here, well I had started to make a name for myself a little bit ... I existed in the press, in the magazines ... each time there was an event or a telethon or something on the television, I was invited [...] I was very lucky because I didn't have to go knocking on doors myself, 'please can you give me some songs?' etc. so frankly, all the doors were opened for me and everything ... but I realized everything that was offered to me to sing, wasn't necessarily me. [20] (Kiwan's and Gibert's interview with Oum, April 2008, Casablanca)

Oum explains that after two years of toing and froing between France and Morocco she decided that she would return definitively to Morocco to pursue her musical career. For her, the 16 May 2003 terrorist attacks in Casablanca and Morocco's success in the African Cup of Nations football tournament were linked to her decision to resettle in Casablanca permanently:

Oum: And I already had a name [in France] ... and then one day, when I was coming back from France, it was a strange year ... so many things were happening ... well, there were the 16th May attacks ...

Marie: 2003 then?

Oum: That's it, there was the African Cup of Nations where Morocco got to the final I think ... or semi-final ... well, basically, there were lots of feelings of Moroccanness if you like ... and that's it, I was a little bit sensitive ... and at the same time, I met, um ... that's it, I was sensitive, I told myself um ... it would be good if I did some things here now ... but at the same time ... it came about because I knew that I didn't have everything that I wanted in France. [21] (Kiwan's and Gibert's interview with Oum, April 2008, Casablanca)

Another significant feature of Oum's 'return' was her meeting with fellow Casaoui soul singer Barry. Oum explains that Barry's teaming of dialectal Arabic (*darija*) lyrics and non-Arab, Western-influenced rhythms and instrumentation (guitar) was something of an artistic revelation for her and was part of a broader realization on her part of the aesthetic and political possibilities available to her in a Moroccan and Muslim context:

> That we were coming back to the 16th May stuff, actually, as a girl I wanted to get up on stage and sing ... and dance and say Hamdullah and there's nothing wrong with that, especially ... during my period where I had taken a while to accept that I could be really happy here, and sing things here ... but which I had borrowed from there, you see. That is, that I had never understood why in gospel, for example ... they sung the love of God, they sung ... they went into a trance and all that, and they danced and all that, whereas I mean yeah I am more or less Muslim, culturally and everything [...] I've got an enormous amount of faith, and I also wanted to say that, wearing what I wear, with my style ... and perhaps by singing in English, and by dancing ... but to say Hamdullah, especially after this stuff, the 16th May etc., that added to the fact that ... at the time there weren't that many girls yet. Well, even today, but ... today it's a little bit better ... so if you like, because for me, we've nevertheless got a mission ... it's not about having fun on stage and earning a little bit of money and all that ... the fact that we should be useful, not necessarily that people identify with us, but that we should have a certain way of thinking, all that, that we should bring something ... and I felt ... I still feel that role. I am happy here ... I have my convictions ... I love Islam, and besides, for here and for elsewhere, I want to sing about this Islam, and to sing about it really freely. [22]
> (Kiwan's and Gibert's interview with Oum, April 2008, Casablanca)

So in Oum's case, her return to Morocco after a brief two-year spell of toing and froing between Casablanca, Rabat and Paris is bound up in her desire to be part of an innovative and somewhat tumultuous cultural and political context in the post-2003 period. Her performative stance on Islam in particular suggests a clear sense of attachment to a certain 'marocanité' (a term she uses) which is nonetheless inscribed within a broader cosmopolitan frame which draws on her varied and transnational influences and relationships. Her first album *Lik'Oum*, which was released in May 2009 and self-produced, has been made possible by her transnational links, since while Oum wrote all the lyrics, the music was composed by Italian (Udina-based) composer and arranger 'Kermit'.

Khansa Batma

Khansa Batma is another singer who, although she is currently predominantly based in Casablanca, did spend a significant length of time outside Morocco. In Khansa's case, after releasing two albums in Morocco she spent three years in Istanbul working in television and, like Oum, made frequent trips back and forth between Turkey and Morocco during this time. In 2005–6, Khansa, who is the daughter of the late Mohamed Batma, founder of the well-known 1970s group Lemchaheb, and niece of the late Larbi Batma, leader of the mythical Nass El Ghiwane, decided to make a 'return' to music and to Casablanca and started working with her composer brother Tarik Batma on her third (rock) album, due out in 2010. In a similar manner to Oum, Khansa talks about how following the cultural and artistic developments in Morocco from afar somehow compelled her to return in 2006:

Khansa:	I was very full up … I had to let it all out, I was very full up … I had to let it all out, and people didn't stop saying 'Khansa, Khansa, Khansa', people were asking for me, people in the street, things like that, on blogs or stuff like that, silly things like that … and then I was going back and forth all the time … I could see the developments from afar … I could see how things were happening … afterwards I had the offer from this company Click, and I said to myself why not? And I wanted to as well. I wanted to be … this time, I had spent three years behind the camera, I wanted to be in front of the camera a little bit.
Nadia:	You say that you were observing the developments from afar … in what sense? In terms of the media … I don't know … the infrastructure?
Khansa:	Everything. The mentality of people who are the leaders in Morocco, the media, this boom with the liberalization of the audio-visual landscape, especially radio stations …
Nadia:	Which dates from 2000?
Khansa:	2005. 2005–6. 2006.
Nadia:	That's when there was the liberalization of the airwaves?
Khansa:	Yes. And then all the festivals, all the cultural events which started to emerge … Dakhla Festival, festival of this, festival of that.[5] [23] (Kiwan's interview with Khansa Batma, April 2008, Casablanca)

The emergent cultural effervescence in Morocco is clearly tied up with Khansa's return and her sense of optimism regarding the future.

It can be argued that her enthusiasm is couched in somewhat patriotic terms, although she rejects outright any nationalist motivations. Nevertheless, it is fairly striking that Khansa, like Oum, articulates a highly cosmopolitan and transnational existence (in 2008, at the time of interview, Khansa was still flitting back and forth between Istanbul and Casablanca) with a more grounded attachment to Morocco, to the extent that one wonders if these musicians can be seen as part of the broader development in the new Moroccan music scene of what we have called 'alternative nationalism'.[6] The nature of Khansa's attachment to Morocco is hinted at in any case in the following extract:

Nadia: But in spite of all that, even if you came back, if you're carrying on, if you're recording, that means that you, you see, you remain optimistic about what's happening here?

Khansa: Of course, because I remain optimistic, because it's my country, damn it. Not, not that, I'm not going to give you the spiel 'it's my country', blablabla nationalistic and all those things that I am, but patriotic, if I am, it's normal, but at the same time ... it's ... I've understood something that no matter what success you can have elsewhere, success at home is priceless. It's priceless. And then everything's to be done in Morocco. There's a whole public to bring in behind ... you see, to come. There's everything to be done. It's hard. It's difficult. It asks for a lot of determination. Lots of patience ... strong nerves, getting knocked down, being strong and getting up again ... lots of things like that, because there's everything to do and learn and relearn. There's everything to do. There's a system ... a whole cultural system which has to be changed. Which has to be readapted, to be rewritten. We're in the process of writing the cultural history of Morocco. Young people, us, our generation, we're writing the history of Moroccan musical culture. I'm talking about Moroccan music. And we're doing it. But this time, this time round, the task is a difficult one.[7] [24] (Kiwan's interview with Khansa Batma, April 2008, Casablanca)

Ali Faraoui

It is not only musicians who have been tempted to return to Morocco and play their part in the country's new-found cultural dynamism. This trend also concerns cultural producers and activists more broadly. Ali Faraoui is a sound engineer based in Casablanca and in 2006 he set up a recording studio called Plein les oreilles which has become a sort of reference point for many of the groups which make up the so-called 'nouvelle scène musicale' in Morocco (such as Hoba Hoba Spirit, Fez City Clan, Haoussa, Mazagan and others). After a childhood spent in Rabat then Casablanca, Ali left for Paris in 1979 in order to study architecture there. Alongside his studies, he was active musically and became a self-taught sound engineer. Although he left Paris for personal reasons, Ali also talks about a realization in 1993 that Paris was no longer the same and that things had started to change in Morocco as well, both factors spurring him on to return:

> I left Paris in '93, we weren't laughing any more ... we had been at the Place de la Bastille in '81 with Mitterrand, and in '93 it wasn't a barrel of laughs any more in Paris so ... at the same time sound was opening up here [...] and it was opening up in terms of advertising in Morocco, it was opening up a little bit and everything, and so I said OK then I am going to go home to my country ... and I came back to Morocco. [25] (Kiwan's and Gibert's interview with Ali Faraoui, April 2008, Casablanca)

Amel Abou el aazm

The notion of bringing certain professional skills and know-how back to the country of origin after a period of residence abroad is a fairly ubiquitous one and can be seen as an example of what Levitt has called social remittances (Levitt 1998, 2001, but see also our critique in the Introduction); our 'case-study' artists and cultural producers clearly had such skills before departure but nevertheless built on them as a result of their migration experience. Like Ali Faraoui, French-Moroccan student Amel Abou el aazm left Rabat in order to undertake her higher education in Poitiers, Lyon and Paris, and after obtaining a Master's in politics and international relations in 2006 (she wrote her dissertation on the relationship between politics and music in the new Moroccan music scene), she returned to Morocco to take up a job with the Fondation de Fez, working on the Slam and Klam music and spoken word festival. In parallel to this job, Amel started to manage one of the main emergent groups of the new music scene in Morocco, the fusion outfit Darga (reggae, ska, gnawa). After six months of working in Fez, Amel decided to devote all her energies to managing Darga, who from 2006 onwards had begun to make a significant impact on the festival circuit in Morocco and in Spain and beyond (for example Belgium, France, Italy, Sweden). The partnership with the association Fábrica de ideas in Madrid was particularly important in the international promotion of Darga within the 'world music' scene. Since the release of the group's second album in 2008 things have slowed down for the group and some of the original members have had to be replaced. Nevertheless, Amel continues to be active in the cultural scene, and has been involved in theatre and dance projects as well as the establishment of an association called Lawnouna ('our colour') which was established in 2004 to encourage cultural and musical exchange between young Moroccans and young sub-Saharan Africans living in Morocco. She was also behind the setting up of a cultural enterprise known as AB Sawt in 2008 (a play on words – *sawt* in Arabic meaning 'sound' and 'sawt' sounding similar to 'south' in English). Indeed the slogan of AB Sawt is 'Écouter le sud' or 'Listen to the South' and it was set up by Amel in collaboration with Badre Belhachemi (Darga guitarist and vocalist) in order to contribute to the professionalization of the emergent urban music scene in Morocco and to facilitate the mobility of artists from the South within the South. The principal dimensions of AB Sawt's work concern cultural programming, distribution and communication, and public and media relations, and they are currently promoting a selection of Moroccan and Algerian musicians based in Morocco, Algeria and France (including Hocine Boukella, also known as Cheikh Sidi Bémol; see Chapter 3). Beyond AB Sawt, Amel has now become heavily involved in theatre and is director of the Fondation des arts vivants in Casablanca, which organizes theatre education workshops and high-profile theatre festivals. While Amel is clearly very active in various cultural scenes in Casablanca, she remains fairly reticent about the recent cultural effervescence in Morocco, arguing that in Darga's case it was the group's link with the Spanish tour organizer (and Fábrica de ideas) that allowed the group to survive in a context where only a select few musicians and groups can manage to keep afloat in a Morocco which may have many summertime music festivals but which, during the rest of the year, can be a rather more subdued place in terms of concert dates and venues:

> People think that Darga is the super group, etc., but we're actually really fragile. We are trying to structure it as much as we can, but it's really difficult when we know that for six months we had zero dirhams, and that we are totally in deficit. So yes of course it's good, of course it's great, of course yeah there are all these radio stations etc. but for me that's nothing ... it's nothing serious, we've not really built anything ... the Boulevard which has existed for ten years and on which everyone counts, well, from one day to the next, it could

no longer exist any more. And we don't know if there will be the resources ... what they'll do ... so it is clear that, in relation to Darga, already it's been more than two years that we've known ... what saved Darga, is that we could start touring abroad, and that there was this Spanish tour agent who straightaway put her confidence in the group, who saw that it could work, and who invested a lot ... but if there hadn't been this Spanish tour agent, today we would have nothing. [26] (Kiwan's and Gibert's interview with Amel Abou el aazm, April 2008, Rabat)

So while Amel has clearly invested a great deal of her creative energies into Morocco's urban cultural scenes, and is propelled in her work by a concern for broader South–South, African agendas (the Lawnouna and AB Sawt ventures testify to this), she is very much part of a cosmopolitan, transnational network which draws on her multiple contacts in France, Spain and the UK too. She acknowledges that these transnational networks have enabled her to carry out her work in Morocco.

Conclusions

In this chapter we have shown how artists' networks across Europe and the 'South' are often inscribed in multiple locations beyond the highly visible concentration of diasporic musicians in capital cities (see Chapter 3). Our discussion has focused on the phenomenon of multi-sited individuals and groups who are simultaneously located in capitals and provincial towns and cities across Europe, but also in countries of origin, and on the resettlement of migrant artists and cultural producers in their countries of origin. These phenomena and our varied case studies highlight different, but interrelated, dimensions of cultural globalization, in as far as it concerns relations between North and South. What seems to emerge from the musicians' and cultural producers' stories is a highly complex articulation of the narratives of transnationalism and alternative nationalism. In other words, they simultaneously inscribe their work within a transnational/cosmopolitan frame yet all the while are subscribing to a groundedness and attachment to a strongly culturally inflected sense of place.

Part 3
Mutual Support

5
Mutual Supports: North <> South

In this chapter we will focus more closely on national cultural institutions in the North and the role they play in the facilitation and activation of transnational cultural networks. To what extent do institutions such as the British Council, the Institut français, the Goethe-Institut and those associated with them in the South such as the Cercle germano-malgache/Goethe Cultural Centre, the Alliance française, the Centre culturel Albert Camus or cultural divisions of various embassies engage in 'top-down' initiatives with North Africa and Madagascar and to what extent do such initiatives work in tandem with other local cultural actors based in the South? This chapter will also focus on the complex nature of the relationship between cultural institutions attached to the former colonial power (that is, the Institut français in the case of North Africa and Madagascar) and cultural actors (for example festival organizers, musicians) who are based in the former colonies. The first section of the chapter will provide a brief overview of the historical and political contexts surrounding the establishment of these institutions, before going on to consider the main ways in which such bodies intervene in the various cultural scenes in Morocco and Madagascar, taking as our focus a number of key case studies drawn from our field research with musicians, cultural producers and institutional representatives. Our field research in both Morocco and Madagascar suggested that although the cultural policy contexts are quite different in these countries, the roles that cultural institutions such as the Institut français, British Council, Goethe-Institut and CGM play are in fact fairly similar: namely they serve, partly, to facilitate the emergence of home-grown sustainable cultural scenes and, at the same time, also work towards the transnationalization of such scenes, through network-capacity building across transnational spaces. Hence, in both cases, the work of such cultural institutions has an inward and an outward dimension which combines the translocal with a transnational optic.

This chapter will also consider some of the ambiguities of the intervention of such institutions in the cultural field. In particular, we will ask whether some aspects of the cultural capacity-building agenda of organizations such as the British Council or Institut français are somehow tainted with broader neocolonial agendas, which in the case of Morocco (and the Middle East and North Africa in general) are also tied up with the democratization pressures which inform the foreign policies of Britain and France. Clearly linked to this ambiguity is the lack of clarity concerning how the original remit of such nationally defined organizations such as the Institut français, the British Council and indeed the Goethe-Institut (the promotion of French, British and German cultures abroad) is articulated with the more recent orientations which place more emphasis on the development of the cultures/ cultural scenes of the countries of the South.

Historical and political antecedents

France has a long-established tradition of a strong state-led cultural policy and although the Ministry of Cultural Affairs was only set up in 1958, French cultural policy has historically been closely articulated with France's foreign policies and, most significantly, its imperial expansion. Hence culture has always been a prominent feature of France's conception of international diplomacy, and the projection of France's cultural identity/influence abroad (the *rayonnement* principle) is thus part and parcel of the missions of the Ministry of Foreign Affairs. France has a dense network of cultural institutions abroad, comprising 161 cooperation and cultural action services, 209 cultural centres and institutes across 130 countries, and 459 subsidized Alliances françaises.[1] Beyond these cultural centres, France's ambassadors are key to the implementation of France's cultural policy in a whole range of locations. Within Francophone Africa there are 30 cultural institutes and 5 more in non-Francophone African countries (Ager 2005: 60). While the network of Alliances françaises are independent local associations, they are heavily subsidized and are linked to the Alliance française in Paris. The dense network of cultural institutes and Alliances organizes cultural events such as film screenings, concerts, exhibitions, seminars and workshops where local artists as well as artists residing in France are invited to perform. There is also a strong linguistic dimension to these cultural institutes, which also serve as libraries and French-language teaching centres.

One must situate the current state of affairs in the broader context of decolonization. In the wake of most of Francophone Africa's independence in the 1960s, France sought to maintain close ties with its former colonies and protectorates and one of the key ways of achieving this was through both French-language education and what Ager calls 'cultural aid'. Ager further shows that in terms of the French language, the stakes were regarded as particularly high and in 1966 the newly established Haut comité pour la défense et l'expansion de la langue française (High Commission for the Defence and Expansion of the French Language) was placed under the tutelage of the prime minister. Georges Pompidou and Valéry Giscard d'Estaing presided over Franco-African summits in 1973 and, from 1981 onwards, François Mitterrand also saw to it that Africa was central to his foreign policy (Ager 2005: 58). In 1984, the Haut comité pour la défense et l'expansion de la langue française disbanded into two organizations: the Haut conseil de la Francophonie (The Francophone High Council) and the Haut commissariat de la langue française (The High Commission of the French Language), and in 1986 the first summit of Francophone countries was held ('Sommet de la Francophonie'). The OIF groups together 56 member states which all share the use of the French language and, according to the website, 'universal values' as well. In 2002, Abdou Diouf, the former president of Senegal, was elected as Secretary-General of La Francophonie. The OIF, which officially became known as such in 2005, has its roots in the 1970 Treaty of Niamey, which led to the establishment of the Agence de coopération culturelle et technique (Agency for Cultural and Technical Cooperation). Today, its objectives include, among others, the promotion of democratization, human rights, the French language, education, cultural diversity and sustainable development (see www.francophonie.org/, accessed November 2010). Given the linguistic dimension of the OIF, it has unsurprisingly been active in the cultural field. Of particular significance was its establishment of the satellite television channel TV5Monde in 1984 which now broadcasts to over 200 countries from its headquarters in Paris via a number of regionalized channels covering Europe, Asia, the Pacific, Africa and the Americas.

While the days of 'la Françafrique' – the term used to denote the 'special relationship' between France and Francophone Africa – are gone, President Chirac did nevertheless maintain a close interest in the fortunes of several Francophone African states. However, from 2002 onwards these interests were increasingly defined in economic and financial terms, as opposed to the political and military terms of the Françafrique era, reflecting the newly globalized policy environment (Chafer 2005).

Since President Sarkozy's rise to power in 2007, some commentators have characterized the France–Africa relationship as being one of 'new interventionism', which would also suggest some form of continuity in the notion of a 'special relationship' linking France and Africa (see Charbonneau 2008).

So it is evident that despite the demise of the French empire (and indeed, perhaps *because* of the latter's demise), the French state occupies a fairly significant position in the international cultural scene. It is able to do so through a clearly defined cultural policy which aims to promote French culture and language abroad, against American or 'Anglo-Saxon' cultural hegemony. (France was one of the leading nations in the move to set up the UNESCO Convention on Cultural Diversity in 2005.) It sets out to achieve its objectives through its Ministry of Culture and Communication and the Ministry of Foreign Affairs, which work in tandem with the semi-autonomous organization known as Cultures France (formerly AFAA or the Association française de l'action artistique/French Association for Artistic Action), and, of course, through the dense network of cultural centres located in a range of countries across the globe.

German cultural policy abroad

The cultural and educational equivalent of the Institut français for Germany is the Goethe-Institut (GI). Named after Johann Wolfgang von Goethe, a true polymath and one of the towering figures of eighteenth- and nineteenth-century German literature and European cultural life in general, the GI was set up in 1951 as a non-profit cultural institution. Though politically independent it is nevertheless closely linked to the German government, from which it receives its main funding and whose ethos it represents abroad. Its main purpose is the promotion and study of German language and culture worldwide, and to encourage cultural exchanges. There are at present 136 fully accredited Goethe-Instituts and 11 liaison offices in 92 countries, including Morocco and Algeria, as well as a further 30 official 'Goethe-Centres'. In Madagascar the Goethe-Institut is represented by the so-called Cercle germano-malgache (CGM) which was set up in 1975 and which in the year 2000 received in addition to its associative charter in Madagascar the status of a 'Goethe-Centre', based on a cooperation treaty whereby the CGM agrees to pursue its language and cultural work 'nach den Grundsätzen und Qualitätsmaßstäben des Goethe-Instituts' – in line with the principles and quality standards of the GI (official website www.goethe.de). On the

German Foreign Office's official website the significance of the CGM for German–Malagasy relations is listed as follows:

> Important elements in cultural relations with Madagascar are the work of the bilateral cultural institute Cercle germano-malagasy (CGM)/Goethe-Centre and academic contacts, especially in the natural sciences and German studies. With some 520 German pupils, the Goethe-Centre contributes to the dissemination of the German language and *has for decades now, despite its very modest funding, organized a wide range of events countering the French influence on the country's culture.* Since its establishment, it has been funded from the Federal Foreign Office's cultural budget. With funding for Africa having been generally augmented, the Goethe-Centre's budget was also substantially increased last year [2008], enabling activities to be further expanded. (www.auswaertiges-amt.de/diplo/en/Laenderinformationen/01-Laender/Madagascar.html, accessed 16 May 2010, our emphasis)

At the time of writing (November 2010), official political relations between Madagascar and Germany are still suspended, following the seizure of power by Andry Rajoelina in spring 2009, although diplomatic relations continue to be upheld through its embassies. Cultural relations are not affected by this – hopefully temporary – freeze, and the CGM continues its activities unimpeded by the general crisis in the more formal realms of economic support. We highlighted the lines from the Foreign Office's own text about the CGM to draw attention to a somewhat bizarre formulation about the CGM's success in 'countering the French influence on the country's culture' 'despite its very modest funding'. The hardly intended connotation of a Franco-German cultural turf war whereby the CGM erects its German flag on the building in Anakely to counter the French domination of the CCAC and the Alliance française elsewhere in Antananarivo may answer to the perception of the Foreign Office's own view of cultural relations in Madagascar, and its wish to strengthen German cultural influences, but hardly fits with the much more broadly conceived cultural activities of the CGM and its long-standing director Eckehart Olszowski. One of the advantages of being merely affiliated to the Goethe-Institut lies in the fact that the position of director is not regulated by the same principle of usually three to six years' circulation which is the rule for GI employees and ambassadorial or near-ambassadorial staff. Hence Olszowski has been in charge of the CGM for 30 years, enabling him not only to learn to speak Malagasy fluently – he even co-edited a two-volume German–Malagasy, Malagasy–German dictionary (Bergenholtz et al. 1991, 1994) – but also to become intimately acquainted with Malagasy culture and Malagasy artists. Nor does he see himself as a German bastion; indeed, the directors of the other cultural institutes – the CCAC and the Alliance française – are regular visitors to the CGM's concerts, just as Olszowski will not miss out on important events organized by the French institutions. Of course, the CGM regularly organizes activities and events that follow the brief of the Foreign Office's declaration: they conduct German-language courses, host visiting artists and scholars from German-speaking countries, run symposia and workshops; they celebrate a 'German' Christmas with an advent wreath strung from the ceiling; and most recently in November 2009 hosted an embassy event with a graffiti-covered copy of the Berlin Wall in the main hall of the CGM, which was subsequently and somewhat dustily taken down in celebration of the 20th anniversary of the fall of the Wall in Berlin. However, what has given the CGM such a significant place in the cultural life of Madagascar is its vital support for Malagasy roots musicians, for 'la musique du terroir'. A quote from Madanight.com posted in 2006 gives quite a different and much more appropriate flavour of the CGM's multiple roles:

> The German Goethe-Institut, also known as Cercle germano-malgache since 1975, better known as CGM, made a name for itself as the most convivial of all the cultural institutions of Antananarivo. Since its opening in 1960, it has always been a place for artistic exchange, musical discovery and language studies. Nowadays, the centre offers different activities including the teaching of the German language of course but also drawing and music. Its small concert hall is a place for music lovers to meet, especially during the Madajazzcar Festival. The CGM also promotes local music. The great personalities of Malagasy music of the likes of Ricky, Rossy, Dama, Silo, Rakoto Frah, Feo Gasy and Solomiral owe a great deal to this cultural centre. The CGM also offers a platform for Malagasy poets, who gathered within the 'Faribolana Sandratra' society. Apart from its cultural and didactic activities, the centre also became a proper information centre about Germany. [1] (www.madanight.com/articles/diplomatie/783-madagascar-allemagne-une-cooperation-bilaterale-epanouie.html, accessed 16 May 2010)

How much more to the point in describing this lively hub of activity! We have already discussed the CGM's vital role in Chapter 2, with quotes from Mbasa (of the group Salala), and when we analysed the ways in which key individuals, vital institutions and the geo-social infrastructure act together to turn the capital city into a cultural hub. For musicians, the CGM is one of the most important cultural institutions in Antananarivo, alongside the CCAC and the Alliance française, with many artists from all over the country often receiving their very first opportunities to perform, to join forces with others and to build up their careers. Mbasa's unsolicited account of the vital role that Olszowski played in his career sums up best of all what we have heard from many other musicians, including Ricky Olombelo, Samy and many others, and underlines our own collaboration with him during the TNMundi cultural event in November 2007:

> Well, I could go so far as to say that Salala owes a great deal, 50 per cent or more, of its artistic style to Olszowski. Because I mixed, I did a cappella but I also did music with instrumental accompaniment, but it was Olszowski who told me 'You choose, you choose, because you underestimate that your group has a certain groove, but you need to opt for one direction, because that's how you gain much more attention in relation to the other groups.' At the time I was not at all convinced. Because at the time we thought that perhaps one day we would make some kind of career out of music, and so we thought to keep all the options open. But Olszowski told me, 'Voilà, you stop doing rose-tinted songs, stop doing things with a guitar, and all that, stop using women, women in the centre of your group. Work together just the three of you.' And so I tried. I wasn't convinced, but he was. He was convinced. And he took me to see others who were of the same opinion. So I thought to myself, well if it's someone of Olszowski's calibre who says that, if the Goethe itself tells me that this is what is interesting, then I'd be stupid to contradict them. That's how it was in the beginning. And after that he organized a concert for us with Ricky. And the people became enthusiastic, but at the time we couldn't even fill the little hall of the CGM. So yeah, it took some effort to make it relatively professional. And the CGM at that time was by far superior to the Ministry of Culture as far as the promotion of the culture and especially the music of Madagascar was concerned. I think there are quite a number of groups just as Salala who would have long since disappeared if the CGM had not offered some proper structures. [2] (Meinhof's interview, April 2009, Nantes)

The CGM's role is limited to Antananarivo, although through its support for migrant musicians from all over Madagascar as well as from abroad, it is continuously constructing a translocal and transnational cultural space that allows artists to increase their networking capacity and thus to facilitate sustainable cultural development. The Goethe-Instituts in North Africa, although blessed with more official representations with two fully accredited GIs in Morocco – Rabat and Casablanca – one in Algiers/Algeria and one in Tunis/Tunisia, have far less visibility for North African musicians than the CGM has in Madagascar, if our interviews with North African artists are anything to go by. Here the French, Spanish and the British cultural institutions seem to be more involved in cultural networking than their German counterparts.

Facilitating home-grown sustainable cultural development

The Boulevard

The Boulevard des jeunes musiciens Festival (discussed in Chapter 2) which is held annually in Casablanca, Morocco started out as a small-scale urban music festival in 1999 and has grown to become one of the largest, if not the largest, urban music festivals in Africa. The festival showcases hip-hop, fusion and heavy metal/rock music from around Morocco, bringing together emergent national musicians and international stars invited from abroad. The event is a prime example of how an alternative cultural movement moved from a marginal to a central position within the broader cultural landscape. Indeed, the Boulevard is the result of the collective efforts of a group of friends (activists, artists, journalists, etc.) who moved from being cultural 'outsiders' in late 1990s Morocco to becoming 'a cultural reference' in 2010. Despite receiving sponsorship from foreign cultural institutes (the British Council, Institut français, the French Embassy in Morocco – the Service de coopération et action culturelle/The Cooperation and Cultural Action Service), private companies such as Nokia and Coca-Cola, and most recently from King Mohammed VI (in 2009), they have nevertheless managed to maintain an 'underground' or 'alternative' image. Indeed, what is particularly interesting about the Boulevard is its ability to successfully ally public and private, national and transnational interests within the same event. (For more specific details on the emergence of the Boulevard, which is far more than a festival, but can be considered as one of the major current cultural movements in contemporary Morocco, see Chapter 2.)

In terms of the institutional support that the Boulevard has generated for its activities over the years, the Casablanca Institut français has undoubtedly played a key role in supporting the festival. The Institut français in Casablanca has often served as a venue where related workshops and conferences have been held. For example, in 2006 the IF Casablanca hosted a discussion panel on the use of *darija* in Moroccan urban music in parallel to the festival itself and in 2007 it hosted a panel on the theme of language and new technologies. Furthermore, the Institut français in Casablanca has also hosted the annual Musical Documentary Festival since 2007. Beyond the hosting of related events, the Institut français in Agadir has also been involved in artistic residence projects such as the one involving the Marseille group Watcha Clan and Agadir groups Amarg Fusion and Style Souss. This residence project led to a performance at the 2007 Boulevard in Casablanca.

Since 2002, the British Council in Morocco has also been a key partner in the activities of the Boulevard and has funded the participation of musicians based in Britain in the 2005 and 2006 programmes (for example hip-hop artists such as Pogo, Ty and Black Twang and Ninja Tune's VJ Hexstatic). In 2007 the British Council was a particularly visible partner of the Boulevard since it funded a transnational music residence known as Music Matbakh, the aim of which was to bring together young musicians from the North Africa and Middle East regions for a three-week residency in London, followed by a UK and international tour of North Africa and the Middle East. What is interesting about the Boulevard–British Council link is the fact that it became much more than an institutionalized funding partnership. This clearly had something to do with the fact that the British Council arts officer, Hicham El Kebbaj, was himself passionate about urban music (especially hip-hop) and became a freelance manager for a number of the groups who gravitate around the Boulevard (Hoba Hoba Spirit and H-Kayne being just two prominent examples). El Kebbaj left his post with the British Council in 2008 and it appears that the 2010 sponsors of the Boulevard Festival do *not* include the British Council. Nevertheless, the relationship between the British Council and the Boulevard could certainly be thought of in terms of *mutual* support because not only has the festival benefited enormously from the funding of British-based artists in the festival programmes, it could be argued that the arts officer was also able to develop certain skills as a cultural entrepreneur because of his close work with the Boulevard team. Indeed, the arts officer in question became a sort of Boulevard activist, and contributed to the team during both the festival and its planning stages. The British Council also awarded Momo Merhari, co-founder of the Boulevard, the Young Music Entrepreneur of the Year prize in June 2006. Momo won £7500 prize money to be used in the development of a music project fostering greater links between the UK and Morocco.

So it could be argued that the above examples of the involvement of the Institut français, the British Council and the CGM demonstrate the ways in which national cultural institutions of the North can be quite instrumental in the development of home-grown cultural scenes in the South.

This evaluation of the role of national cultural institutes in Morocco is generally one which is reinforced by the musicians as well. The majority of musicians we met point out that institutions such as the Institut français, the Instituto Cervantes, the CGM or the British Council were instrumental in the development of their careers, since these cultural centres often provide aspiring musicians with precious rehearsal space, often free of charge or at heavily subsidized rates. The network of the Institut français in particular supports young unknown musicians in this way. The same can be said for the role of the Alliance française in Madagascar which through its 6 major offices in provincial towns (*pôles régionaux*) and 22 others has a network in place which enables it not only to support local artists but also to construct a translocal space for touring. Thus valiha player Rajery as well as Justin Vali have in turn been able to create 'orchestras' with lesser-known musicians from different corners of the island and group them together for national and even international tours. Justin Vali in particular is musical director of the so-called Ny Malagasy Orkestra which lists as co-producers the three key representative institutions for France in Madagascar: the French Embassy, the Alliance française and the CACC (Centre culturel Albert Camus). In 2009, and again in 2010, the Orkestra has been touring France, thus gaining the first international recognition for a group of largely unknown musicians, many of whom live in the provinces, such as the formidable lokanga violin player, singer and dancer Remanindry, whom we visited in his house in a district of Toliara in 2009.

In Morocco, guitar and singer-songwriter, and Boulevard activist, Hicham Bajjou points out that his early musical career with metal and rock bands Total Eclypse and, later, Dayzine was closely linked to the Casablanca branch of the Institut français, and that he also worked regularly with the Instituto Cervantes and the British Council.[2] In addition, Hicham Bajjou is now one of the main instigators of the annual Film Documentary Festival which takes place in Casablanca each spring and it is also significant that the documentary which screens films from around the world has been held at the Casablanca Institut français since it was established in 2007. In a similar vein, musician Badre Belhachemi from fusion Casablanca-based group Darga also notes that the Institut français and Instituto Cervantes 'culturally, get things moving a bit in Morocco' [3] (Kiwan's interview with Badre Belhachemi, April 2008, Rabat).

Beyond the Casablanca–Rabat strip, as well as outside Antananarivo, the network of the Alliance française and the Institut français are just as, if not more, significant in provincial towns such as Meknes or Agadir in Morocco, or the many distant towns in the Malagasy provinces. We just quoted the case of the Malagasy Orkestra as only one of several examples that are sustained or even owe their existence to the support of these cultural institutions. In Morocco, Ali Faiq, the lead singer from the group Amarg Fusion, highlights the fact that, in his opinion and experience, the Institut français and the artistic residencies that have been organized there have allowed groups like his own and others categorized as being part of the 'nouvelle scène' to 'professionalize' (Kiwan's and Gibert's interview with Ali Faiq, April 2008, Agadir). The desire to professionalize is similarly characteristic of the relationship that the Meknes-based rappers H-Kayne have with their local Institut français. H-Kayne are one of the most significant and well-known rap groups to have emerged in the new Moroccan scene, thanks in part to their triumph at the 2003 Boulevard Tremplin competition. They continue to reside in Meknes and have taken it upon themselves to set up their own association, 'Urban Style', one of the aims of which is to cultivate and foster other up and coming talents in the local Meknes scene. And for those who are lucky enough to be selected at the prestigious Boulevard Tremplin competition, the H-Kayne group members organize a pre-Tremplin, to allow the contestants to hone their on-stage skills. These pre-Tremplin sessions take place at the Meknes branch of the Institut français, and Othmane and Hatim point out that after lobbying the director they were able to gain access and have maintained good working relationships with successive directors since.

Facilitation of transnational cultural development

While the above examples show that national cultural institutes such as the Institut français, the British Council or the Instituto Cervantes provide valuable support in accompanying the emergence of a young, urban 'new music scene' within Morocco, we must not lose sight of the fact that these institutions principally work transnationally. They are therefore involved in the facilitation of cultural scenes which reach beyond Morocco (and North Africa) or Madagascar. A key example of this transnational dynamic is the British Council-sponsored project known as Music Matbakh.[3] Music Matbakh was a three-week music residency which took place in the UK in May 2007 and it brought together 12 musicians from Morocco, Tunisia, Lebanon, Egypt and Syria and three musicians from the UK. The project was conceived by the British Council (Hicham El Kebbaj and Leah Zakks) and produced by Serious, an international 'world music' and jazz production organization based in London. The residency, led by Robert Plant's guitarist Justin Adams, also brought together a wide range of musical genres such as rock, metal, electronica, hip-hop and more 'traditional' Arabic music repertoires. Following the three-week residency, which saw the group working and performing together in London, Cambridge and Gateshead, the musicians went on an international tour of the North Africa and Middle East regions over the summer, starting off with a performance at the 2007 Boulevard des jeunes musiciens in Casablanca.

The British Council, which operates as 'an executive non-departmental public body', is nevertheless sponsored by the UK government's Foreign and Commonwealth Office. Its broad aims are as follows: 'to build mutually beneficial relationships between people in the UK and other countries and to increase appreciation of the UK's creative ideas and achievements' (www.britishcouncil.org/new/Documents/About-us/ FCOManagementStatement.pdf, accessed August 2010). With specific reference to the Music Matbakh project, the objectives of the British Council could be summarized as pertaining to the promotion of British art, cultural exchange, the challenging of stereotypes, support of local (non-British art scenes) and the broadening of artistic collaboration processes beyond bilateral national exchange.[4] While the reactions of certain musicians involved in the project suggested that the 'top-down' nature of the residency was at times regarded as problematic ('the only thing, which was a bit weird for me, was Arab musicians but an English musical director'; 'It's a bit sad that this programme wasn't initiated by a country from the Arab World'; Gibert's interview with Ousso, May 2007, Gateshead; Hiba, quoted in *London Project*, 28 May 2007) there was a general sense among many of the participants that the project had been a worthwhile learning experience (in terms of both musical 'discovery' and developing their professional skills):

> It's none the less an opportunity to have very very enriching exchanges [...] So it's things like that as well ... new social networks bring new musical, cultural, artistic colours. [4] (Gibert's interview with Skander, May 2007, London)

So I'm learning something very very good, not on the musical level but on the ... Actually something more important than the musical level you know: how to work in a team. If you're not able to do this, you're not able to do this music. (Gibert's interview with Ousso, May 2007, Gateshead)

A key objective of the residency, aside from the creation of four unique concerts within the UK, and then the international tour, was the facilitation of professional networking for the musicians. Musicians were asked by the British Council and Serious representatives who they would like to meet in the UK music industry (music producers, distributors, media contacts, training opportunities, other musicians, etc.) and a special showcase concert of the Music Matbakh project was organized at the Spitz Gallery in London on 22 May 2007, to which representatives from the media and music industry, cultural institutions and diplomatic representatives were invited. Following the residency, one musician, Ousso, moved to the UK to undertake further jazz music training (Serious organized an interview for Ousso at the Royal Academy, although he ended up studying at a private establishment), and MCs Bigg and RGB were able to showcase their work in a number of London's hip-hop venues thanks to the networking of the Moroccan-based British Council arts officer Hicham El Kebbaj.

The Music Matbakh project clearly faced certain challenges linked to the broad range of musical genres it brought together and the short timeframe it provided for the production of a musical set and multiple performances. The group also encountered some difficulties once they left the UK context. The lukewarm reception at the Boulevard des jeunes musiciens, where the young Moroccan public was far more keen on hearing Bigg as the commercially successful solo artist than seeing him as part of a broader artistic project along with other musicians unknown to them, also suggests that the creative process which the musicians were so enthusiastic about when in the UK did not necessarily translate into public acclaim in their respective countries of origin.[5] Nevertheless, Music Matbakh has enjoyed something of an afterlife and a number of its participants came together to form Music Matbakh (Independent), a sort of offshoot of the original experience. This reduced group of six musicians from Morocco, Egypt and Jordan got together once again for two performances in Cairo and Alexandria in February and March 2008. Their reunion was the result of the initiative taken by Egyptian guitarist Ousso, who also organizes the underground music festival SOS Music in Cairo, where the re-formed Music Matbakh (Independent) played.

So the Music Matbakh example shows how cultural institutes such as the British Council are working fairly effectively in the facilitation of transnational cultural development. What emerges from the Music Matbakh experience is that what was an initially 'top-down' initiative took on a sort of life of its own, and although the project faced several challenges due to certain elements of its design, it led to the development of new transnational networks among musicians from the Middle East and North Africa. Music Matbakh is thus an example of how top-down initiatives led by cultural institutions can produce unexpected results.

The TNMundi project

A further example where cultural institutions supported transnational development comes from our own work with the TNMundi project. Having developed in part from a previous EU-funded project, Changing City Spaces,[6] where we first experimented with a cultural event in Saint-Ouen outside Paris in 2005, TNMundi organized three cultural events: in Antananarivo in 2007, in Rabat in 2008 and in Southampton in 2009 (Figures 5.1, 5.2).

Figure 5.1   TNMundi event in Tana (© Ulrike Meinhof)

Figure 5.2 TNMundi concert in Southampton (© Turner Sims Concert Hall)

For each of these events, the aim was to bring together all the constituencies of our research and to demonstrate in practice and to a wider public the multiple effects of musicians' transnational networks. Hence in all three events researchers from the university sector debated with cultural policy-makers, members of NGOs, media and music industry representatives and, most importantly, the artists themselves. The highlight of these days of debate were specially devised concerts, all three curated by the Malagasy musician Dama, where after several days of artist residencies musicians who had never played together would give one or in some cases two public concerts. TNMundi was not interested in producing a top-down fusion of musical styles but rather to make visible the processes and possibilities of collaboration between artists who were presenting and sharing their work with one another. Hence, apart from organizational matters, we withdrew from all the preparation for the concerts with only Dama acting as the cohesive link between all three musical events and the diverse musicians. This series of collaborations was only feasible because financial support from a range of different public and private agencies allowed us to invite artists from the different nodes of their transnational networks – from Germany and France and Malagasy provinces to Antananarivo; from England, France, Madagascar and other parts of Morocco to Rabat; and from Madagascar, Morocco, France and Germany to Southampton. Altogether TNMundi produced five concerts, all preceded by artists' residencies, which enabled the artists to get to know one another and develop a joint programme based on their own decisions as to how and when to collaborate.

Under the musical direction of Dama, the first event in Antananarivo included 15 Malagasy-origin musicians from Europe and different regions of Madagascar, with one of the two concerts being broadcast live on Malagasy national television; the event in Rabat comprised six artists of Moroccan background resident in Europe and Morocco; and the final event in Southampton brought together 15 artists, 7 of Malagasy, and 8 of North African origin. Thus we were able not only to present and discuss the relevance of academic findings with a wider public, but also to demonstrate in practice – and symbolically – some of the more positive possibilities of cultural globalization.

Understandably, none of the non-academic activities could be funded from our research grant, so we had to rely on different kinds of sponsorship. This came for instance from the CGM in Antananarivo, which not only hosted the two-day symposium on its premises free of charge, but also liaised with private sponsors and the national TV station which in turn hosted the concerts. For the event in Rabat, both the British Council and the Institut français supported the international flights and local travel of musicians, while the Faculty of Letters, University Mohammed V of Rabat, hosted the event,[7] and for the final and most ambitious event in Southampton, the Arts Council South-East provided an additional grant for the two public concerts at the University of Southampton's Turner Sims Concert Hall. These musical encounters would not have been possible without the support of the respective cultural organizations, setting in motion new and now independent artistic ventures between some of the artists in question. Thus – and only to give some brief examples of many other connections subsequently formed – the very first event in Saint-Ouen in 2005 created the first opportunity for the Madagascar All Stars – then only a group of five individual artists – to meet up with the influential German radio producer Werner Fuhr of the WDR (Westdeutscher Rundfunk), who subsequently invited the group to the Cologne studio from where their career snow-balled. The event in Antananarivo enabled Mfa Kera, Berlin-based gospel and jazz singer who left her native Madagascar at the age of six, to return for the first time to Madagascar and meet up with other Malagasy musicians, with many collaborations having followed since then. Rabat created a link between Dama, the London-based musician Farid from the Moroccan group MoMo and the Paris-based Binobin, which subsequently was reconfirmed in their collaborating in the final event in Southampton. And the event in Southampton itself sparked off a new connection between Paris-based oud player Yazid Fentazi from Algeria and Régis Gizavo from Madagascar.

Challenges/ambiguities

What these developments underline is the vital role of cultural institutions in supporting artists who do not easily survive in competition with the fast-changing fashions of Western pop music. But there are ambivalences which we cannot ignore. Of course, the involvement of the British Council in a non-Anglophone, non-post-colonial cultural space such as North Africa further underlines the cosmopolitan dimension of music, so that a Moroccan-origin musician resident in London such as Farid Nainia can become fundable and thus indirectly a representative of his new country of residence irrespective of ethnic background. We have already shown the ways in which this can work on a regional level in France, where both Edgar Ravahatra and Mamiso were selected to represent their French region of residence in national competitions. Similarly, the songs and films by Turkish-origin musicians and film-makers are regularly entered as Germany's contribution in the Eurovision Song Contest and international film festivals.

However, we must consider the question as to the extent to which this is a positive development away from narrow ethnicization and national identity politics towards a much more open and cosmopolitan imaginary, or purely an appropriation by the national markets of cultural diversity as and when it seems strategically useful, only to be dismissed when it ceases to fulfil that role. Thus, while cultural institutions such as the British Council, the Institut français or the Alliance française undoubtedly provide crucial mechanisms of support for sustainable home-grown and transnational cultural creativity in both North Africa and Madagascar, their activities do bear some significant ambiguities. For example, although the British Council is a charity and an executive non-departmental body, operating at arm's length from government, it is nevertheless linked to broader UK government policy agendas, particularly with regard to geopolitical issues in the Middle East, Near East and North Africa regions. The UK Secretary of State for Foreign and Commonwealth Affairs must account for the operations and performance of the British Council to Parliament, and the Foreign and Commonwealth Office (FCO) is the British Council's Sponsoring Department. Given this context, it is perhaps unsurprising that the British Council's 'Intercultural dialogue' operation currently prioritizes a focus on the Middle East, North Africa, Central and South Asia, with Iraq, Saudi Arabia, Egypt and Pakistan being given a special mention in the British Council's 2008–9 annual report, whereas Madagascar has even lost its British embassy to neighbouring island Mauritius. The British Council clearly states that its work in the field of intercultural relations is to engage with and influence young people in order to forge a 'safe and secure culturally diverse world'. In concrete terms, the intercultural work of the British Council will focus on three main initiatives known as 'Connecting Classrooms', 'Active Citizens' and 'Global Changemakers'. The Active Citizens plan sets up UK–overseas partnerships to provide 'a new framework to help young people understand how they can contribute more fully to their societies and the global community'. What the nature of this 'new framework' is exactly is not made clear in the annual report. But it does appear to suggest a politically prescriptive agenda. The term 'democratization' is not used but one could easily substitute the word for the phrase 'a new framework'. The 'Global Changemakers' programme has a more explicitly political objective, namely to 'create new networks of leaders in society', offering 'highly motivated young professionals' the opportunity to 'influence policy formulation'. It would perhaps be an exaggeration to argue that the intercultural dialogue programme of the British Council is part of a broader neocolonial agenda for the world's developing countries. Nevertheless, the explicit objective to influence young people and 'those who influence young people' does bear the hallmark of some sort of 'civilizing mission' which ultimately is designed to serve the 'UK's long-term interests'. Note that the UK's long-term interests are not spelled out in this section of the report but one imagines that they are linked to the building of 'international relationships based on trust and understanding' in a context of growing global economic crisis and conflict (British Council annual report 2008–9, www.britishcouncil.org, accessed 7 May 2010).

Global financial and geopolitical instability also forms the backdrop to the elaboration of the British Council's activities under the creative and knowledge economy heading. The 2008–9 annual report states that: 'Our work also seeks to share the benefits of the creative and knowledge economy as a very powerful response to global insecurity, financial crisis and isolationism.' Priority countries for the British Council's work in the creative and knowledge economy include Brazil, China, Russia and India, but Central and South Asia, sub-Saharan Africa, the Middle East, Near East and North Africa are also cited as important regions where the British Council aims to develop 'dialogue through access to English' and to 'tackle misconceptions, support innovation and trust'. In terms of plans for the future, the British Council report lays out its objectives to initiate a new global programme known as 'Cultural Leadership International' which aims to foster 'the development of and interaction between cultural leaders' in both the European and Near East and North Africa regions. The leitmotif of the British Council's creative and knowledge economy strategy is 'capacity-building' and it is certainly a theme that was prominent in the Music Matbakh artistic residency discussed above. Capacity-building gets at the notion of infrastructural development and it clearly frames much of the British Council's work under the rubric of the creative and knowledge economy. The development of a stable and sustainable creative infrastructure is posited as being beneficial for both the UK and the countries it has partnerships with. Nevertheless, it could be argued that the capacity-building agenda, like the intercultural dialogue programme, is ambiguous to the extent that it does seem to be enmeshed with broader geopolitical concerns such as global insecurity, and one wonders whether the focus on the NENA region (Near East and North Africa) is also bound up with a democratization agenda. The ambiguity stems not from the pro-democracy approach itself, but rather from the symbolic challenges that such work entails, not least the possible perception shared by young people in the NENA region of a foreign Western cultural institute which is somehow 'meddling' in their internal affairs and 'peddling' a benevolent yet Eurocentric vision of what constitutes 'healthy, well-functioning societies' (British Council annual report 2008–9, www.britishcouncil.org, accessed 7 May 2010).

This of course links to a broader question that arises in our examination of North–South mutual support in the cultural field. Just who is supporting whom? To what extent can one argue that twenty-first-century cultural relations really enable a two-way process where both the North and the South mutually benefit and support each other? In the case of the network of French Institutes and cultural centres (the 'réseau culturel français à l'étranger'), this is certainly an ambiguous issue, particularly in the light of the fact that one of the main objectives has always been and remains the promotion of French culture abroad. Certainly, within the field of contemporary popular music, the emphasis has been placed on efforts to defend and promote French music (chanson, electronica, 'world music made in France') in the face of Anglo-American domination. In the realm of cinema, it is well known that France was one of the leading countries to push forward for a UNESCO Convention on cultural diversity in 2005, arguing that cultural products such as films and music are not commodities like any other so should benefit from special protection from WTO regulations on free trade. Such a position was reiterated in a governmental statement made by France in December 2009 (*Pour une nouvelle stratégie culturelle extérieure de l'Union européenne/* For a new extra-EU cultural strategy).

Nevertheless, France has, in a sense, been forced to use the language and the logic of the market to be able to continue to defend its presence on the international cultural scene, and as far as contemporary popular music is concerned, the Ministère des affaires étrangères et européennes teams up with Cultures France, the Bureau export de la musique and the network of French cultural institutes and centres abroad in order to promote French artists and music sales through tours, residencies and festivals. The main genres of music concerned are electronica, chanson, world music 'made in France' and jazz. And it would seem that the French language is no longer a significant marker of the 'Frenchness' of the music since many of the artists promoted by the French government and its partners write and sing in English, or non-European languages (world music), and the largest export market for French music is currently the United States, rather than the French-speaking

Benelux countries. Given the linguistic policies of successive French governments in relation to language use both at home and abroad, this is nothing less than a major paradigmatic (perhaps pragmatic?) shift in attitude. And even if the inclusion of world music 'made in France' into the French government's music policy and export agenda does signal an openness to a diverse and complex image of 'Frenchness' (in order to be promoted abroad through the Bureau export, for example, French musicians do not need to be French nationals; the only criteria is that their music is signed to a French-based record label), the fact remains that the main *raison d'être* of French cultural policy abroad is the promotion of France and the presentation of French-based artists to the world. This overarching objective was made evident when the TNMundi project first approached the Institut français in Rabat for sponsorship of one of our cultural events there; the IF director at the time made it fairly clear that the musicians we should invite to our event should be based in France and the idea of co-sponsoring the return to Morocco of the British Council-funded Music Matbakh group (one of our initial ideas for the artistic programme of the TNMundi Rabat event mentioned above) was excluded. So, at times, this overriding 'national' principle is difficult to reconcile with the notion of transnational reciprocity or the facilitation of home-grown creativity in the global South.

The mismatch between policy agendas of foreign cultural institutes and organizations and the objectives of artists in Morocco and Madagascar can stem from an institutional approach which is, at times, too 'top-down' in character. This is a critique which has been made of the EU Delegation in Morocco, which, since the 1995 Barcelona Declaration, has been working on reinforcing the political, economic, cultural, social and human dimension of a Euro-Mediterranean partnership. The Mediterranean countries involved in this partnership are not concerned by adhesion to the EU, but, according to the Barcelona process, culture is regarded as being a vector of social integration. The backdrop to this process is one which is founded on dialogue and cultural exchange as well as mutual understanding. To this end, the EU Delegation in Morocco along with the EU member states' cultural institutes and embassies has been the instigator behind a jazz festival held in Rabat on an annual basis. The festival, known as 'Jazz au Chellah', is an opportunity for jazz musicians from Europe and the Mediterranean to work and perform together over a four-day period, usually in June. The festival was established in 1996 and the 2010 festival focuses on bringing together jazz musicians from a range of EU member countries with diasporic Moroccan musicians based in France and Germany.

The festival is a fairly high-brow affair; for example, the Moroccan musicians who were chosen for the 2010 event are relatively unknown to a wider public but were described as being 'prestigious'. In the run-up to the 2008 festival, the Moroccan musical director, gnawa fusion musician Majid Bekkas, pointed out that the process of musical creation and encounter between musicians from different traditions should not be folkloristic or result out of superficial musical curiosity: 'the issue at stake is to really make the encounters successful and to not fall into the trap of anecdotal encounters [...] otherwise we can call it a jam session, no problem' [5] (Kiwan's interview with Majid Bekkas, April 2008, Rabat). In order to achieve this aim, Bekkas revealed that some of the musicians who have been chosen to perform together are actually already working or touring together. Bekkas makes an effort to distinguish the Chellah Festival from other events which bring together Moroccan and European musicians, which he describes as 'touristic' as opposed to 'cultural' (Kiwan's interview with Majid Bekkas, April 2008, Rabat).

Conclusions

While foreign cultural representatives in Morocco and Madagascar undoubtedly provide crucial support for artists in these locations, in local and transnational terms the snapshot of the Jazz au Chellah Festival invites us to reflect on the very notion of the national cultural institution. The Jazz au Chellah Festival is the result of a collaboration between several EU member states acting under the aegis of the EU Delegation in Morocco. The watchword of the event is Euro-Mediterranean partnership and, indeed, the role of the national cultural organizations such as the British Council, the Institut français or Goethe-Institut may become increasingly challenged in the broader context of developing postnational, regionalized agendas such as the Euro-Mediterranean partnership.

A further challenge to the historical role played by national cultural organizations such as the British Council and the French cultural network overseas is that of cultural and political globalization. This is perhaps more visible with regard to the French case since the worldwide dominance of the English language and American cultural products casts a long shadow over attempts to maintain French as an important world language and Francophone cultural output, especially in the field of music and cinema.

Finally, in considering the supportive and facilitating role played by organizations such as the British Council, the Goethe-Institut and the French cultural networks, one is inevitably led into asking the following question: to what extent are supra-national organizations (for example the EU), infra-national and transnational organizations superseding some of the work carried out by the traditional foreign cultural institute? The case of infra-national and transnational organizations is a particularly interesting one. The final chapter of this book continues this theme in examining North–South relationships between civil society organizations and musicians.

6
Mutual Supports: South <> North

In this chapter we will investigate an almost completely undocumented relationship existing or emerging between actors in civil society movements and socially engaged Malagasy and North African musicians. The civil society organizations in question are European-based NGOs and other more loosely structured associations and their transnational offshoots or links, whom we've encountered as a result of our work with individual musicians. Our own awareness of such links and what we will be able to document empirically in this chapter comes as one of the surprising results of our theoretical and methodological approach to the study of transnationalism. As discussed before, we are describing and analysing transnational networks as flows of individual actors rather than focusing on clustered diasporic groups in fixed locations. Only by extending beyond a study of spaces, places and localized groups of people were we able to discover links which at first sight had little to do with the musicians' primary activity as transnational artists. Hence the combination of following individuals and conducting multi-sited ethnography at what we defined as 'hubs' was particularly fruitful in uncovering artists' links to civil society movements and associations.

To throw some light on this phenomenon and to narrow down the wealth of empirical material we have collected it will be useful to concentrate on specific types and examples of organizations that play important roles in artists' life trajectories. On the one hand, there are those associations which largely or exclusively emerge from the same ethnic groups as the artists themselves. Their attention is mainly directed towards their own diasporic community with a firm bridge to country of origin, which allows them to retain a dual, bi-cultural, 'bi-focal' perspective (for example Portes 2000). For transnational musicians these associations constitute a considerable social capital (Halpern 2005).

Their support for artists living in Europe and in their country of origin is highly significant, since they can create an infrastructure for mobilizing audiences outside the music industry's more commercialized and often inaccessible or restrictive practices (see also the discussion of 'trans-cultural capital' in the Introduction to this book, as well as Meinhof and Triandafyllidou 2006: 200–2).

On the other hand, there are local and national European associations with no or very few migrant members. Examples of these include the Friends of Madagascar based in Munich, the associations Baobab and Welthaus in Austria, and Azafady in London. Their *raison d'être* is to lend support to particular developmental projects in parts of Madagascar or North Africa. The intriguing fact that these particular organizations have established close connections with specific musicians from these countries or their associated diasporas is the result of a series of coinci-dences rather than any underlying initial interest in the arts. It is their links with artists which is virtually undocumented, since by definition they fall completely outside any research on diasporas. Nor are they particularly typical for NGOs or charities in general, who may employ artists for occasional fund-raising purposes but who do not form a deep and on-going connection with specific artists. Hence one major focus of this chapter follows our artists' engagement with this second type of association and analyses what we have come to see as a truly symbiotic relationship in North <> South interaction.

Finally, there are European associations which are based in the South and which often work in combination with European and local staff. Azafady's office in Fort Dauphin, already referenced in Chapter 1, is an example of the latter. We shall later introduce examples for the Moroccan situation which show a related pattern of engagement.

Diasporic associations

Ethnically defined associations by and for specific diasporas cover a wide range of types of organizations and size of membership, ranging from more formalized NGOs with statutes, membership fees and official charity status to loosely organized groups of individuals. For Francophone Africans most of these are locally organized associations in France and to a lesser extent the neighbouring Francophone countries of Belgium and Switzerland: hence Paris as well as other provincial towns, where the largest number of people of Malagasy and North African origin in Europe live, typically house one or more such groups. Such associations emerge from relatively dense diasporas in towns and suburbs, where membership is drawn from the local migrant community whose purposes they serve. However, ethnically defined organizations also exist in other parts of Europe where migrants of a particular origin are much more dispersed. Their formation depends on virtual networks with only occasional face-to-face encounters, most typically during festivities such as Independence Day or New Year's Eve parties where artists are invited to perform. For all associations – whether they work through local or translocal networking – virtual forms of communication via email and other internet-based facilities are essential, either complementing or replacing face-to-face encounters. As was already shown in Part 2, the supportive role of these organizations for artists cannot be stressed enough. Even where their main purpose is not directed towards the promotion of the arts at all, ethnic networks often provide artists with the first stepping stone into an artistic career, offer continuing support through their capacity to mobilize audiences without expensive promotion, and in some cases – and often with considerable personal risks being taken by individuals – even manage to turn themselves into amateur tour operators. We would now like to introduce two such associations for a more in-depth account of their place in artists' networks, one Malagasy and one Moroccan. Both case studies also link to the topics discussed in Chapter 4 since their existence and radius of work mostly lead away from the capital city to provincial networks, allowing artists to diversify and become more independent from the *passage obligé* of Paris.

Madagascar in Castelginest

Our first example of such a small relatively informal association is based in Castelginest, a small town of just over 10,000 inhabitants about 6 miles (10 km) outside Toulouse. We encountered the founders of the group because we were following a French tour of the Malagasy environmental and cultural project Voajanahari, which was jointly organized through the collaborative effort of several local associations in southern France, in places such as Castelginest/Toulouse, Marseille, Montpellier, Lyon and other non-Parisian locations. How can we explain the motivations of key individuals in these associations that drive such considerable investment of time and effort on behalf of 'their' artists? If we listen to the activists' own stories we find first clues in the ways in which they perceive and construct the connection between themselves and their country of origin, which often had been left at a very early age. A superficial glance at their activities and *raison d'être* could suggest a somewhat inward-looking, exclusive agenda and an overemphasis on cultural essentialization. There is no doubt that the diasporic view back to Madagascar often has nostalgic, romanticizing and indeed essentializing elements, something which also finds expession in the lyrics of many of the artists' songs.[1] But we will argue that nostalgia is only part of the story. Interviews with two of the founders of this small association – two sisters of a family of five siblings all resident in the same small town of Castelginest – give a more diverse and complex picture of the impetus that drives these activists' continuing involvement with Madagascar.

Both sisters experience their dual affiliation to Madagascar and France as an opportunity and a challenge. On the one hand they do see themselves as mediators between their two countries in a somewhat stereotypical way: as a bridge across perceived cultural differences, where they are cast in the role of ambassadors for their country of origin in a host country largely ignorant of and/or indifferent towards it. But on the other hand they also construct an agenda of similarity and shared purpose that cuts across any cultural distance, through the appeal to more global issues about environmental destruction and protection. This becomes most sharply focused in connection with their association's promotion of the Voajanahari project and its concert plus debate structure, which articulates cultural social and environmental concerns more directly than a more usual concert-only performance would allow. The sisters' account of the range of involvement by their association – from the first concert promotion to the organization of whole tours and projects – gives us a good insight into the ways in which ethnic organizations have multi-layered motives and serve multi-layered purposes.

The extracts below show the ways in which the two sisters position themselves through their own life stories, from the rediscovery of Madagascar right up to the articulation of shared global concerns. Their accounts challenge any view of diasporic associations as ghettoized and inward-looking, while at the same time confirming the enormous significance of ethnic ties.

Rediscovering Madagascar

In the first extract the younger sister, Domi, narrates her initial reaction to life in France when she arrived as a young girl. Fully integrated into a French community without any other Malagasies in the region, it was mainly due to her father that the Malagasy language remained the language spoken in the family. This she initially resents, but accepts as part of her everyday home life, although she does say elsewhere that she *understands* the language better than she speaks it. However, as she gets older she regains an interest in the language and her country of origin. To her, this represents a 'rediscovery' rather than a continuity:

Domi: When I was five ... For a while, I did not want to speak Malagasy at all. But my parents always insisted that we should speak Malagasy, and I could understand the language perfectly well anyway, so that was not a problem at all. They insisted and at some very special point, I don't know but it was ... One does not really ask oneself why all of a sudden one wants to get closer again to Madagascar. It started to happen during my adolescence. We were living in Auch, roughly 70 km [40 miles] away from Toulouse, and we were not at all part of the Malagasy community, we were really integrated within the French society but at some special point ... well anyway my parents, and especially my father, he is ... he always kept the Malagasy traditions and his Malagasy origin alive, he never lost it. So it all came back. Of course, at some point, we wanted to be with Malagasy people, to go to Malagasy events, listen to Malagasy music, to rediscover Madagascar ...

Ulrike: And do you remember ... The first friends you made, were they French or did they come from somewhere else?

Domi: No, mostly French ... We were really integrated into the society ... We mastered the language perfectly, hmm ... We did not feel different, we were integrated but there was this Malagasy side that was calling us at some special point – I don't know but that's how I felt it – this need to know where one comes from. So all of the sudden, we became passionate about Madagascar and ... and that was that and voilà! [1] (Meinhof's interview, Castelginest, December 2006)

What is interesting in this passage is not only the story itself, but also the grammar through which it finds expression. When Domi describes her earlier rejection of the Malagasy language she is the agent of that wish, placing herself in the subject position – '*I* did not at all want to speak Malagasy' – against her parents' insistence to keep the language going. But her reconnecting with Madagascar is described almost as a sudden revelation by a force beyond her control 'mais y'a un côté malgache qui appelle à un moment donné' ('there was this Malagasy side that was calling us at some special point'). Having joined her siblings who are all now resident in and around Toulouse and Castelginest – something which she recounts at another part of our conversation – her rediscovery of Madagascar not only offers her a new community for sharing music and social activities, it also links her back to the Malagasy traditions of her parents, especially her father who by then had left his wife and returned to Madagascar. The regaining of an aspect of a Malagasy identity becomes a form of self-discovery, of knowing her roots: 'on a besoin de savoir d'où l'on vient', rather than being couched in the terms often associated with ethnic affiliations, namely that of an escape from a hostile host society into a safe haven.[2]

Engaging with Malagasy networks

From the beginning, the 'rediscovery' of their Malagasy heritage by this generation that entered France at a young age is both in-group and out-group directed. It has an inward-looking perspective in the sense that rediscovery now becomes the sisters' motivation for further engagement with Malagasy associative networks and they have found a renewed interest in Malagasy culture. But in its efforts at cultural bridge-building and social engagement it has an equally strong outward-looking perspective.

For Domi and her sister Hangotiana the first step of getting involved comes via a local Malagasy association that is largely youth-oriented, with sports, dance and other similar self-organized activities in its centre. In that sense it is like any other youth club. But when the organizers become more ambitious and try their hand at organizing a concert with Malagasy musicians the evolution of a social club into a cultural association starts:

> Domi: In fact, we started because we were part of this association called Taredy; all of us: my sister was the president, I was the secretary and so on. At first, it was an association for young Malagasies. We did some sports, etc. And we did some dancing ... And we were wondering, why not organize our first concert? Because we were always attracted to Malagasy artists, etc. So for a while we organized events, small events you could say, around Toulouse. But we were ready to change and move a bit faster so we needed more money, needed to get more involved, etc. We did the first concert ... and it was a success. And we enjoyed it a lot! [2]
> (Meinhof's interview, Castelginest, December 2006)

It is at this point that the organization splits. Whereas the majority of the Malagasies organized in Taredy finds this cultural turn too taxing, the sisters and other members of the association leave to set up a second association, now entirely devoted to supporting the arts. Hence the group progresses from a purely activity-oriented association of young Malagasies in the locality to one which now takes on the promotion of major artists from the diaspora and from Madagascar. Domi explains:

> Ah, why did we create a second association? It was because in Taredy there were quite a lot of people and not everyone was ready to carry on with the artistic activity. It required lots of money, time and involvement ... And so, at some point, there was a split. But well, if Taredy would not carry on with this, we just had to create our own association ... So we did only that, we were only working with artists, our approach was always artistic, whether it was for an exhibition of paintings or a concert or ... It could be theatre, literature ... everything that related to the arts and to Madagascar. [3] (Meinhof's interview, Castelginest, December 2006)

Their new association is now entirely devoted to the promotion of Malagasy art, an engagement that entails considerable economic and administrative risks. With this move the association also begins to reach outwards, attempting to attract the local French population as well. This is partly a strategic move, since without a bigger audience that includes non-Malagasies as well the costs of bringing artists to their small town or even to Toulouse would be too great – an obvious difference to the situation in Paris where large concert halls such as the Malagasy community centre Tana Orly or the Espace Chevreuil in Nanterre can attract an audience of hundreds or even more than a thousand purely from the Malagasy diaspora.

Ambassadors of culture

But apart from the strategic necessity to attract the local population as audiences for their cultural events, there is an additional strong desire to mediate their own newly discovered interest in Madagascar to the host society, to counteract the negative images of poverty and deprivation by an alternative perspective. Both sisters stress that they see their role as mediators: to introduce a French population, who knows very little of Madagascar, to the activities and talents represented by the migrant populations living in their midst and to the cultural resources they offer through their transnational connections.[3]

Hangotiana: We also wanted to insist that it was about ethnic diversity, as she said in the newspaper. We really wanted to insist upon this. That is to say we wanted plenty of the inhabitants from Castelginest to be with us, the Malagasies. Not only us Malagasies on our own. Our aim is not purely the diaspora; we want to open up to other people. And it is more interesting to explain Madagascar to people who have no idea about it than to Malagasies who say: 'I know that, all right? You're not going to lecture me about my country!' It is more interesting ... So we worked along with the mayor from here, to put posters everywhere in the village. And the mayor also wants this to work because I told him: 'My aim is not to do something communitarian only, for us to stay among ourselves. Not at all. It is really about opening up. We live here, we've settled here, so we want the inhabitants from Castelginest to come and meet us and let go of preconceived ideas. For them to discover Madagascar because so many of them have never heard of it.' So many of them have no idea, because there is no media coverage for Madagascar, isn't that so? Other places get good coverage but Madagascar is still ... Little by little, you can see something sometimes but not much. And in any case, we get always the same images: pictures of misery and poverty. And it's true, we get worked up, because it's only about that, and yet we have our own enormous wealth ... we have a real joie de vivre. [4] (Meinhof's interview, Castelginest, December 2006)

The two sisters in Toulouse are not alone in their ability to combine a European and cosmopolitan perspective with a rediscovery of their origins. Nor are they untypical in their desire to challenge the often highly restrictive view of Europeans of countries in Africa caught between images of poverty, corruption and threat on the one hand and exoticism on the other. Madagascar in particular has recently been put on a fantasy map of dancing lemurs through the highly successful animation films *Madagascar* 1 and 2.[4] Other Malagasy informants, such as Laterit film producer Marie-Clémence Paes,[5] travel agency director Josielle Randriamandranto, the singers Rachel Ratsizafy and Edgar Ravahatra in France and Mfa Kera in Berlin, also share a position where their *re*discovery of Madagascar inspires them with a desire of *re*-representing their country of origin that would challenge both prevalent clichés about Madagascar: one that stresses the natural paradise populated by lemurs and endemic species – albeit under threat – but ignores people and culture, and another that stresses the extreme poverty of its people and deplores their deprivation.

Sharing a social and environmental global agenda

Introducing the enormous variety and richness of Malagasy cultures and natural resources to a European public without stereotyping it, while simultaneously alerting the same public to the genuine difficulties faced by the people and countries in the South, is a complex double act. The association's collaboration with artists enables both threads to be woven together in an engaging way, by creating an agenda where both shared pleasure and shared concern link Europeans and migrants in a network of global similarity rather than North <> South difference. Hence their choice of artists, such as the group Mahaleo, Lolo and Erick Manana, and in particular the project Voajanahari already reflects this double purpose.

Yet, combining artistic pleasure and social concern is not without its hurdles. It is one thing to introduce well-loved successful artists to a new public and leave it to their songs and their performance to try and engage the audience in wider concerns. It is much more difficult when the performance attempts to become part of a wider social platform. In the case of the project Voajanahari, brought to Europe by Dama, Ricky and Hajazz, the attempt to link a specially produced film with a live concert and a subsequent debate represents a much higher risk of turning off the audience, and raises important issues about the ways in which 'audiences' become 'engaged' publics.[6]

Hangotiana describes very well the difficulties which she herself faced when confronted by Dama with his wish to link a concert with the showing of a video and a debate:

> In fact, it is a project, Voajanahari, that we ... The day we started to talk properly with Dama, he showed us a video. At the time, it's true that no one was really interested, there was my sister, me, my mum. We were not interested but we watched it. It was like a film we were watching. But for me it was special because it was an answer to something I was looking for. Because, so far, we had organized concerts: we had put artists on stage, and we'd sing, because it's songs that we love. But there was something special about Voajanahari that

moved me. I was very touched. I don't know why, it was my land. Something made me deeply want to be part of this, to be part of this journey. So we all talked, we talked about it with Dama: 'What is it exactly, what do you have, is it some kind of movement, what exactly is Voajanahari?' We asked Dama, what is it exactly? And he explained it to us. And they were saying: 'We know Dama, we know Ricky, but what is this here? What's going to happen? Because it looks like, hmm ...?' Well, for most people to understand, we simply said that we were trying to make people aware of environmental protection. But also of our cultural environment, our traditions, not only about nature but about the relationship between these two worlds which have to coexist but not ... Anyway, with what's going on in Madagascar nowadays, and even there in Madagascar, it is quite difficult to convey the message. People need to live, to eat ... When people are hungry, they don't care if a tree is burning ... So how is it possible for all of this to coexist? Because if we only philosophize, no one will be interested. People need something concrete ... That is what has been difficult for us, trying to catch people's attention nevertheless. We even used marketing to attract them; that is to say, ask them to join the project Voajanahari, to tell them that it is dynamic and that we won't fall asleep. [5] (Meinhof's interview, Castelginest, December 2006)

The ambitious multimedia concert plus debate approach of Voajanahari to the raising of environmental awareness is thus not without its problems, and it is doubtful whether the project would succeed in the way it does were it not for the charisma and fame of the two leading artists Dama and Ricky Olombelo. Using music as a bridge to stimulate wider social and environmental debates is a much harder exercise than simply attracting audiences for live music with or without engaged lyrics. The special deep involvement by the two sisters in promoting the project Voajanahari rests on a deeply felt identification with the particular project's concerns and the artists involved. More generally, the most significant support for artists rendered by ethnically based associations remains information flow, concert promotion and organization of events, and the support of arts and crafts exhibitions with an implicitly rather than explicitly constructed social and environmental agenda. However, the fact that Voajanahari could stimulate such full engagement by the network of local ethnic associations right across France allows us to understand better the complexity of motives behind such formations.

Moroccan music and civil society

The NGO context regarding Morocco is significantly different from that in Madagascar, and although the country faces enormous challenges such as low literacy levels, poor water and electricity supplies, bad transport links and poverty rates, particularly in its rural and mountain locations, Morocco is in a stronger economic position than Madagascar. A glance at some key statistics reveals the contrasting circumstances of the two countries. For instance, the GDP (purchase power parity) for 2009 in Morocco was estimated at $4600 compared to Madagascar's $1000, and the proportion of the population living below the poverty line in Morocco is 15 per cent compared to Madagascar's 50 per cent.[7] Nevertheless, despite these two contrastive pictures, one finds that there are similar dynamics at work concerning the transnational convergence of musicians and civil society organizations. Thus in relation to our fieldwork on Moroccan musicians, cultural producers and their transnational networks, it is possible to identify three types of civil society organization which engage with musical and broader artistic creativity in Morocco and Europe: multicultural European-based associations; European-represented organizations based in Morocco; and Morocco-based organizations which radiate northwards to Europe. Of course, typologies are not an exact science and it must therefore be acknowledged that these categories overlap to a significant extent.

Let us consider our first Moroccan case study, the Geneva-based association called Mosaik Production. Mosaik Production was set up in April 2005 by Amina, a Moroccan-Swiss DJ based in Geneva, and two other co-founders. Mosaik's principal aim is to create links and creative partnerships between Swiss and African musicians, with a particular focus on Morocco. Since 2006, Mosaik has been working with the Casablanca Boulevard des jeunes musiciens Festival and provides workshops during the festival's Tremplin competition (for more details on the Boulevard, see Chapter 2). In 2006, 12 members of the Mosaik association travelled to Casablanca to volunteer and lend a hand to the organization of the festival, and from 2007 onwards Mosaik has offered writing, rap, graff (graffiti art), photography and DJ'ing workshops during the festival in partnership with local Moroccan associations, targeting young adults and children. Mosaik has also promoted its own Geneva-based artists and, in 2007, members of the Mosaik association, Jonas and the Taxi Brousse Orchestra performed at the RUC stadium, and then in 2008 Anuar and DJ Twista performed at the festival. In 2009, Mosaik returned to Casablanca, its 15-strong team made up of Algerians, Swiss-Lebanese, Swiss-Iranians, Italian-Swiss and Swiss members. In fact, Amina explains that she was the only member of Moroccan origin to take part in the Boulevard workshops. In September 2010, Mozaik Production brought over Casablanca and Rabat acts Haoussa and Mobydick as well as Casablanca-based graphic artist Molotov to Geneva's La Bâtie Festival. The Boulevard des jeunes musiciens Festival organizers were also invited and a special documentary film about the Boulevard, made by Geneva-based USF Prod, was screened and discussed in a workshop (www.mozaikproduction.ch/, accessed November 2010).

In a similar manner to the Malagasy sisters in Castelginest, Amina, the founder of Mosaik, discusses her motivations for setting up the association in terms of a 'reconnecting' with her past. Amina (who has Sahraoui origins) was born and brought up in Casablanca and came to Switzerland in 1979. She is now a Swiss national (and has been for 26 years) but regularly returns to Morocco (at least twice a year to visit family and to take part in the Boulevard des jeunes musiciens Mosaik workshops). Below she reflects on her trajectory and the reasons for launching the association:

So Mosaik Production has existed since 2005, it's actually me and two other people, we moan that nothing ever happens in Geneva ... so the idea is always, among our, um, cultural and artistic activities ... we're always in contact with the different communities here, in general Africans and North Africans, and we said to ourselves that we would, um ... well try to set up an association, but from the outset the objective has been to make links with Africa. Because, we're steeped in Africa, we feel it ... well, we need this link, in order to be able to survive in the urban jungle [laughs] ... so there you go. It's a very strong link. [6] (Kiwan's interview with Amina, July 2009, Geneva)

Although Amina was brought up in Morocco, she grew up in a French linguistic and cultural environment: she attended the French Lycée Lyautey in Casablanca and spoke French at home. Her father left Morocco for political reasons and hence Amina's family relocated to Switzerland where the family already had some links (Amina's sister and aunt were based in Switzerland). Amina explains how it is only over the past decade or so that she has actively sought to re-engage with the country in the cultural sense:

The first thing is that I, it's been 30 years since I left Morocco, so I live in Geneva, so the Morocco of today no longer has anything to do with the Morocco which I left behind ... so I left in '79, approximately, and at the time ... it was Nass el Ghiwane, all that movement [...] ... but it's there that it stopped, that's it, we locked the door ... and they locked it and threw away the keys in fact, and it stopped there. Culturally nothing was happening in Morocco any more. Well, me, being here ... so that was that. I went back to Morocco from time to time, but with no cultural link ... I went to see my parents ... and I came back ... so it's now been about ten years since I reconnected with Morocco, with the new state, government, a new king, innovation and an opening up ... tolerance, a democracy in inverted commas, which is being put in place, I mean, there you go. And so with all that, and what was interesting, is that we've nonetheless ... the opening up has been brought about by young people, who have made themselves heard little by little, with their differences, with their musical and cultural references, so Morocco is a country of contradictions, there are those who look towards the east, and there are others who look towards the west ... and ... but it works and there you go! It's a relationship which is in full knowledge of the facts, so it works. [7] (Kiwan's interview with Amina, July 2009, Geneva)

Despite the fact that Amina's affective links with Morocco in particular and Africa in general are, clearly, major motivations for her involvement with Mosaik, she is nevertheless wary about the various labels that are often applied to this sort of association – whereby it is either considered by policy-makers as being an organization working towards 'integration' of diverse migrant populations or one which celebrates diversity in a superficial 'multiculti carnival' sense:

Because here, ah, Morocco, Africa ... there is a lot of prejudice ... and so, I was a little fed up with this prejudice, and I didn't want to be ghettoized, labelled either ... yes, um ... it's a cultural association, so an integration association, so everything that that implies ... so ... I'm fed up with that label ... I refuse it, and so I told myself, um ... that's it, we set up a cultural association which actually targets Africa, which targets urban arts, because we are, we can't deny that ... and fed up also with this label of traditional Africa, grass skirt, African dress, couscous etc. ... so. We're going to change things ... we're going to try to see things differently and ... give something different. There's never been a dynamic like this one here ... so we're going to create it ... we're going to give ... and ... since we've been active ... a lot of things have changed. [8] (Kiwan's interview with Amina, July 2009, Geneva)

Amina thus argues that Mosaik is a 'different' sort of association and indeed what is interesting about this organization are the ways in which it has become involved in the Boulevard des jeunes musiciens and thereby engendered a mechanism of mutual support between artists and cultural activists in Geneva and Casablanca. At several points in our discussion, Amina alludes to the friendship and mutual trust which developed between the Mosaik team and Momo and Hicham's Boulevard team. She also points out that there was no expectation on the part of the Moroccans that a Swiss organization, based in the North, would merely become a cash cow for their projects:

> It was 2007 ... so, I was there before, for the Tremplin, so I was there to help out ... for the Tremplin ... I was there ... I could see, if you like ... I know a bit about festivals about different cultures and ... every time that I'm there, and um ... really it's difficult if you like for ... I find it incredible that a festival like that ... of that size ... um ... can put their confidence in me ... that there's this openness and that ... there you go, it's not always said, you know, if ... but here, if you don't know people, you can't be backstage ... even as an artist ... there you go. So ... that, there was a ... a confidence which developed little by little. [...] But what is nice, is that there is really ... that I recognize that what is very, that what is well, deserved by the organizers is that they never asked for anything. The objective is not ... 'yeah there are some Swiss people coming, we'll ask them for' ... no, never! ... and it was an equal relationship, which was fabulous for us. It was really very important ... it's that which made us more involved ... we said to ourselves hold on, these are people who ask us for absolutely nothing ... we're there, we're from another context and everything ... we bring a little ... so, that's it, the link ... developed, they are really very strong links ... some people stay in contact ... artists ... with Facebook and the internet ... it's a lot easier ... and every time we arrive to the open arms of all the people who are involved in the festival. [9] (Kiwan's interview with Amina, July 2009, Geneva)

Voluntary, non-ethnic aid associations

By contrast to the ethnic associations which build on very strong identification with artists as cultural representatives of their culture, the type of organization to which we now turn is largely or exclusively made up of voluntary or paid-up members from the majority society. While the majority of such aid organizations do not engage with artists beyond hiring them for occasional background entertainment, there are some small-scale charities which do develop much deeper connections. In all the cases we discovered, the relationship with artists arose from a series of accidental encounters with key members of the associations rather than any endemic interest in music or even more broadly in anything cultural. But these encounters had major consequences for both sides, causing what we would like to describe as a virtuous cycle of mutual benefit.

Virtuous cycles of mutual benefit

In order to understand the nature of this virtuous cycle it will be useful to reflect on some of the problems and pitfalls of encounters between people of the richer northern and the poorer southern hemispheres. Whether experienced through tourism or aid, such meetings are almost always fraught with various legacies of inequalities. These may be the legacy of colonial/post-colonial relations or simply extend from extensive economic inequalities, insufficient mutual understanding and different declared or hidden agendas. Hence the relationship between the aid-receiving local populations in the South and aid-givers from the North, be they NGOs and other voluntary charities, or large-scale aid organizations such as the World Bank or Oxfam, is often marred by misconceptions, misunderstanding and disillusionment (see also Grillo and Stirrat 1997; Goedefroit and Revéret 2007). Recent developments in aid discourses prioritize local agency and participation, as well as sustainability beyond the life cycle of aid (Pottier *et al.* 2003: 24–5). Yet, in practice, the relationship remains structured through expert vs nonexpert discourses and actions that often exclude local knowledge and expertise from setting the agenda and from defining the target group's own needs. This in turn exacerbates problems of the non-sustainability of aid projects. It is here where the relationship between socially committed artists and equally minded aid associations becomes unusually fruitful and interesting. We will show below the impact which such encounters between aid-givers from the North and artists from the South can have in redressing the inequality between the rich who give and the poor who take, by creating a common purpose where each gains from the other in a virtuous cycle of interdependencies. As before, our Malagasy examples focus on artists from the group Mahaleo and another musician, Ricky Olombelo. These are artists whom we have defined as 'human hubs' in transnational networks; that is, they are enormously influential musicians with a strong social agenda who carry others in their wake, but who themselves are the central focal points through which the networks organize themselves. What we will argue is that the involvement of these artists from 'the South' with aid agencies of 'the North' challenges stereotypes of givers and takers and creates a new relationship of mutuality where each is both giver and taker. The exchanges and events that we witnessed between musicians and key members of the charities were invariably marked by dialogue, curiosity, mutual support and respect, a desire for and a pleasure in their encounters. They were thus very different from other more usual settings where NGOs occasionally enlist artists to form an entertaining background for fund-raising activities. As we will show below, it is this much richer and meaningful relationship which creates cycles of mutual benefit.

There are several aid organizations that we encountered in following the network of the musicians we were researching, and who themselves have projects in place to sustain local initiatives in Madagascar. In Austria these include among others the association Baobab (named after the iconic tree of Madagascar), and an association attached to the Catholic church called Welthaus – literally 'House of the World', and in Francophone Switzerland an NGO called Nouvelle planète. They all share an interest in developmental projects in Madagascar: Baobab and our German case study the Freunde Madagaskars exclusively so, whereas Welthaus and Nouvelle planète have only relatively recently extended their interest to the Red Island. But for all of them the encounter with the musicians proved pivotal in expanding or redirecting their involvement. Again we will adopt a case-study approach to give some of the flavour of these interactions. Hence as our key example we will take a small NGO with a seat in Munich, Germany, with the name Sakaizan'i Madigasikara-Freunde Madagaskars (Friends of Madagascar).

Sakaizan'i Madigasikara-Freunde Madagaskars (FM)

Set up in 1993 with the aim of supporting a primary school and the education, health and nourishment of local children in Belo sur Tsiribihina, a small isolated town in the west of Madagascar, the association has sustained its activities for 16 years, with generations of primary school children in the district of and around Belo benefiting from regular education and annual bursaries. FM has also undergone changes and further development in the kind of support it now gives to the people in Belo and a few other regions of Madagascar. Some of these further developments were inspired by a growing friendship between the current director and his wife, Erich and Anne Raab, and the musicians Ricky and Dama. It is this type of relationship between musicians and NGOs that we have described elsewhere as an 'inspirational triangle' (Gibert and Meinhof 2009).[8] What follows are extracts from several taped interviews conducted with Erich Raab from July 2007 onwards, which typically show the impact that a connection between musicans and NGOs can have for mutual benefit. As is the case for many 'northerners' in small non-profit aid organizations, the Raabs' own involvement with Madagascar began with tourism. His amusing account of the beginning of their love affair with Madagascar shows the accidental nature of what subsequently became a deeply absorbing full-time involvement:

Ulrike: How does an Erich Raab from Munich get involved with Madagascar?

Erich Raab: Well, Erich Raab and his wife had climbed Kilimanjaro and then they rewarded themselves with one week's holiday on Mauritius and as we were flying over Madagascar we looked down and said, ah yes, let's go there one time and have a look at that country, and a few years later we did just that, that was 1987, our first journey to Madagascar, and we travelled all over the country with a rucksack without any organized plan and we fell in love with the country and got stuck there, got to know some people and the year after we returned again. And so for the last 20 years we've been going to Madagascar on a regular basis, once per year, even twice sometimes ... Last time I counted the old visa entries in my old passports, and I think the last journey we made was number 22 ...

Once we'd asked for the umpteenth time for a new visa at the honorary consul of Madagascar, this consul phoned us up and pointed out that there was this German–Malagasy association, a nationwide organization. And since we'd been travelling to Madagascar such a lot did we not wish to join them. So we went to the next meeting of the German–Malagasy Association ... and at this assembly there was a young colleague from Munich who gave a report about a newly founded association in Munich, and we picked up our ears, established contact right away and immediately became members of that association [Friends of Madagascar]. And that association came into being because some other people from Munich, from the same district of Schwabing, where we also live, had travelled to Madagascar and had encountered the Principal of a primary school in Belo Tsiribihina, and he had showed them the school and the poor conditions in which the children were being taught there, and these people decided to support this school by sponsoring materials, which they took there on their next journey, or sent there. And we became members of this association and were directly involved in building up the project from scratch. [10] (Meinhof's interview, Munich, July 2007)

The association quickly set about building up the infrastructure of the primary school by tackling the most immediate needs such as connecting the building to water and electricity supplies, repairing the roof, building benches and creating sanitary facilities.

Raab remembers that in the beginning 'the school director had to roll up the cables at the end of the lessons so that nobody would pinch electricity, well yes, the conditions were very tough'. Later, and with the help of a specially employed teacher, Adolpho, the association rented a house to set up an educational centre with a library, and developed a programme for supporting the families and their children so that they could go to school. From 2002 onwards the Malagasy government started to provide more material help for schools, thus enabling the association to shift its attention to a pedagogic programme, providing scholarships for selected students. There were however difficulties of communication, false starts, uncertainty about direction and overambitious demands for new additional projects by the teachers. Raab says of these difficulties: 'For many years now I have had the experience that procuring financial support is often easier than finding sensible ways for spending the money.' It is here where the encounter with the musicians becomes crucial.

Initially the developmental work of FM in Belo and the invitation to the musicians of the Voajanahari project to perform in Munich were two quite separate activities. The first belonged to the charity's own statutory aim to support the children of Belo and their educational needs, the second was a more spontaneous wish to share the immense pleasure in the performance of outstanding Malagasy musicians with their local community in Munich:

Once apropos of an independence day celebration in Berlin we met a Malagasy musician who was playing there ... and through him we established contact with his brother Ricky in Tana, and ... when Ricky performed for the first time the project Voajanahari with Dama and Hajazz – I think it was in Bergisch Gladbach – we went to listen, and made friends with them, drank some glasses of wine together, and that connection developed, and now we have brought Voajanahari twice to Munich, once at the BUGA [National Gardening exhibition], once at the One-World-House in Munich, once to a community centre in Eching, and last year a second time to Munich at the Moffat Hall. [11] (Meinhof's interview, Munich, July 2007)

Up till that moment there is nothing as yet unusual in this encounter. A dedicated aid organization works on a project in Madagascar and at the same time enlists some Malagasy musicians touring in Germany to give concerts. But as the relationship starts to develop into one of mutual trust and friendship, Raab sees a new form of collaboration opening up. He now enlists those two musicians, who are extremely famous in their own country, to perform a charity concert in Belo in support of the association's development project there:

And then we asked Dama and Ricky if they would be interested in accompanying us to Belo and give a concert there as well, and they agreed and organized a wonderful concert in Belo, and it was so difficult to organize: since there is no amplification there we had to fetch it all ourselves – first Dama drove it in his pick-up truck from Tana to Morondava, and there our Adolpho collected it and brought it to Belo. And the biggest problem for Adolpho's organization was that he had to persuade the representative of Gerama, the energy supplier, not to switch off the electricity during the evening of the concert, because normally electricity gets cut off in the evening, and that worked out fine ... well with such a VIP event, people told us this was the biggest cultural event in the whole history of the town, when such famous musicians as Dama and Ricky come to give a concert, then he's got to guarantee the electricity supply ... And the public were all dressed up in their best clothes, with all the VIPs of the town present as well, and in the end there were 500 people or so. [12] (Meinhof's interview, Munich, July 2007)

After this huge success in the town of Belo the association's status and credibility as well as Raab's own recognition grows in both Madagascar and Germany. In Madagascar connections expand in Belo itself, but now also include influential diplomats and opinion-makers in the capital city; whereas in Germany the connection with the Malagasy musicians opens the door to the Malagasy diaspora, which up till then was completely outside its radius. But it has further and still on-going consequences for the direction that the association's work is now taking. Rather than seeing the children and their educational needs in isolation, the association now opens its eyes to a much more holistic appreciation of the integral needs of their parents and village life as a whole. Given that the majority of Malagasies still live a peasant life in the countryside, questions of agricultural sustainability, eco-farming, environmental destruction and rural exodus now become part and parcel of the association's approach to their pupils' educational needs.

> During our last visit in connection with the concert of Dama and Ricky in Belo, the representatives of the peasant associations came to the hotel where Dama was staying and for an entire morning Dama had to discuss the problems of the peasants with them. And that's when we noticed that our restriction to the target school, teacher, children was not sustainable in the long term, but that instead we needed to tackle a broad spectrum, and since 90–95 per cent of the population are peasants, the children's education is directly linked in with the problems of agriculture, we understand now that this is absolutely central, and now we try to include this for example by covering adult topics in our library. [13] (Meinhof's interview, Munich, July 2007)

It is at this point where the relationship comes full circle and becomes a genuine exchange of equals with mutual benefit to one another's aims, sustained by a deepening personal involvement, friendship, even passion. A charity from the North has gained local mediators with considerable know-how, and through the nationwide status of the musicians acquires higher status for their association at point of delivery as well as at home. With their more frequent concerts and their participation in the private and formal meetings of the associations, the presence of Malagasy musicians attracts members of the diaspora. These factors in turn create new interactions that broaden the membership profile and extend and sustain the transnational networking. Hence in place of a one-sided relationship of a North to South aid-flow on the one hand, and a South to North artistic flow on the other with separate aims, we find instead a complex and constantly renewing cycle of South <> North and North <> South interactions. Not only do the artists increase their opportunities for performances in the more lucrative settings of European concert halls, they also support the associations' aims at their multiple sites of engagement. They in turn find their own social projects in their own countries supported by European associations.

Once again this is how Raab explains this broadening of the agenda:

> Our statute states as the target the children of Belo but it also says that these concerns can be expanded upon, but of course we can only do that when we increase our resources and there is not enough capacity in a small association like ours. We did however start a new collaboration with Dama, and his eco-farm, that we want to continue to expand upon, the collaboration with Dama's Centre, because that's an obvious next step since we're always going past his farm, and we also managed to win Dama as advisor for our projects – that brings in a new perspective already. [14] (Meinhof's interview, Munich, July 2007)

We have used one case study to demonstrate a truly symbiotic relationship between developers in the North and artists in the South connecting in mutual multi-directional flows of sustained and expanding transnational networks. These examples, though still quite unusual, could nevertheless be replicated by several other similar links. In our own research the connection with the Austrian and Swiss associations proved especially interesting here (see Gibert and Meinhof 2009 for a more extensive exploration of these). In all cases it is the pivotal role of particular artists with a pronounced social agenda and a keen interest in their own country's fate which matters most, in turning the unequal relation between the North and the South into a much more egalitarian one based on friendship and respect. Hence the emphasis on the musicians from Mahaleo or projects like Voajanahari.

An interview with Heribert Ableidinger, director of the Welthaus organization in Linz, confirms this relation from the perspective of a primary aid-related church organization:

> During the first years we only had the collaboration via music and culture, because the members of Mahaleo kept on stressing that their primary aim was to establish a globalization of friendship, and friendship must function without money and without any dependencies. However, after some time went by we did suggest that we were an organization to finance projects and that if they could propose some projects we would be very happy to evaluate these. And this is how little by little we ended up doing developmental

work with development projects with them. [15] (Meinhof's interview, Linz, September 2007)

The artists of Mahaleo and selected others may be exceptional in the scale of their commitment and the extent of their transnational involvement, but they do show the potential for interactions based on what both Heribert from Welthaus and Dama refer to as a 'globalization of friendship' (Meinhof 2005: 132).

Voluntary, non-ethnic associations: the case of Morocco

Whereas Amina from the Mosaik association in Geneva emphasized how confidence, trust and mutual support emerged fairly spontaneously in the relationship between the Boulevard and Mosaik teams, it is possible to argue that organizations in Morocco represented on the ground by Europeans may, at times, present rather more challenging trajectories. It can be argued that this sums up some element of the experience of the French association Éclats de lune in Marrakesh. Set up by French-Moroccan actor Khalid Tamer in 2005 (Tamer was born in Casablanca but now lives and works with the Paris theatre troupe Graines de soleil), the Éclats de lune association, which works on developing the artistic and cultural offerings in Marrakesh and a number of nearby villages, is represented in Morocco by Claire Le Goff. The activities of the association include providing professional training for cultural producers (*opérateurs culturels*) in Marrakesh and its rural environs, and co-producing cultural and artistic events in the area with a particular focus on theatre, dance and 'traditional and heritage arts' (*les arts traditionnels et le patrimoine materiel*: www.awalnart.com/spip.php?rubrique16#art, accessed 1 June 2010). Since 2007, Éclats de lune has also been responsible for producing an annual festival known as Awaln'art in Marrakesh and several nearby rural locations (Tahanoute, Tamesloht, Aït Ourir, Aghmat) and there is a long-term plan to set up a cultural training centre (*centre de formation*) in Marrakesh. The Awaln'art Festival focuses on providing a showcase of contemporary Moroccan creation by focusing on street theatre, circus arts, music and storytelling and prides itself on its emphasis on the 'africanité' of Moroccan culture, thus favouring the development not only of encounters between Moroccan and European artists, but between Africans as well:

> When we started working on the festival, we really opened up to all street arts ... but with a really local and African flavour. The idea is not to import the way we see street arts ... in France and in

Europe ... it's really to leave ourselves ... to ... to explore what there is here ... what existed and what still exists ... to do it ... to link it to what exists in Africa, and so, to revive this all a little bit, to make all of this visible ... So the objective of the festival is exactly that, it's to provoke encounters ... between contemporary European and Mediterranean creation, and what exists in Africa and in Morocco. [16] (Kiwan's and Gibert's interview with Claire Le Goff, Éclats de lune, April 2008, Marrakesh)

However, Éclats de lune's concern with Moroccan artistic and cultural development in provincial and rural contexts is not without its difficulties and, for example, Claire Le Goff points out that the association's work with a group of young Marrakeshi percussionists threw up significant challenges due to the divergent expectations of the association and the percussionists themselves. It is worth citing our discussion with Claire Le Goff at some length in order to capture some aspects of the obstacles that Éclats de lune faced in its work with local musicians:

Nadia: And the music ... the group [...] can you say a bit more about that?

Claire: So they have ... they are part of the founding members of Éclats de lune. And so ... it's with them that we started working on employment opportunities ... so basically, it's made up of percussionists, a number of whom come and go ... and jugglers. Well, in fact it's not really structured and most of the time they work in ... nightclubs. So what we tried to do was to work with them and to bring them into a process of ... a much more artistic creation process, um ... but we didn't succeed [...] It's part of ... it's part of the process of setting up the training centre here, we can't, basically we realized that through the work that we did with them, that we can't impose a process on young people, a process which they are not part of ... [...]

Marie: And so as a result has that made you question a certain number of things, in the construction of the centre and ...

Claire: Yes, completely. That's it, we have said to ourselves, that we had, that we had to really be really careful about who we work with ... we had to be careful about the process ... how we engender the process ... I mean ... [...] and now we have told ourselves I think that it's important that we work with young people, that's why I was talking about 16–25 years old ... and even 25 is almost too old already, basically it's really so as to be able to take them from the start of their artistic trajectory. In order to really accompany them from the outset. When we work with young people who are more qualified already ... there we have to be more cautious ... and even have selection phases so that it's really the young people who want something ... rather than the other way round. [17] (Kiwan's and Gibert's interview with Claire Le Goff, Éclats de lune, April 2008, Marrakesh)

The misunderstanding between the association and the musicians stemmed from the divergent perceptions of the work to be undertaken and thus highlights one of the potential pitfalls involved in the interaction between a 'non-local' professional association and the local artist population. Despite such challenges, the association nevertheless held the fourth Awaln'art (17–20 June 2010) and the enduring success of this event is surely a testament to the association's capacity to develop meaningful relationships with artists, policy-makers, audiences and publics in the Marrakesh region. The festival has funding partnerships with both public and private European and Moroccan organizations, ranging from the Organisation internationale de la Francophonie, the Institut français and the Instituto Cervantes to the Moroccan Ministry of Culture, the Conseil de la communauté marocaine à l'étranger and the Marrakesh Conseil régional du tourisme. Furthermore, the association's concern with a credible articulation of artistic and local historical/territorial dynamics suggests that the main premise of Éclats de lune's activities is underpinned by a sincere desire to foster local artistic creativity, thus seeking to provide a support mechanism for local emerging artists whether they are located in urban or in rural contexts ('basically, the idea is to train artists um ... who are capable of setting up their own organization [...] to lead them to become aware of their role as an artist in a place' [18] (Kiwan's and Gibert's interview with Claire Le Goff, Éclats de lune, April 2008, Marrakesh)). In turn, the local Amazigh- and Arabic-speaking population supports Éclats de lune by becoming cultural mediators who represent Éclats de lune in the villages near Marrakesh:

Nadia: And so how many are there of you in the team?
Claire: The team is really small ... well ... it's being built up, so there are four artists, cultural mediators, let's say, so they are ... work on the festival, for example, they are in charge

of all the cultural action ... and they are in charge of the performance sites ... that means that they are in contact with the associations who are our partners in the festival, and with them they prepare for three or four months before the festival, they prepare the arrival of the festival. They mobilize the teams, they build the teams ... they make sure that the association leaders are in contact with the public authorities so that we have everything we need for the festival ... so it's what we call cultural action. They work on upcoming festivals ... through, on a number of things and it really depends on the associations we work with ... it's different at every site. For example, Aghmat, we work with an association which wants to valorize the local village material heritage ... so the artist is working on the development of the public square. There you go, at the moment he's working on that. And this approach mobilizes the troops, in fact. Like that, when the festival starts, we've got a whole population which is really into it ... which is mobilized ... and the ideal in the end ... the idea is that it will be them ... that it will be those associations which are the local organizers of the festival. [19] (Kiwan's and Gibert's interview with Claire Le Goff, Éclats de lune, April 2008, Marrakesh)

The cultural mediators who work with Éclats de lune are not simply providing support for the association, they are also chosen to be mediators so that they can use the experience of cultural mediation as a form of professional training, as Claire explains below:

Nadia: And as a result, the workshops which take place in the villages, the children, do they speak French, or does it take place with tutors who are, who speak *darija* ...?

Claire: In that case, we have partners, we have one of our artists who really speaks ... either Berber, or Arabic, and ... a participant in French or if it's not one of our artists, they are a member of the association in question. It's interesting, because if, well ... every experience is a learning experience as well ... the person who is precisely going to do the translation ... we'll choose him so that ... this experience can be a training experience, it can be a young person, for example, who wants to develop their skills in terms of leading workshops, and so who will be in contact with artists, ... he'll learn about workshops ... about the pedagogical process. [20] (Kiwan's and Gibert's interview with Claire Le Goff, Éclats de lune, April 2008, Marrakesh)

This two-way mutually beneficial relationship between the association, the artists and the local population makes it possible to see the case of Éclats de lune in terms of mutual South–North support.

South–South associations radiating northwards

Such mutually beneficial relationships which articulate cultural/artistic and territorial concerns also underpin the work of our final Moroccan case study, ASIDD, an association based in Tassemmitt in the mountains of the Middle Atlas. ASIDD, which means 'light' in Amazigh, stands for Association pour l'intégration et le développement durable and was set up in 2002 by journalist and writer Amale Samie, also known as 'Tonton', who, although based in Casablanca, grew up in Beni Mellal – the nearest medium-sized town to the otherwise remote Tassemmitt region. ASIDD's main goal is to work towards the sustainable development of Tassemmitt – an isolated mountainous area grouping together 200 or so households in the douar of Bou Imoura – through improving access to education and healthcare, and developing a locally appropriate model of sustainable development, eco-tourism and cooperative agriculture. This has been partially achieved, notably through the building of two schools, the first one opening in 2005 and the second in 2009. In addition, the association's activists have been involved in a fight to stop the local government from developing a sheep reserve in Tassemmitt. Such a development would have effectively forced them off their land. Most recently, ASIDD's local activists who live in Tassemmitt and who are part of the Aït Slimane de Tassemmitt community are working with Tonton to develop an eco-tourism (*tourisme solidaire*) project which has seen the construction of an eco-gîte to house tourists trekking in the mountains. This very different type of tourism is aimed at providing the local inhabitants with a sustainable source of income which will work in symbiosis with their environment.

From the outset ASIDD has been closely linked to the Boulevard des jeunes musiciens movement; Tonton was one of the first journalists in Morocco to write about the Boulevard Festival and a close friendship developed between Tonton, Momo and Hicham. And, indeed, the first school to open its doors to 120 pupils in Tassemmitt in 2005 was funded in large part by the musicians who gravitate around the Boulevard. Groups and individual musicians such as Haoussa, DJ Zayan Freeman, Barry, Reborn, Darga, Dayzine, Hoba Hoba Spirit, Naked Monkeys, Dust'n'Bones and Total Eclypse (many of these are mentioned in previous chapters, especially Chapter 2) recorded two ASIDD compilation albums and gave a free concert at the Casablanca Institut français (Hoba Hoba Spirit, Darga and Dayzine), all of which allowed for the collection of 60,000 dirhams.[9] The association also has a presence at the Boulevard Festival's 'Souk associatif' where a range of NGOs and associations have stands promoting their diverse projects to the festival-goers. Tonton is part and parcel of the Boulevard organizing team, and the musicians and organizers of the Boulevard Festival are also closely involved in the ASIDD association; they regularly travel to Tassemmitt, using it as a sort of creative retreat, as Hicham Bahou explains:

> In Tassemmitt, it's become a place, well a second, a sort of little hideout, it's sort of become our home, we know practically all the families from the region – it's not, in fact there isn't a village, it's some houses spread out over a large space, there's a hamlet so the musicians used to go up there on a regular basis. [21] (Hicham Bahou speaking at a panel at the TNMundi conference in Rabat, 'Music and Migration: North African Artists' Networks across Europe and Africa', Rabat, 13–14 November 2008, Faculty of Letters, Mohammed V University, Agdal, Rabat, Morocco)

So the collaboration of musicians and the ASIDD activists of Tassemmitt is part of a broader dynamic of mutual support whereby the local inhabitants gain access to vital infrastructure (for example the schools) and the musicians are able to develop new creative projects outside their usual Casablanca context. The ASIDD experience is certainly not one which is characterized by musicians making one-off appearances at charity concerts and events which serve to provide emergency funds in the form of 'aid' to Tassemmitt and its inhabitants. Rather, the relationship between the Boulevard artists/organizers and the Aït Slimane community is guided by the principle that Tassemmitt's inhabitants should become autonomous, not only vis-à-vis ASIDD but also vis-à-vis their local surrounding region (and, in particular, Beni Mellal). Hicham sums this principle up well in the extract below:

> But the aim of the association, the aim of ASIDD, is not only to build a school, or to assist, or to bring back funds, to undertake little

emergency operations, by bringing clothes before the winter or, the goal is really to think in the long term about how the people can work locally and have an income, and to look after themselves without having to go down to Beni Mellal or going, crossing the straits, because the region is actually in the famous triangle of death [...] which supplies the majority of candidates for emigration ... to Italy mainly and Spain, and the aim was to convince the residents, to say to them, 'listen, it's a very beautiful place, it's a small paradise, it's true that there's poverty but it's here that you can do things ... you don't need to go elsewhere'. [22] (Hicham Bahou speaking at a panel at the TNMundi conference in Rabat, 'Music and Migration: North African Artists' Networks across Europe and Africa', Rabat, 13–14 November 2008, Faculty of Letters, Mohammed V University, Agdal, Rabat, Morocco)

The notion of a virtuous cycle of exchange between the artists and the local inhabitants through the activities of the ASIDD association is particularly apparent through the cultural tourism project which is currently being elaborated there. The development of an eco/cultural tourism dynamic in Tassemmitt will provide the locals with a source of income which allows them to escape some of the chimeras of internal and transnational migration which Hicham refers to above, and as far as the Boulevard artists are concerned, such cultural tourism will also provide them with the opportunity to develop creative networks with local regional artists:

So these residents, it was necessary to help them become aware exactly of the potentiality of the region ... it's very simple, it's better that the residents benefit out of it or others and others, there are lots of them [...] now there's a cooperative which exists which came out of the association and which is entirely managed by the residents, so the president is a resident, effectively, it's someone who is from the region who lives near Beni Mellal, so now they are autonomous and so the region is becoming, well, it's pretentious to say developing and ... but I think that a part of the objectives have been achieved ... Amale Samie is developing a little gîte there – and the goal is just that, we were talking about cultural tourism, is that it may also be a door for artists ... a place for artists ... and we're working on connections, let's say with all our common connections at the Boulevard, it's a time, whether it is a place where we go up to with artists where we can work, where we can develop these things, um, there's a local group, Hindouss ... and just this year we are planning to work together on an artistic creation residency project. [23] (Hicham Bahou speaking at a panel at the TNMundi conference in Rabat, 'Music and Migration: North African Artists' Networks across Europe and Africa', Rabat, 13–14 November 2008, Faculty of Letters, Mohammed V University, Agdal, Rabat, Morocco)

Although ASIDD is very much focused on the local setting of Tassemmitt, it is an association which also has a transnational dimension, radiating outwards and northwards. A branch of the association was set up in Bordeaux by a group of Moroccan students led by Mounir Kabbaj, a Casablanca musician (guitar and bass player) who had been involved in the Boulevard as a musician. While studying at university in Bordeaux (he left Casablanca in 2004) he decided to set up a branch of the ASIDD association with fellow Moroccan students so as to be able to 'do something' for their home country (Gibert's interview with Mounir Kabbaj, June 2009, Marseille). The Bordeaux branch of the association no longer exists but Kabbaj has gone on to set up another association – 'Music Against Ignorance' or MAI – in Marseille, where he is now based. MAI has established a partnership with the Dakhla Festival in Morocco whereby the international musicians performing in the festival take part in a number of music workshops with local schoolchildren, the aim being that in the long term the local children will not only be introduced to certain instruments but will be able to learn to play a variety of musical instruments. Musicians such as Khalid Moukdar from the Casablanca group Haoussa or Hindi Zahra (a Paris-based French-Moroccan singer) have taken part in these workshops which have now been held for the fourth year in a row.

Conclusions

The discussion of the Malagasy and Moroccan case studies above clearly shows that although these two countries present quite different developmental pictures they nevertheless offer significant points of comparison as far as the transnational convergence between musicians and civil society organizations are concerned. In both cases we have seen that, despite real challenges, it is possible to identify a dynamic of mutual support whereby the notion of the North 'giving to' the South becomes outmoded. It is arguable that our work was only able to uncover such processes of mutual South–North support because of the very nature of our 'network' research design. That is, by tracking the transnational networks of individual musicians and cultural activists we were led to encounter connections with civil society organizations which we would not necessarily have come across had we set out to study localized 'communities' of migrants and their descendants. In this way, our research has given us greater insight into the creative and innovative ways in which African artists and cultural activists and their extensive transnational networks contribute to a redefining of cultural and social relationships between North and South. The significance of such interactions is not lost to other activists[10] working, for instance, on the preservation of Madagascar's natural environment and points to the need for a much broader and more holistic appreciation of culture in the North's developmental agenda.

Appendix: Interview Extracts in the French and German Original

NB All extracts relating to the North African material were translated by Nadia Kiwan. Extracts relating to the Malagasy material in French were translated by Ulrike Meinhof and Oriane Boulay, those in English were translated into French by Ricky Olombelo, and those in German were translated by Ulrike Meinhof. All interviews were transcribed verbatim, regardless of linguistic errors by non-native speakers.

Introduction

1 Tu sais nous les musiciens nous sommes des idéalistes [...] Et moi je me suis très attaché à la terre [...] Et bon je voudrais que, les trucs que je chante, que j'ai composé, que je les mette en pratique sur le terrain. Mais heureusement on a trouvé des partenaires [...] C'est-à-dire pour pouvoir réaliser les rêves et la réalité, voilà [...] L'idée c'est ça, c'est-à-dire que y a beaucoup de trucs à faire dans le sud. Y a beaucoup d'argent dans le nord. Comment associer les deux? Donc je crois que bon, si le sud trouve des partenaires sérieux, le nord trouve des partenaires sérieux dans le sud, je crois que c'est à travers ça que l'on peut parler de développement [...] C'est pas une aide pour être dépendant mais ce sont des coups de pouce. (Meinhof's and Gibert's interview with members of the Mahaleo group, June 2007, Paris)

Chapter 1

1 Mais moi quand je chante je pense que je chante dans le sens traditionnel ... Traditionnel c'est une chanson vraiment vivre dans ton sang, pour moi, parce que c'est traditionnel, tradition, c'est ton original. C'est quelque chose original. Donc c'est là que tu fais sortir ton esprit et quelque fois c'est une chose de quelqu'un d'autre aussi a déjà fait [...] Donc comme si tu es Antandroy tu chantes le banaiky, si tu es Antanosy tu chantes le mangaliba [...] Le salegy, ça vient du Nord, le centre c'est le Hira gasy et le tsapiky – Tulear, c'est le traditionnel de Tulear, donc c'est comme ça. Donc je fais les traditionnel un peu mixé, je prends deux, je fais mangaliba ... et je fais jihe aussi, c'est un peu comme le rythme beko j'ai composé ça avec une guitare et j'ai fait comment se sentir bien avec la musique. (Meinhof's and Gibert's interview, October 2007. London)

2 Ce processus [identitaire] accompagne le double mouvement du tsapiky de la ville vers la campagne et de la campagne vers la ville. (Mallet 2009: 15)

3 Le tsapiky unifie l'espace de la ville. Il transcend le temps quotidien et donne sens aux différentes manifestations festives: sports, concerts, bals poussières, cérémonies. Pratique musicale, il est indissociable de la danse et du chant. Langage partagé, miroir de la violence et de la misère. (Mallet 2009: 126)

4 Dama: Tu sais la musique traditionnelle n'est pas aussi traditionnelle que
          ça. Pourquoi je dis ça? J'écoute, par exemple Mama Sana jouer

dans le village [...] pour moi, c'est une musique de maintenant, contemporaine. Quand elle était vivante, c'était au 20e siècle elle était vivante, elle joue et elle raconte la vie de maintenant dans les chansons. Et comment comment dire que c'est une musique traditionnelle, du folklore, tu vois, c'est dépassé, au contraire, c'est une musique actuelle, vraiment comment appeler ça – du terroir quoi. Et c'est dynamique. Et elle raconte tout ce qu'elle voit, et après, parce qu'il y a pas de texte définitif, tu vois c'est comme les ... les ... les ... jijy ce que font les jijy là ... ils racontent tous les événements qui se passent dans le village dans la chanson. Et demain, quand ils chantent cette même mélodie, mais avec d'autres événements qui se passent dans ...

Régis: Ah mais c'est ça, c'est ça l'évolution ...

Dama: Oui, c'est pas une tradition, un truc de musée. (Conversation between Meinhof, Rasolofondraosolo and Régis Gizavo, December 2005, Paris)

5 Moi je joue pas de la musique, je suis pas instrumentiste, donc chaque fois que je fais appel à un guitariste, forcément, c'est quelqu'un qui joue la façon guitare classique, donc folk, carrément Mahaleo, et c'était là que je me suis dit, non je viens du sud, je suis Tandroy, j'écoutais du beko donc je suis ça quoi, je suis la terre rouge, je suis le soleil brûlant du sud, donc si je chante, il faut que je sors une voix rocailleuse au lieu d'une voix mielleuse. Donc je me suis dit tout ça dans ma tête et ça m'a guidé dans mes compositions afin de ne pas, comment dire, être prisonnier en quelque sorte de son amour. Parce que l'amour c'est Mahaleo. (Meinhof's interview, April 2009, Nantes)

6 Dama: Parce que tu as dit, y a pas un rythme de référence, pour distinguer, pour savoir, pour identifier, ça, c'est la musique du [Fort-Dauphin] [...] Donc le mangaliba maintenant est devenu la musique de référence de Fort-Dauphin. C'est ça?

Daday: Oui, c'est ça. Euh, depuis le rythme de Fort-Dauphin, c'est déjà là. Mais ce n'est pas, ce n'est pas mangaliba. C'est moi qui donne le mot mangaliba pour appeler ce rythme.

Dama: Et l'histoire des mangaliba?

Daday: Les mangaliba? Bon, à chaque fois, je joue à Tuléar, à Beheloka, à Morombe et il y a beaucoup de gens qui demandent, quel est le rythme de Fort-Dauphin parce que à Morombe c'est banaky, à Tuléar c'est tsapiky, pecto, à Diego c'est salegy, à Fort-Dauphin y a pas. Donc je commence à chercher le rythme de Fort-Dauphin et de valoriser le rythme de Fort-Dauphin. Je choisis l'humeur Mangaliaba pour renommer le rythme de Fort-Dauphin. (Meinhof's and Rasolofondraosolo's interview, December 2009, Fort Dauphin)

7 J'ai commencé la musique à l'âge de cinq ans. Yeh. Mon père c'est instituteur et paysan en même temps. À Fianarantsoa. Et ma mère 100 pourcent paysanne. Donc la musique est pour moi, j'y suis né avec, la musique. À la campagne, vous savez très bien, les chants, ça fait partie de la vie totale des peuples paysans. Quand nos parents nous emmènent pour travailler la terre et tout ça [...] là-bas, on

chante beaucoup [...] et on nous a élevés aussi dans le milieu du christianisme, on est catholiques, et ce qui m'intéressait beaucoup aussi là-dedans, de le début on chante beaucoup à l'église, et dans ma famille tout le monde chante. Et mon père, en même temps instituteur, il joue l'orgue. Il joue l'orgue à l'église. C'est lui qui a joué l'orgue.

À Ambalavao, c'est la le tombeau de mes parents. Donc, la musique j'ai commencé à l'âge de cinq ans, quand mon père tous les soirs, il nous raconte des contes, tous les soirs avant qu'on dorme des contes et en même temps il joue la guitare et à l'époque quand il finit jouer la guitare, j'ai pris la guitare, et au moment qu'il joue la guitare, je regarde souvent. La main, comme il fait et il dit oui ça sonne bien avec toi comme ça. Donc, chaque fois qu'il fait, il passe la guitare, à cinq ans, six ans. (Meinhof's and Rasolofondraosolo's interview, April 2009, Lyon)

8 Ricky: Ça c'est vraiment quelque chose de connu très connu à Mada ... Le nom du quartier, c'est 67 Ha ... quartier vraiment des différentes ethnies à Madagascar ... Et presque toutes les différentes ethnies à Madagascar ils sont tous là-bas ... Mais à 80 pourcent des émigrations, des gens, c'est au 67 Ha. Et ça c'est le réseau des artistes, côtières tu vois, et encore ...

Ulrike: Donc ça c'est vraiment la région des émigrants de la nation. Et c'est vrai pour toutes les ethnies différentes ou seulement pour quelques unes.

Ricky: Non c'est vraiment différentes [...] parce qu'y [sont] les Antandroy, y a côté les Mahajanga, y a côté nord de Diego, Nosybe et sud-est de Madagascar, tu vois c'est, c'est bien, 67 hectares. (Meinhof's and Rasolofondraosolo's interview, December 2009, Fort Dauphin)

9 Non Senge ... Il a pris ces morceaux là et il est parti parler à la radio, je vais monter un groupe, voilà, takati, takata, et ensuite il m'avait appelé. Est-ce-que tu peux venir là, parce que j'ai trouvé une date, le 27 avril, au CGM, et je dis ok. J'ai monté à Tana, j'ai habité chez le cousin à 67 hectares, mais à l'époque Jean Ramanambintana, les gens qui étaient avec nous dans le Senge, ils travaillent et ils finissent à 17 heures. Donc on commence la répétition vers 20 heures, 17 heures ... Comme ça. Donc moi, j'ai fait à pied tous les jours 67 pour aller à Ankatso. Tous les jours, et rentrer à 10 heures du soir, parce que qu'on a pas l'argent pour prendre le bus, tous les jours j'ai fait ça – ça représente quelle distance? Une heure et demie à pied, tous les jours je viens à 18 heures ou comme ça, et on commence la répétition, on arrête vers 10 heures, et je mange un peu avec eux et je repars pour rentrer à 67 hectares. (Meinhof's and Rasolofondraosolo's interview, April 2009, Lyon)

10 Quand Tsiliva va commencer, se lancer dans son truc, le 90 pourcent du public qui était venu au concert à Tsaman, c'était le public du quartier que j'ai cité [...] Donc c'est 67 hectares, c'est côtier partout. (Meinhof's and Rasolofondraosolo's interview, Toliara, December 2009)

11 Marie: Et tous les autres musiciens, là, les douze, ils sont tous de Morondava?

Tsiliva:	Oui.
Marie:	Et ils sont tous partis à Tana ...?
Tsiliva:	Ouais. Ils sont tous déjà là-bas quand j'ai créé mon groupe. Et ce sont tous des, des cousins.
Ulrike:	C'est toute la famille?
Tsiliva:	Des copains, d'amis d'enfance, voilà. Ce sont tous des jeunes. (Meinhof's, Gibert's and Kiwan's interview, November 2007, Morondava)

12 Tsiliva:	Et quand j'ai eu mon bac je monte à Tana [...] On travaillait ensemble.
Marie:	D'accord! C'est à Tana que tu as commencé à jouer dans ces groupes-là, en fait.
Tsiliva:	Ah ouais, c'est à Tana. Apres ça. Mais quand, quand j'étais ici, c'est mon vœu le plus cher. Mon objectif c'est que d'être chanteur, et célèbre, tout ça. C'est ça mon objectif.
Ulrike:	Et ça ne marche pas ici? Si tu restes ici, ça marche pas?
Tsiliva:	Ça marche pas! Il faut se déplacer un peu.
Nadia:	Il faut aller sur Tana, c'est ça, pour euh?
Tsiliva:	Il faut sur Tana. Parce que ... Nous le groupe Tsiliva c'est le premier artiste qui vient d'ici euh, qui vient d'ici, qui a – comment dirais-je?
Juno:	A être accepté par le public ici?
Tsiliva:	Voilà! Qui est accepté. Et on l'a prouvé hier! Parce que j'ai quitté Morondava 2002. C'est pour ça qu'ils, qu'ils nous acceptent. Parce que faut pas rester ici si, si, si on veut exploser, euh, à Morondava, il faut te déplacer, faut travailler ailleurs. (Meinhof's, Gibert's and Kiwan's interview, November 2007, Morondava)

13 Après, Senge et Jean, ils m'ont trouvé des caves. Là-bas, ça je vous dis, vous pouvez pas vivre là-dedans, c'est comme des tombeaux. Donc. Il dit on va améliorer ça, ils ont dit on va acheter des planches. On a été acheter des planches. Pour faire une petite cloison. Et on a monté des lits aussi avec ce truc-là. Et il m'a prêté son matelas, et comme ça j'avais une [couverture] ouais. Ça c'est là où j'ai habité. C'est crado, à côté c'est les poubelles. J'ai habité là-dedans. J'ai failli avoir une [infection = la toux]. Et les souris, c'est mes amis. Beaucoup de rats. Et j'ai resté dans cet endroit-là pendant deux ans. Quand on a commencé en 96, 97 et 98, et là ça me permet de travailler comme il fait, même quand j'ai vécu dans ... là pour moi, je connais la difficulté dans la vie ... je connais ... je connaissais, à l'âge de 11 ans. Mais quand je raconte actuellement comme ça, mais j'ai vécu là-dedans, j'ai jamais, j'ai aucun complexe, j'ai amené mes amis là-dedans, même les copines, si vous venez venir chez moi, viens, y a pas de souci, je répète avec ma guitare, je répète ma voix, tout le monde me connaît, j'ai habité là, y a pas de souci. Et là, Senge, on travaille le soir, et le matin, on se lève à 5 heures et demie, et nous trois, Senge, on fait le travail de chorégraphie et à 6 heures du matin, on travaille la voix. On fait la voix. C'est comme ça parce que Jean il travaille, à 7 heures il faut qu'il part. Donc nous, c'est le soir et le matin qu'il faut qu'on travaille. (Meinhof's and Rasolofondraosolo's interview, April 2009, Lyon)

14 Anna: Moi j'ai envie d'aller à Tana pour faire le *Pas à Pas*, mais je ne sais pas quoi, quand ... on va commencer le nouvel casting.

Ulrike: Donc c'est surtout Tana qui vous attire?

Anna: Mais oui! Parce que le *Pas à Pas*, c'était bon, hein! (Meinhof's interview, November 2007, Fort Dauphin)

15 il n'y a pas de décentralisation au Maroc ... surtout dans le domaine artistique ... toutes les sociétés, tout est à Casa [...] aucune salle de spectacle à Fès ... (sauf maison de la jeunesse). (Otmane) (Kiwan's interview with Shabka, March 2008, Fez)

16 quand tu vois si tu vois les artistes qui participent dans cette compilation, c'est juste des rappeurs de Casa, de Rabat et de Salé. Il n'y a pas de groupes de Fès, pas de groupes de Tanger, pas de groupes de Marrakech, d'Agadir ... c'est pour cela je te dis tous les événements se passent à Casa–Rabat, Casa–Rabat, c'est ça, tous les médias sont basés à Casa–Rabat, tous les organisateurs, les boîtes de com, tout se passe à, on est ici à Fès, un peu marginalisés mais il y a des bons groupes à Fès, il y a Fez City Clan, Shabka, un autre aussi ... et ces groupes font des énormes efforts [...] ici à Fès, mais notre musique c'est pas mieux que Casa, mais c'est acceptable ... l'accent fassi est accepté au Maroc par rapport à l'accent casaoui ... parce que Fès, capitale spirituelle, et ici à Fès les familles sont très très respecteuses 'mouhafiz'. (Otmane) (Kiwan's interview with Shabka, March 2008, Fez)

17 un rêve ... ça fait plaisir. (Kiwan's interview with Fez City Clan (extract Simo), March 2008, Casablanca)

18 Casablanca, c'est plus une ville plus créative que Fès. (Kiwan's interview with Fez City Clan (extract Simo), March 2008, Casablanca)

19 Hatim: On se rend compte que même en étant H-Kayne et tout et machin, c'est pas qu'on a du mal, mais il y a des groupes ici à Meknès, de Fès, mais on sent vraiment que c'est super centralisé sur Casa–Rabat ... les radios, les machins [...] la radio qui est censée être ... Hit Radio, on l'a pas sur Meknès, on l'a pas sur Fès [...] Nous – ils nous appellent venez faire des interviews, j'ai fait ceux-là, ça a jamais passé [...] moi ça ne m'intéresse de passer si les gens de ma ville ... m'entendent pas tu vois, si vous voulez arriver à ma ville, pas de problème je ferai une interview ... mais ouais, c'est c'est, il y a rien ici sur Meknès, il y a rien, il y a rien.

Nadia: Au niveau médias, il y a pas une radio locale?

Hatim: ... Il y a une radio locale, il y a une radio locale, ça commence à – c'est une filiale de la RTM, SNRT [...] ça commence à 14h, ça termine à 19h je crois ... eux ça va ils passent des groupes d'ici et tout mais personne l'écoute tu vois, mais ouais que ce soit aussi même pour les boîtes de com, tu vois, les boîtes de com ils ont un truc, par exemple, ils vont ont avoir le choix entre un groupe de Fès ou de Meknès et un autre qui est de Casa ou de Rabat, je pense que rien que par proximité et tout, ça va plus pencher vers le gars qui vient de Casa, les journalistes pareil ... les journalistes genre le gars qui travaille le matin machin, ils sont sur Rabat, sur Casa, il a envie de faire un sujet sur le rap, directement il va le faire à Casa, il va voir les rappeurs qui sont sur Casa. Ils vont pas descendre jusqu'à je sais pas où ... donc nous on ressent ça mais, nous nous, en tant que H-Kayne ça nous affecte pas, nous on joue nos morceaux, qu'on soit de Casa ou pas, on nous appelle pour des grands festivals et tout. Moi je parle pour des groupes qui gravitent autour de nous – Mehdi K-Libre ... des gens qui sont là depuis longtemps, qui ont fait leurs preuves, qui ont sorti leurs CDs ... mais tu te rends compte que voilà, les médias s'intéressent pas vraiment, tu vois. (Kiwan's and Gibert's interview with Hatim and Otmane, H-Kayne, April 2008, Meknes)

20 Ali: Avant, il y a six ans au Maroc, la majorité de groupes ne savent pas qu'il y a un dossier de presse, qu'il y a une affiche [*sic*] technique, comme ça, qu'il y aura des relations avec des musiciens inter-nationaux comme ça, maintenant, on arrive à le concrétiser. Et avant on jouait qu'aux gens de notre région, de notre ville [...]

Nadia: Et au niveau de votre formation musicale, enfin vous chantez depuis toujours? Comment ça se fait que vous êtes venus à la musique?

Ali: Vraiment, pour moi je chante depuis toujours ... c'est vrai que parce que nous avons cette habitude de cérémonies tradition-nelles chez nous ... les mariages et tout ça ... c'est notre école de formation. (Kiwan's and Gibert's interview with Ali Faiq, April 2008, Agadir)

21 Nadia: Et vous l'avez enregistré à Agadir?

Ali: À Agadir, oui. Parce que toujours on travaille par nos moyens, parce que c'est très difficile d'aller à Casablanca et de vous dire voilà le pre-mier, voilà le quinzième jour donc il faut finir des chansons comme ça. C'est très difficile, donc nous on a choisi un studio dont on a déjà réalisé le premier album, donc ça a évolué l'expérience, et aussi ça nous donne confiance de faire ce que nous avons déjà. (Kiwan's and Gibert's interview with Ali Faiq, April 2008, Agadir)

22. Ali: Pour nous, on a choisi le ... parce que il y a aussi cette variété culturelle au Maroc, il y a des patrimoines c'est plus un seul patrimoine, il y a, c'est une richesse, nous, nous avons choisi les rwais, les rwais ce sont des troubadours du Souss, ils ont leurs caractéristiques personnels, et aussi les rwais, vraiment, ce que, ils sont, les caractéristiques de leur musique, de leurs chansons, en est en voie de disparition comme ça. Donc nous on fait réponse à l'appel de l'UNESCO ... surtout de préserver ce patrimoine, surtout qu'elle est en voie de disparation, au niveau des modes, au niveau de la métrique, au niveau de la poésie, mais aussi au niveau de, au niveau de ... c'est-à-dire que les gens n'arrivent plus, surtout les générations d'aujourd'hui, n'arrivent plus à écouter ce patrimoine, donc nous, on a essayé de le formuler, de le réveiller en quelque sorte.

Nadia: Quand vous dites je reprends un peu vos mots, que c'est en voie de disparation, c'est ...?

Ali: C'est-à-dire la chanson des rwais a des caractéristiques spéciales surtout les modes. Les modes ils sont anciennes, donc maintenant les gens n'arrivent plus à chanter dans ces modes ... les rwais nouveaux, ils arrivent plus à chanter dans ces modes, ils arrivent à créer leur boulot ... d'interpréter de prendre chez les autres, les modes, et de chanter, comme ça, je suis dérangé, hein. J'entends la musique comme ça ... c'est pas grave, c'est pas grave [...] Donc ce qui est en disparation ... comme j'ai dit tout à l'heure, il y a un appel, de l'UNESCO, 15 octobre 2002, ou 2001, je crois, qui disent qu'il faut préserver les musiques de la Méditerranée, et parmi ces musiques, il y a la musique des rwais, qui est ancienne, qui est ancienne donc nous, on est conscients on sait que les rwais sont plus comme ils sont dans les années ... au début du siècle, au 1900, ou en 1880 comme ça, la génération de Hajj Belaïd, et de Aboubakr Anchad, les gens n'arrivent plus à garder ce patrimoine, nous on dit pas qu'il faut le garder tel qu'elle est, mais il faut mettre là-dedans la création et la créativité ... Ce que nous avons fait à Amarg Fusion [...] Nous on a essayé aussi de préserver un instrument ribab, cet instrument lui aussi il est en voie de disparation. (Kiwan's and Gibert's interview with Ali Faiq, April 2008, Agadir)

23 C'est-à-dire c'est pas pour préserver les modes. C'est pas de ... de chanter les chansons comme les rwais ont fait ... sur le mode ... le mode est de créer nous-mêmes ... de créer, de composer des chansons sur ça, donc comme ça on va le préserver ... nous on veut pas un patrimoine figé ... c'est-à-dire qui risque tou-jours folklorique, pour les touristes et tout ça, nous voulons un patrimoine que nous voulons bien partager [...] Et aussi on n'a pas imité les rwais ... nous on imite pas les rwais. On le joue à notre façon. Mais on dit que ça c'est la musique des rwais, mais à notre façon. (Kiwan's and Gibert's interview with Ali Faiq, April 2008, Agadir)

Chapter 2

1 Rachel: Mais du coup, je me suis rendu compte que je connaissais plein de chansons d'eux [les Mahaleo], les paroles, les – c'est comme ça que j'ai appris à parler Malgache, en fait, en écoutant des paroles, en essayant de comprendre, en demandant à ma famille 'Qu'est-ce que ça ça veut dire? Et ça, ça veut dire quoi?' J'ai même un dico malgache [rire]. Et voilà, c'est ...

Marie: Et maintenant tu parles Malgache?

Rachel: Oui, je parle. Je parle pas le Malgache littéraire, mais en tous les cas on me comprend [rire] ... et je me débrouille très bien! Ouais, ouais ...

Marie: Et là tout ce qu'ils disaient pendant le concert, tu comprenais sans problèmes?

Rachel: Ouais, ouais ... Après, quand c'est des termes très ... très précis, ou des mots très compliqués, j'ai un peu plus de mal, mais je comprends dans le contexte, dans le ... Par exemple, tout ce qu'ils chantaient, je comprends... je comprends les sujets, donc, qu'ils vont évoquer, tout ça, quoi. (Meinhof's and Gibert's interview, June 2007, Paris)

2 Dama: Les musiques que je fais ... ce sont des chansons qui reflètent toujours la vie à Madagascar. C'est ça. C'est ça. Je fais des chansons qui racontent la vie à Madagascar. Et voilà, la vie des gens. Ce que je pense aussi moi, par rapport à ça. Je fais des chansons. Et moi je pense que ça reflète, ça reflète que je ne suis pas déconnecté des réalités de là bas. Que je suis là-dedans. Et que je vis là-dedans. Donc quand je compose ... c'est toujours un reflet de ce que je vis, de ce que je pense, ce que je sens. Qu'est-ce qui me fait mal, qu'est-ce qui me fait donner de l'espoir. Et je le chante. Parce que je suis parmi la population de Madagascar. Mais je peux pas composer des chansons comme ça, qui tombent du ciel. Je chante ce que je sens. Ce que je vis. Ce qui me fait vibrer. Ce qui me fait mal ... voilà, donc je crée par rapport à ça. (Meinhof's interview, June 2003, Paris)

3 La musique, c'est le lien, qui fait vraiment le lien, parce que je sais pas si les Malgaches ici ils ont le temps pour la musique, pour eux c'est toujours la musique de Madagascar. Ils se retrouvent toujours dans leur pays. Par rapport à cette musique ... Donc ... on a fait une synthèse des différentes facettes de la vie de Madagascar, de la vie des gens. Donc tous nos espoirs, nos espérances, c'est comment, à quelle référence il faut se tenir, quelle valeur culturelle on a. Donc l'importance de la tradition, l'importance des héritages culturels que nous avons eus, l'importance de notre diversité culturelle, l'importance de ce que nous appelons le système d'entraide, l'importance de ce qu'on appelle la solidarité. Parce que la solidarité est devenue un mot qu'on utilise à n'importe quelle sauce quoi. Mais, il y a cette notion de solidarité qui s'organise au sein des villages ... par rapport à la culture du riz, par rapport au travail de la terre, y a le système d'entraide, les gens discutent, y a une démocratie locale, les gens discutent comment construire un petit barrage, comment construire une petite école, et comment construire une petite route. Les gens discutent comment gérer le village. Comment se défendre par rapport aux voleurs de zébus. C'est tout un système qui est déjà là. Donc ça, ce sont déjà des richesses culturelles, des richesses civiques comme on dit, oui. C'est le civisme local qui est déjà là qu'il faut prendre en main, qu'il faut renforcer. Mais le problème c'est toujours, on dit la solution est toujours de l'autre côté. Alors que la solution est déjà à Madagascar. La musique remet toujours en place ... bon ... il faut partir de ce que nous avons déjà. Et les autres ça va renforcer ce que nous avons. C'est un peu toujours comme ça notre démarche ... par rapport à la musique. (Meinhof's interview, June 2003, Paris)

4 Je suis monté à Tana, le rêve mais vraiment le rêve inespéré pour moi, c'est de voir en chair et en os sur scène les Mahaleos. Et j'ai eu plus que ça. Donc Mahaleo [he still calls Dama by his first name Mahaleo here] habitait dans le même couloir que moi à l'université. Et chaque fois que l'on se rencontre dans le couloir, je savais pas quoi dire ... oui oui ... je savais pas quoi dire ... Je voulais parler mais je savais pas qu'est-ce qu'il faut que je dise. Et ben voilà pendant un certain temps je suis comme ça, et puis plus tard, comme Mahaleo est l'homme simple qu'il est, donc certainement il est conscient de ça quoi. Et donc chaque fois qu'il me voit, il me dit ah bonjour, petit frère, et donc ça m'a débloqué, et puis voilà on a fait pas mal de fois des choses ensemble. Par exemple la première sortie de Salala par

exemple, c'était avec le Goethe-Institut, au CGM, Olszowski, et on était dans la même équipe que Dama et d'Gary, Samy et Ricky. Donc toute l'équipe qui tourne autour du CGM quoi. [4] (Meinhof's interview, April 2009, Nantes)

5 C'etait dans le contexte de la crise politique actuelle à Madagascar. La population malgache est divisée, les citoyens malgaches sont divisés en deux. Pro, l'ancien président Ravalomanana et pro le Président de la Transition. Et cette division a aussi des ondes de choc si on peut dire comme ça. Cette division se répercute ici aussi en Europe dans la Diaspora, parmi, au sein de la Diaspora malgache il y a beaucoup de divisions. Et le groupe Mahaleo quand on a annoncé notre concert – parce que c'était déjà un concert préparé déjà depuis un an par une grande production de Kanto – [...] y pas mal des gens de la Diaspora sur l'internet qui disent que par rapport à la situation actuelle à Madagascar, 'pourquoi Mahaleo ne dit rien?' Voilà. Donc si Mahaleo fait un concert, ici en Europe malgré les conditions politiques à Madagascar, cela veut dire que ce n'est pas, ce n'est pas innocent, ce n'est pas innocent et que y a même, y a même des informations sur internet qui dit que le concert est un concert pour le HAT, pour le Président de la Transition. Donc c'est Mahaleo ... nous sommes au milieu. On nous tire. Le pro TGV disent que nous sommes pour le TGV les pros Ravalomanana disent que nous sommes pour Ravalomanana ... Donc c'est pour ça que moi j'ai expliqué dans les concerts, nous avons déjà parlé de ça depuis 72, mais en 72 nous étions les acteurs. Mais, mais nous ne sommes pas d'accord de ce système de régime présidentiel qui chaque fois crée des [political parties] [...] les présidents qui se succèdent créent leur propre parti. Donc ça devient un parti d'opportunistes. Les gens veulent tous aller dans le parti du président pour être près du pouvoir. Donc ça commence comme ça. Y a les autres qui ne sont pas dans cette voie, donc ça crée, tous les dix ans ça crée des troubles, des crises. Donc c'est ça qui faut combattre. Ce système de régime présidentiel. (Meinhof's interview, June 2009, Paris)

6 En fait, l'association, je t'explique qui était, c'était l'association artistique qui organisait des événements à la FOL, était composée vraiment en majorité de Français. Alors que normalement, dans les statuts c'est une association marocaine. Donc c'est au moment que nous on est rentrés dans la FOL, et on commençait à organiser des concerts, qu'on s'est aperçu qu'il y avait une association, on avait un cadre, qu'on pouvait utiliser pour organiser plus de concerts. Et c'est là, qu'un directeur de la FOL, qui nous a proposé de rentrer, parce qu'à cette époque-là, l'association, il fallait juste se présenter, et il y avait un vote, et c'est tout. [...] ils étaient pas aussi motivés que nous, nous on, nous on était plein dedans, on voulait vraiment faire des tas de choses. Et donc c'est comme ça qu'on est entrés dans l'association, et puis c'est comme ça que ça s'est détachée après, parce que la FOL n'a pas aimé justement la manière dont on gérait ça ... si tu veux, la FOL est devenue un peu plus populaire, il y avait plein de gens qui venaient, qui profitaient un peu des concerts, et que eux, ils n'aimaient pas ça. (Kiwan's interview with Hicham Bajjou, March 2008, Casablanca)

7 Est-ce que le rôle [du Ministère] c'est de faire des événements ou d'accompagner des événements? (Kiwan's and Gibert's interview, April 2008, Casablanca)

8 On n'a pas des nuits blanches à cause des sponsors, on a des nuits blanches à cause des autorisations, à cause de plein de choses, mais c'est tout, il y a pas de, si tu veux, le problème avec les autorités, c'est que avant ils comprenaient pas du tout ce qu'on faisait, pour eux on on était des extra-terrestres et maintenant ils ont peur des islamistes, ça veut dire, si les islamistes nous attaquent, ils nous ont attaqués l'année dernière au parlement ... donc du coup c'est une nouvelle donne, c'est-à-dire, s'ils nous autorisent ils ont peur de la réaction des islamistes tout ça, et nous, on est au milieu. (Kiwan's and Gibert's interview, April 2008, Casablanca)

9 Ça faisait quarante ans que la jeunesse de ce pays attend de s'exprimer, tu vois elle est en attente, elle voulait s'exprimer, elle voulait avoir des jeunes qui la représentent. Ces artistes-là ont fait ça. Les jeunes de ce pays s'identifient à ces groupes-là maintenant, au lieu de s'identifier à des Américains, ou à des Français ou à des Anglais, ben non, il s'identifient à des groupes marocains, donc du coup, il y a une telle, un retour, une certaine fierté d'être marocain déjà [...] ces musiques-là font partie si on veut d'un Maroc résistant aux obscurantistes, ils font partie de ceux, on fait le même travail que les flics, c'est-à-dire, par rapport à ça, sauf que eux ils ramassent après, nous on les bloquent avant. On touche aux cibles qui les intéressent parce qu'ils [the Islamists] essaient de recruter les jeunes et tous ces jeunes-là qu'on a au festival, c'est-à-dire, qu'il y a à peu près 150,000 spectateurs chez nous, pendant les quatre jours, et c'est des jeunes qu'ils peuvent pas toucher, on constitue une sorte de barrière à leur idéologie fasciste si on veut. (Momo Merhari interviewed for Metropolis, ARTE, 2007)

10 En 2003, Fouzi, le DJ avec qui on a commencé au départ, c'est un gars qui avait un magasin ici, c'était le seul endroit où on pouvait aller répéter, il y avait un micro et tout ... 'les gars il y a un truc, le Boulevard des jeunes musiciens, c'est des gens que je connais, ils font ça, c'est un tremplin, na na ni na na na, na na na', ouais mais nous on prend ça, pouf, on s'en fout nous ce qu'on veut, c'est voilà, on veut sortir notre truc ... 'mais non vas-y ça peut faire, ça peut faire', et on est allés comme ça, c'est-à-dire, lui il nous a dit, 'donnez-moi le dossier, moi je vais l'envoyer, on sait jamais'. Il l'a envoyé, Momo en l'écoutant, il m'a dit, il a dit que, 'ouais pourquoi pas?', on est venus ... [phone interruption] par pur coïncidence ... Momo il a apprécié, il a appelé Fouzi ... il leur a dit 'OK pas de problème ... vous pouvez participer au Boulevard', on est allés ... euh c'était un peu électrique l'ambiance tu vois au début, plein de groupes, regards de travers et tout, 'eux il viennent de Meknès eux ils sont de Casa' ... tu vois ... et voilà on a joué il y avait onze groupes, mais je peux dire, en 2003, c'est vraiment, Momo le dit, c'était là où il y avait le meilleur potentiel, meilleurs groupes, il y avait onze groupes de sélectionné, on a joué, le public il a adoré ... c'est la première fois qu'on montait à cinq sur scène, c'est-à-dire avec Khalid et avec ses nouvelles chansons ... on les a jamais faites sur scène ... ça a donné, on est descendus, on a dit 'c'est vous, vous allez gagner', on a gagné, on était super contents, là c'était vraiment le déclencheur parce que bon, là il y avait plein de journalistes, plein de médias étrangers aussi donc on a commencé à avoir nos premiers articles ... et à partir de là, aussi avec Hoba Hoba qui ont gagné la même année ... c'était le départ, on commençait à entendre parler de la nouvelle vague de

jeunes musiciens, c'est vraiment à partir de là, avant 2003, je pense pas qu'il y avait autant d'engouement autour de ce mouvement ... c'est arrivé, il y avait des réalisateurs en 2003 ... des bons films ... c'était une bonne année 2003, c'était ça vraiment le tremplin, la rampe de lancement c'était ça, et à travers le Boulevard on a pu faire les autres festivals ... auxquels ils étaient plus au moins affiliés, c'est-à-dire, Festival d'Essaouira, les arts populaires je crois [NK: ça c'est Marrakech c'est ça?], ouais, Marrakech et le jumelage qu'ils ont fait avec Garorock et là, Garorock aussi pareil, inoubliable, tu vois, on a fait deux années de suite ... pareil, bonne ambiance, c'était bien ben, de toute façon, le Boulevard, je pense de tout façon, tous les groupes, le Boulevard fait partie de leur passé, je connais pas de groupe qui au jour d'aujourd'hui, on le connaît, qui est pas passé par le Boulevard, j'en connais pas. (Hatim, H-Kayne) (Kiwan's and Gibert's interview with Hatim and Othmane, H-Kayne, April 2008, Meknes)

11 Hicham: Il y a eu un contact je crois à travers le Boulevard, parce que je crois que j'ai dû parler du Boulevard. J'en parle que c'est une plateforme qui est très importante. C'est elle un peu qui joue l'intermédiaire en tout ce qui est festival en général, surtout festival étatique ou festival aussi privé, qui sont faits par des boîtes de communication, ce qui veut dire à chaque fois qu'il y a un festival qui veut inviter un groupe jeune de musique actuelle, il appelle le Boulevard pour qu'on, et puis il lui demande de lui proposer un groupe, ou deux groupes ou trois groupes, ça dépend du style qu'il veut. Donc le Boulevard jouait un peu une sorte d'agence, tu vois, pour les groupes, mais d'une manière un peu indirecte, et pas régulière, c'était surtout pendant l'été, surtout à des occasions.

Nadia: Donc c'était qui l'interlocuteur, ou c'est qui, si ça continue toujours, ce travail d'intermédiaire?

Hicham: Cette histoire marche un peu moins parce que maintenant les groupes, ils sont un peu plus connus, maintenant ils les contactent directement. Avant c'étaient des groupes qui n'étaient pas connus du tout, des gens, enfin, qui étaient connus de quelques fans ici, tu vois des gens qui suivaient un peu les concerts, mais sinon les institutions et les boîtes privées. Ben, ce qu'ils faisaient c'est de contacter Momo et Hicham, c'était là-bas, c'est pour ça que je t'ai ramenée ici. La FOL, tu vois. La FOL, c'est juste en face. Donc là-bas c'était une salle de théâtre, et c'est là-bas où on organisait un peu le festival. Tu vois le portail, le grand, le bleu? Donc là-bas il y a un théâtre à l'intérieur, un petit espace, une cour, où il y a des salles de musique et aussi de danse, d'arts plastiques aussi, et donc là-bas c'était un peu le QG, quoi. Donc les gens ils appelaient, parce que Momo, il travaillait là-bas comme régisseur de la salle, et puis Hicham et Momo, c'était une équipe, enfin une association, en fait une association culturelle qui est fédérée par cette fédération, qui n'est plus d'ailleurs depuis un moment, depuis quelques années déjà, 2003, mais là je parle vraiment de la période Totale Eclypse, donc 1999–2002, 2003, ça marchait encore, tu vois c'était ça un peu le QG – on se trouvait tous ici, des gens ils appelaient pour avoir des groupes, pour avoir ... et puis ils spécifiaient leurs besoins – s'ils avaient besoin d'un groupe de rock ou de métal, ou je ne sais pas quoi, ça dépendait de l'occasion. Donc après ils les mettaient en contact avec le groupe lui-même, et voilà. (Kiwan's interview with Hicham Bajjou, March 2008, Casablanca)

12 Si tu veux sur la programmation, on part sur une sorte de rétrospective si tu veux de dix ans, c'est-à-dire, qu'on on va passer énormément de groupes qui sont marocains ... qui sont passés par chez nous quoi ... toute les têtes d'affiche maintenant ... on peut se permettre maintenant d'avoir des têtes d'affiche marocaines ... ça veut dire des groupes qui peuvent ramener du monde alors qu'avant on pouvait pas se permettre, donc ça sera l'occasion aussi de mettre ça en valeur ... et puis voilà donc il y aura beaucoup moins de groupes étrangers, beaucoup plus de têtes d'affiches marocains avec deux scènes pratiquement pareilles. (Kiwan's and Gibert's interview with Momo Merhari, April 2008, Casablanca)

13 Beaucoup de musiciens travaillent et sont impliqués dans le Boulevard, au fait il est monté aussi en partie par des musiciens, le magazine qu'on sort aussi c'est beaucoup de musiciens qui écrivent qui l'illustrent qui font du graphisme et ... et nous on fonctionne, comment dire, comme une tribu, comme une famille, ça veut dire on donne une priorité aux gens de la communauté quand on cherche quelque chose, ou quand on veut déléguer, quelqu'un pour nous aider pour ces tâches ... on voit d'abord des gens qui nous entourent ... et donc il y a une sorte de cercle qui fait que ça grossit mais en même temps, c'est les mêmes personnes donc il y a le même discours ... il y a le même esprit et ça se voit. (Kiwan's and Gibert's interview with Hicham Bahou, April 2008, Casablanca)

14 C'est un réseau d'operateurs culturels, surtout marocains, qui vivent à l'étranger, ça veut dire des mecs qui ont des salles de spectacle, il y a des mecs qui ont des labels ... des mecs qui sont des tourneurs, des mecs qui ont des associations culturelles ... c'est comme ça, tu vois. Qui sont un peu partout en Europe, et le but c'est voilà, c'est faire la promotion des groupes marocains. (Kiwan's and Gibert's interview with Momo Merhari, April 2008, Casablanca)

15 Avant, par exemple, les organisateurs de spectacles, ils se contentaient des affiches et puis des spots. Moi, quand j'ai fait la communication, moi j'ai fait des reportages, des émissions sur l'artiste. Donc des entrevues, des ... l'historique de l'artiste, tout ça. Donc ça c'est ... et les décors, tout ce qui est autour de l'événement. Donc ça a vraiment créé une sensation auprès du public, et ça a suscité l'engouement du public. Donc le premier spectacle était vraiment un succès. Et puis, j'ai encore réédité un autre spectacle, et c'était encore un succès. A ce point-là, donc, je me disais il faut que je me lance, donc, dans les spectacles. Parce que je trouve quand même que c'est, c'est, c'est ... Ça rapporte pour une société. Et puis j'ai commencé à travailler, j'ai commencé à professionnaliser cette filière, parce qu'avant, c'était pas du tout professionnel. C'est-à-dire que tous les facteurs, tous les acteurs qui sont impliqués dans l'organisation du spectacle sont tous des informels. Par exemple, mois je suis organisateur, mais avant, l'organisateur il est à la fois directeur dans une banque, ou chef de service dans telle ou telle société. Ce qui fait que

y'a pas, y'avait pas vraiment d'organisateurs professionnels. Donc, à ce moment, je me disais, il faut que je me professionnalise dans ce métier, parce que, quand j'ai vu quelqu'un qui organise par exemple un grand concert, donc c'est une association de jeunes ou de travailleurs qui se regroupent le weekend, par exemple, et puis ils ont décidé 'Tiens, on va organiser un concert. Donc, toi, est-ce que tu es disponible demain, lundi?' 'Bah, moi je travaille, je peux pas ...' Enfin, c'est comme ça qu'on a fonctionné avant. Mais, à partir du moment que nous on a travaillé, donc, ça a changé petit à petit. Et puis, ça a commencé comme ça, et ça continue jusqu'à maintenant. Donc nous on fait à peu près trente concerts par an, depuis 2004, 2005, 2006, 2007–8. Et les concerts, on fait ... y'a pas que Madagascar, parce que nous on fait aussi des concerts, euh ... en France et à la Réunion. Et puis on amène des artistes là-bas et on essaie d'organiser, on amène des artistes en France ou à la Réunion, et bientôt à Mayotte ... Administrative, c'est, c'est toujours à partir d'ici. Donc les antennes à Paris, ou à la Réunion, ou à Marseille, ces gens-là ne font que la préparation, disons, matérielle ... Donc, ils font par exemple la réservation des salles. Et même la réservation des salles, c'est nous qui payons les acomptes. Donc eux, ils ne font que la préparation vraiment matérielle ... et puis voilà, c'est tout, hein. Et la vente des billets, c'est à la réservation. Donc, voilà, et la logistique des artistes. Comme nous, par exemple, avec les Mahaleo, quand on arrive là-bas, ces gens là-bas, ils ont déjà fait la réservation d'hôtel, par exemple, assurent les transports ... l'hébergement ... la restauration ... Mais ça, c'est du budget, c'est toujours par ici que, c'est toujours ici à Madagascar, donc c'est-à-dire que c'est Media Consulting qui organise tout. Mais ces gens-là, donc, c'est pour ... pour nous aider à réaliser le projet. C'est ça, en quelque sorte. (Meinhof's and Rasolofondraosolo's interview, November 2007, Antananarivo)

16 Jaobarison: Le problème, c'est que ... au niveau des artistes, y'a des artistes qui ne ... qui ne comprennent pas très bien la situation. Ils pensent que, quand on joue à l'extérieur, donc ils imaginent vraiment un spectacle, euh ... grandiose. Par exemple, y'a des artistes qui sont venus hier ici au bureau. Je les fais venir en France. Et quand on a discuté du cachet, quand j'ai dit 'Voilà le cachet', donc, euh ... c'était vraiment, euh ... c'est à côté de la plaque. C'est ce que j'ai dit. Et il fallait que ... qu'on discute, il fallait que je lui explique comment ça se passe, parce qu'il pense que, quand on joue en France, par exemple, il y a des étrangers, il y a beaucoup, il y a trois mille, il y a quatre mille personnes là-bas. Pourtant, c'est pas ça. Parce que la plupart ... le public est composé surtout ... c'est ...

Dama: De la communauté malgache.

Jaobarison: De la communauté malgache.

Ulrike: Ce sont des Malgaches?

Jaobarison: Des Malgaches. Donc, c'est comme, c'est comme une soirée, mille deux cents personnes, mille cinq cents personnes. Maximum, c'est mille cinq cents personnes ... Des fois même, c'est trois cents personnes, deux cents personnes. Donc, c'est juste pour que la communauté malgache, la diaspora malgache puisse avoir, puisse ... – comment on dit ça? – puisse jouir des spectacles donnés par des artistes malgaches ... Mais y'a aussi des États-Unis. Y'a le Canada. Parce que là aussi, y'a une forte communauté malgache ... Surtout à Montréal. Là, quand on a joué – c'était en 2006 – y'avait à peu près quatre cents, cinq cents personnes, malgaches. Donc, et pourtant, y'avait encore des Malgaches qui n'ont pas pu venir à Montréal, parce que ... on n'a pas bien communiqué. Donc cette fois-ci – ce sera au mois de mai – cette fois-ci, maintenant, dès maintenant, on commence déjà la communication ... pour vraiment sensibiliser ces gens-là. Parce qu'ils ont raté le premier concert. Et ... là, on espère que cette fois-ci, y'aura ... on espère y'aura une plus grande affluence. (Meinhof's and Rasolofondraosolo's interview, November 2007, Antananarivo)

17 Avant tout je suis musicien de temple sacré parce que on est formé là-dedans comme toute la famille, donc à partir de là ... on a fait des petits concerts au village, mariages, fêtes de l'école, et tout ça ... mais je ne suis pas connu du tout à Tana, en ville, pas du tout, rien du tout, sauf oui, par contre, j'ai été commerçant de la valiha, comme tous mes frères et tout ça ... Et c'est de là [Tana] que j'ai rencontré un ... bon un tourneur disons, qui essayait de former un groupe folklorique pour venir en France. Donc on a fait le concours, les sélections, etc. et tout ça. Donc je suis élu par les autres joueurs de la valiha, on était quatre et voilà ... donc l'aventure commence là. (Meinhof's and Rasolofondraosolo's interview, May 2006, following the concert by the Madagascar All Stars at the Traumzeit Festival in Germany)

18 Deux ans avant, je me suis dit, mais, bon, je vais essayer ça. Moi je voulais quand même être ici [Paris], quoi, partir de Madagascar pour essayer de voir autre chose, quoi, et je m'suis dit bon, j'ai des compos, bon, je vais aller ... j'étais déjà a Tana, j'ai essayé de trouver un studio c'était pas évident ...
Et là ... j'ai rencontré Kiki ... oui, l'oncle à Rageorges ... J'suis allé chez eux et, bon, j'ai dit, 'mais bon, je veux enregistrer, je veux participer à un concours, mais ... J'ai rien ... Est-ce que vous pouvez me prêter votre studio ... juste pour un après-midi ou un jour, ou une journée?', et là, ils m'on dit 'oui' ... Rageorges, il m'a dit 'sans problème' ... donc après, 'il faut parler avec Kiki' et tout, mais Kiki, il était encore jeune, jeune, jeune ... Encore, on a essayé de faire, de monter ce projet ... et puis bon, j'ai réussi à faire une chanson ... Après, on a fait deux, trois, comme ça ... Et après, on a envoyé la cassette de Madagascar ... Et moi j'attendais rien, hein, moi j'attendais ...
Et après, un soir, j'étais devant un poste de télévision ... et j'ai vu mon clip qui apparaissait sur la 'Deux', c'était en 1990. Et là, bon, sur Antenne 2, à 20 heures, moi, j'ai vu ça ... et: 'qu'est-ce que je fous là?' ... les artistes qui avaient gagné le prix, et RFI, et tout ça, et j'étais dedans ...
Et après, RTM, la radio RTM ... m'a appelé, comme quoi, et après, j'ai gagné un prix ... c'est parti comme ça ... Et puis, on m'a envoyé un billet pour la remise des prix un an après ... Et là, je suis parti de Madagascar, c'était ... Le début de l'aventure. (Meinhof's and Rasolofondraosolo's interview, June 2006, Paris)

Chapter 3

1 Bon j'ai l'impression que tout le monde est parti de là-bas ... toute ma génération [...] il y a plein de musiciens qui avaient débarqué dans les années 90, pratiquement tous les musiciens de la place d'Alger ... étaient venus ici. Alors à l'époque il y avait tout le monde, beaucoup de gens qui partaient de l'Algérie. Et voilà, on s'est retrouvés en fait tous à Paris, avec les mêmes problèmes de papiers ... et tout ça ... et ... c'est un reflexe grégaire quand on part ailleurs, je pense, tout le monde, on se retrouve forcément dans le même lieu ... Voilà, c'est-à-dire, vraiment naturellement le ... les gens ... faisaient de la musique ensemble quoi ... à l'époque il y avait Karim Ziad, Aziz Samaoui, Moustafa Moutawi et tout, tous ces gens ils habitaient par exemple le même appartement à Clichy ... tu vois ... ils partageaient, le même appartement ... avec, je me rappelle, par exemple sur le même palier à Clichy il ... il y avait deux apparts' qui étaient loués, et c'est que des musiciens algériens, il y avait six ou sept musiciens ... parce qu'à l'époque ils venaient d'arriver, donc quelqu'un a un plan pour un appart' parce qu'à l'époque on venait d'arriver, c'est comme ça. (Kiwan's and Gibert's interview with Hocine Boukella, February 2008, Ivry, France)

2 En gros le fait d'être comme ça ... euh en collectif, tu vois, ça dans un sens ça nous a obligés à vraiment voir tous les aspects de notre travail quoi, tu vois, bon comme il y a pas tellement de boîtes de production qui s'intéressent à notre travail, ben on a décidé de créer une boite, un label de production. (Kiwan's and Gibert's interview with Hocine Boukella, February 2008, Ivry, France)

3 Et c'est vrai que ça a ... vraiment de '98 jusqu'à 2008, ça a été vraiment une très, très bonne expérience ... parce qu'il y a eu pas mal de rencontres, et mine de rien c'est dans ce lieu qu'on a tous ... si tu veux ... euh ... fait avancer notre travail quoi aussi bien l'Orchestre national de Barbès que Gaâda que Sidi Bémol ... il y a eu plein de groupes qui ont été montés là-bas aussi. Des jeunes groupes et euh ... et en plus euh ... c'est-à-dire il y a, on a une très, très bonne aura si tu veux en Algérie, dans le milieu des musiciens et tout ça, à Alger tous les musiciens connaissent Louzine ... ils pensent d'ailleurs que c'est euh ... c'est un gros truc ... je sais pas si tu es venue dans le lieu ...? [...] C'est un local ... tu verras dans le documentaire, c'est très vieux ... donc il y a des musiciens qui venaient d'Alger, et bon qui avaient l'adresse et qui arrivés là-bas, ils étaient étonnés de voir ce gourbi un peu! et euh voilà donc ... justement ... Louzine nous a permis aussi de nouer vraiment des contacts avec l'Algérie ... on a eu des contacts avec donc Belda Diffusion par exemple ... qui est un jeune éditeur à Alger [...] ça nous a permis de nouer des contacts avec des gens comme ça, et puis avec des groupes algériens surtout ... comme Index ... un jeune groupe qui s'appelle Djmawi Africa. (Kiwan's and Gibert's interview with Hocine Boukella, February 2008, Ivry, France)

4 Et moi je pense que le ... enfin, moi personnellement, arrivant ici en France, je sais que c'est plus facile de trouver par exemple les disques des chanteurs algériens, pendant que moi, j'aime bien un chanteur qui s'appelle Cheikh Hammada, c'est un chanteur bédouin, en Algérie j'avais un disque de lui et j'ai cherché, mais là-bas je n'ai jamais trouvé ... ici je l'ai découvert! Slimane Azem c'est pareil. C'est un chanteur kabyle qui était interdit en Algérie, tu vois ... C'est

ici que tu vas le découvrir ... tous ses disques [...] Mais en gros toute la musique algérienne vient d'ici, hein. Parce qu'en Algérie il n'y a rien ... tous les groupes de musiques qui sont à Alger, ça veut dire dès qu'ils commencent à avoir un peu de notoriété, ils vont ailleurs ... ils restent pas en Algérie, parce qu'il y a pas de concerts. (Kiwan's and Gibert's interview with Hocine Boukella, February 2008, Ivry, France)

5 Parce que Barbès est un quartier d'immigration, c'est un quartier de rencontres, et, surtout pour les Maghrébins, bon, ça commence à changer. Nous et surtout ceux qui sont venus avant nous, il y avait plein d'immigrés [...] C'est le quartier, avant de venir à Paris, je connaissais ni le 15e, ni le quartier chinois, le 13e, le quartier le plus célèbre chez les gens novices comme moi j'étais avant, c'est le premier quartier. Après la tour Eiffel, on connaît Barbès [...] et puis c'est un passage obligatoire de transition. (Kiwan's interview with Taoufik, February 2004, Paris)

6 Le but en fait, je voulais pas faire un truc à 100 pourcent maghrébin, algérien. Je voulais plutôt dans ma musique du métissage [...] quand je suis tombé sur des musiciens complètement différents que moi, avec une culture musicale complètement différente que la mienne, le but c'était ça, de monter une formation [...] chacun me donnait sa touche musicale qui est à part [...] Un côté celte – ça c'est mon coté berbère qui sort. Le gnawa, le populaire algérien – c'est aussi ma culture. (Kiwan's interview with Karim, El-Gafla, October 2003, Paris)

7 De l'Algérie à Paris, en passant par le Cameroun ou la Pologne, les sept membres d'El-Gafla forment une sorte d'Orchestre International de Ménilmontant, coin de Paris métissé et populaire, comme leur musique. De bars en squats et de salles en festivals, le bruit court et la caravane passe, suivie par un public large et fidèle, réunissant tous ceux qui apprécient l'énergie de Gnawa Diffusion, la douce mélancolie de Souad Massi ou le franc parler de Zebda. (www.louzine.net, accessed 1 December 2009)

8 J'aime beaucoup cette ville, je pense pas que je pourrais quitter cette ville [...] en plus j'ai fait des rencontres hallucinantes à Paris [...] sur le plan musical surtout [...] la France c'est le métissage de toutes ses cultures [...] Je me sens très très bien dans Paris. (Kiwan's interview with Karim, El-Gafla, October 2003, Paris)

9 On avait les pieds là-bas [Algeria] et la tête à Paris. (Excerpt from interview with Karim Ziad on www.algeriades.com, accessed 2 December 2009)

10 Ah oui, je suis parti, c'était horrible. Il y avait ça aussi ... qui m'a mis les coups de pieds au derrière [...] il y a eu ce mouvement effectivement, ce, ce, il y a eu plein de départs d'Algérie de musiciens, parce que effectivement en Algérie on avait du mal à faire de la musique. A vivre, en tout cas, de musique. (Kiwan's interview with Karim Ziad, July 2008, Paris)

11 Maintenant dans des groupes de jazz, qu'on entend actuellement, je reconnais la touche que j'ai ramenée en France. C'est-à-dire maintenant tous les batteurs,

tous sans exception, travaillent ma partie. Elle fait partie des écoles. [...] et il y a de très bons batteurs, qui sont sur la place de Paris et qui jouent ça, et c'est le seul pays où il y a des Européens qui arrivent à jouer de la musique du Maghreb, efficacement, par exemple on ne retrouve pas ça ni en Angleterre, ni aux États-Unis, ni ailleurs. Il y a qu'en France. Pourquoi ça aussi? Parce qu'effectivement ça fait quatre ou cinq ans que j'enseigne dans cette école. (Kiwan's interview with Karim Ziad, July 2008, Paris)

12 En fait, le premier endroit où j'ai répété à Paris, c'était Louzine, et vu que t'as l'ONB qui répétait là-bas, pleins de groupes, donc tu connais forcément tout le monde, tu vois. (Gibert's interview with Hichem Takaoute, February 2009)

13 Le pourquoi de toutes ces soirées, de toutes ces actions, c'est ... vient d'une attitude, d'une conclusion par rapport à un état de fait, c'est-à-dire que je suis d'origine algérienne, l'idée c'est que en tant qu'individu, j'ai une double culture qui est forcément algérienne et française, parce que je suis quasiment né ici, je suis venu en France, j'avais quatre ans, et l'idée c'est qu'en tant qu'artiste, cette double culture, on peut l'exprimer, moi je l'exprime en tant qu'individu quotidiennement par rapport à mon mode de vie, mais en tant qu'artiste, on doit l'exprimer, j'allais dire par une musique qui est forcément un petit peu nouvelle, par un mouvement musical qui intègre, je dirais les influences des deux rives de la Méditerranée. (Kiwan's interview with Mohand Haddar, December 2003, Paris)

14 C'est ça aussi l'avantage de Paris, c'est que ... on peut ... si on veut faire de la musique d'origine marocaine, on n'est pas obligés de jouer avec des Marocains uniquement. Parce que les autres aussi ont écouté des trucs, donc déjà ils ont ... il y a une ouverture. De ce côté-là, Paris c'est un peu l'idéal pour les fusions. Et du coup on a eu l'occasion de jouer avec des Français bien sûr, franco-français déjà, Marocains, Algériens, mais aussi des Réunionnais donc on disait toute à l'heure, [...] Ivoiriens, Sénégalais, Polonais ... donc ... et chacun apporte sa sensibilité bien-sûr, enfin au niveau de l'interprétation. (Badr Defouad – Kiwan's interview with Badr and Adlane Defouad, July 2008, Paris)

15 J'avais en tête, cette idée que le métissage pouvait être fluide musicalement ... et ça pouvait créer autre chose, c'est pas juste du collage [...] c'est-à-dire, quand je dis ça, c'est-à dire une nouvelle culture musicale qui n'est pas stérile [...] c'est, elle donne un nouveau départ, comme si on était en train de parler de nouvelles musiques, d'un monde nouveau etc. qui était ni quelque part, ni enraciné dans un pays ou dans un autre et que l'idée qu'on a derrière et qu'on voit finale-ment [...] comme beaucoup de mes copains de l'époque ... on se sent de plus en plus citoyens du monde. (Badr Defouad – Kiwan's interview with Badr and Adlane Defouad, July 2008, Paris)

16 D'origine malgache, une des significations du mot Kanto est la 'perfection', une qualité essentielle que nous souhaitons attribuer à toutes nos activités. La société est dotée d'une équipe dynamique, créative et rigoureuse, lui permettant d'évoluer dans les domaines du marketing et de la communication événementielle. (www.kanto.fr/, accessed 25 April 2010)

17 En parlant de New Morning, ce que j'organise, j'essaie de toujours par exemple de vendre des billets à la Fnac, mais, les concerts sont référencés dans les journaux parisiens, dans *Nova Magazine*. J'essaie d'ouvrir en fait, j'essaie d'ouvrir mais il faut une base communautaire pour amortir les spectacles, en termes financiers donc on fait Croissance, Sobiky, et les mailings aussi … Sobiky.com c'est plus ouvert, plus jeune, c'est intéressant en fait. (Kiwan's interview, April 2003, Paris)

18 Mon concept de ce que je fais, c'est partager, c'est essayer de […] partager quelque chose […] je me dis pas je vais organiser un concert pour la communauté. J'organise un concert parce que j'aime l'artiste en fait. Mais bon il y a toujours ce souci de popularité. Je veux pas. Ça m'est arrivé d'organiser un ou deux concerts, où j'adorais les artistes comme Edgar Ravahatra et personne le connaissait et on se retrouvait 5 ou 60 au New Morning alors que Erick Manana on y va a 500–600 personnes. Donc c'est surtout ça qui motive, j'aime bien la musique, j'aime bien l'artiste et c'est l'affection, l'affection. (Kiwan's interview, April 2003, Paris)

19 Ulrike: J'aimerais bien bien que tu me racontes un peu qu'est-ce qui s'est passé depuis le temps de Mahaleo à Olympia. C'est comment que tu as continué a …

Lova: À travailler?

Ulrike: À former toutes ces connexions?

Lova: En fait, Mahaleo, c'était vraiment le départ parce que comme je t'avais dit lors de la première interview. On travaille déjà avec la diaspora, dans des petites salles plutôt, en banlieues qu'on … on voulait travailler maintenant sur de grandes salles pour vraiment faire une vraie promotion et Mahaleo c'était vraiment le point de départ, et depuis Mahaleo en fait on a continué y'a un an ici à La Cigale avec Lolo et puis en septembre on a fait Jaojaoby ici à l'Olympia. Donc là on revient avec les Mahaleo deux ans après La Cigale, c'est-à-dire, depuis à peu près deux ans et demi on a fait quatre, on va faire quatre concerts à l'Olympia, parce qu'on vient avec Erick Manana en novembre. On a fait quatre concerts à l'Olympia et deux à La Cigale. Donc, euh … on travaille, on se rend pas compte. Mais, c'est vrai qu'on continue à travailler. Mais, ça … ça commence à prendre. Mais on n'a pas encore atteint nos vrais objectifs. Mais on se l'est fixé à cinq ans, on est a mi-chemin. A mi-chemin, et pour l'instant je pense qu'on est en bonne voie pour atteindre un peu ce qu'on veut! …

Au niveau de la communication maintenant, on a tissé notre réseau dans les, dans tout ce qui est un peu diaspora c'est maîtrisé on va dire. Et puis on commence à avoir des partenaires comme RFI, France Outre-Mer, Radio France Internationale, France Inter, ça reste, on commence à rentrer dans des trucs un peu plus internationaux. Donc ça c'est un travail, euh … travail à long terme. On s'est fixé à cinq ans, on est à deux ans et demi maintenant … On nous sol-licite aussi pour produire des gens, mais malheureusement on n'a pas la structure nécessaire pour lancer de nouveaux artistes.

Donc, pour l'instant, on est resté sur Jaojaoby sur des groupes, des valeurs sûres pour pouvoir remplir des … que ce soit bien l'Olympia, ou La Cigale, ou le Morning on peut encore prendre quelques risques, faire des trucs un peu plus conceptuels, comme d'écouter Lolo qui vraiment est les deux auteur-compositeur mais on nous consulte quand même pour dire voilà, y'a des artistes qui vont arriver, est-ce que vous vous pouvez … Mais pour l'instant on a toujours dit non parce que on ne peut pas lancer un artiste comme ça à La Cigale, sachant que aujourd'hui on a une grande, on va dire on est a 70 pourcent de la diaspora encore. Donc 30 pourcentage d'étrangers hors-diaspora. On est encore à 70 pourcent, mais ce sont des choses qui, sur lesquelles on travaille parce qu'on sait que des Mahaleo ne sont pas euh … il ne sont pas toujours là quoi … Vraiment c'est un virage qu'on va prendre sur les deux ans, deux ans et demi à venir. On va essayer de trouver d'autres artistes, des groupes malgaches un peu moins connus mais qu'on va essayer de remplir La Cigale, comme Ricky par exemple, cette génération-là, et peut-être des All-Star aussi, On va essayer de travailler là-dessus, pour les deux ans et demi, trois ans à venir en fait. Trouver autre chose que le Mahaleo, Lolo sy ny Tariny, et Jaojaoby. (Meinhof's and Gibert's interview, June 2009, Paris)

20 Lova: On fait un grand concert par an à Madagascar. Donc, l'année elle est très bien remplie!

Ulrike: Tu, tu fais aussi un concert à Madagascar?

Lova: Ouais, l'année dernière j'avais emmené Yannick Noah, on avait fait Yannick Noah euh … l'année dernière au mois d'avril. Et cette année,

Ulrike: Et tu es allé où à Madagascar?

Lova: Juste à Tana on a fait un concert à Tana … On l'a fait au Palais des Sports. Et là normalement, on doit faire Francis Cabrel le 30 octobre, mais avec les événements, c'est encore en stand-by. Voilà. En même temps on fait un grand événement là-bas. Et ça nous remplit vraiment.

Ulrike: Ah mais ça m'intéresse beaucoup. C'est comment que tu organises ça d'ici? Tu as quelqu'un?

Lova: J'ai une équipe.

Ulrike: Tu as une équipe là-bas? Mais c'est pas le Media Consulting?

Lova: Non, non, non. C'est Kitana Production.

Ulrike: Vous, vous êtes en concurrence avec eux. Donc, c'est ton équipe qui travaille spécialement pour toi?

Lova: Là-bas oui. Mais pas à l'année. Par exemple, ils travaillent grosso-modo, par exemple pour Noah on a travaillé sur trois mois … J'ai un noyau de quatre personnes, et après ça peut aller jusqu'à cinquante personnes quand l'événement se rapproche, mais j'ai une équipe là-bas avec laquelle je travaille. (Meinhof's and Gibert's interview, June 2009, Paris)

21 Régis: Moi, quand je suis arrivé en France, donc c'était pour la remise des prix de ce concours-là, donc je suis allé à … en Guinée-Conakry, bon, avec l'armada de RFI, avec des journalistes presque la moitié de l'avion, et c'était comme ça même à Madagascar aussi, on avait une remise de prix de RFI et je pense que vous avez pu apercevoir les voitures à Tana, Mafy, RFI et tout ça, quoi … mais c'était pareil … Donc, c'était une chance parce que c'est pas tout le temps qu'on

voyage avec les journalistes, qu'on peut avoir un peu des critiques de presse, quoi ... Et, c'était bien sérieux et donc moi, je suis arrivé là-bas, bon ... j'étais accompagné par une formation guinéenne ... Et, c'est là le début, parce que, à chaque événement de RFI, ils invitent toujours les stars africaines. Donc, il y avait Ray Lema, Manu Dibango, et d'autres, quoi ...

Et donc, ces gars là ... ils habitent ici, à Paris, la plupart. Donc, ils sont toujours accompagnés la plupart du temps par des musiciens français, le noyau parisien, quoi ... Et là, il y avait un gars qui s'appelait, qui s'appelle Francis Lassus, et là, il m'a vu jouer et c'était parti comme ça, pour lui, c'était un coup de foudre. Il est passé devant ma loge et il m'a entendu jouer, et là, il m'a dit 'ouais, oui, c'est toi que je veux, il faut que je t'invite à Paris, je vais t'héberger, donc, voilà, quoi, c'est parti comme ça ...

Et donc, moi je suis rentré à Madagascar après, et après, bon, je suis revenu pour la 'Francofolie' de La Rochelle et là, j'étais avec un groupe complet de Madagascar, des musiciens de Madagascar, musiciens malgaches ... Et après, les gars ils sont rentrés, et je suis resté, parce que le gars, il a insisté que je vienne chez lui ...

Ulrike:	Francis Lassus?
Régis:	Francis Lassus. Et là, il m'a hébergé. Donc il a tout fait pour que je puisse ...
Dama:	Rester?
Régis:	Oui, rester. Voilà. Après, on a formé un groupe qui s'appelait 'Bohe Combo' ...
Dama:	Comment?
Régis:	Bohe Combo ... C'est le son de Paris, quoi, un peu, parce qu'il avait Charles Bonnard, qui vient du Cameroun, un guitariste qui s'appelait, qui s'appelle Pascal Danaé, qui vient des Antilles, et Jean-Michel Pile, qui est aussi un des ... un Français juif, ainsi que Salut Lolo, qui était là aussi, la chanteuse qui est maintenant, qui a son groupe ... Et moi, et Francis Lassus et David Mirandon, qui m'accompagne maintenant. (Meinhof's and Rasolofondraosolo's interview, December 2005, Paris)

22 Régis:	La différence entre le groupe Mahaleo et le reste ... Lolo aussi, bon ... il était très connu ... c'est que, bon, c'est autre chose, parce que les Malgaches, ils s'attachent beaucoup à leur histoire et ces groupes-là, ils ont, ils étaient là, quoi, c'est ça, c'est ça. Et pour moi, quand je chante mes chansons, c'est un truc à part vraiment. En plus, il faut me comprendre aussi ... les gens qui voient et ... quand Erick, il joue, les gens, ils chantent ... Parce que c'est ... ce sont des textes que les gens, ils comprennent vraiment. Pour moi, par exemple, les gens, ils ont du mal, sauf deux ou trois chansons qu'ils arrivent à comprendre. Parce que moi, quand j'étais à Madagascar, j'ai passé un an ... et après, je suis allé directement ici ... J'ai joué là-bas que ... Donc, j'étais pas vraiment connu là-bas, j'étais connu à la télé ... j'ai passé à la télé, tout simplement ... Eh mais, c'est ça, bon, je me suis concentré surtout, quoi, la musique, ma musique, ce que je fais, et tout ça, ces trucs nouveaux, très nouveaux, et ... et les Malgaches,

c'est-à-dire que … ils s'attachent beaucoup à la musique vraiment nostalgique, voilà, c'est ça … Ma musique, on peut la danser, mais en même temps, les gens, ils se cherchent un peu … alors, ils veulent … ils veulent écouter l'accordéon … ils chantent … il faut du temps … hein, il faut que … c'est pour ça que moi, j'ai dit tout à l'heure que maintenant, je veux aller vers la communauté malgache et je vais jouer et … même dans les soirées malgaches, pour essayer de …

Ulrike: A-ha, a-ha …

Régis: C'est tout simplement jouer pour eux, quoi. (Meinhof's and Rasolofondraosolo's interview, December 2005, Paris)

23 Rachel: Moi, entre autres, je suis venue à Paris pour faire du, du jazz, enfin, je fais partie d'un groupe de jazz – Jazzpel – et euh, voilà, depuis trois ans, même, trois, trois-quatre ans, trois ans … Moi je suis arrivée à Paris y'a deux ans. Deux ans. J'ai suivi ce groupe, là, de, de jazz et puis on a tourné un peu partout … ici, à Paris. Et euh… Monsieur Olivier-Roman Garcia est apparu. (Meinhof's and Gibert's interview, June 2007, Paris)

24 Il se trouve que j'ai pas mal bossé dans l'Océan indien, notamment à Madagascar, et à la Réunion. Donc j'ai rencontré Leila Negro, qui est une chanteuse de la Réunion. Qui organise des tournées dans l'Océan indien. Et puis un jour … on m'a proposé de partir en tournée, d'accompagner une chanteuse malgache qui s'appelle Tiana, qui est très connue là-bas … Disons moi j'ai dit oui sans vraiment, sans vraiment connaître la musique malgache et euh, quand j'ai reçu le CD, euh … là j'ai eu … la douche froide! Oui, parce qu'y a toute une culture … Y'a une culture de guitare qui est très, très forte. Moi je suis espagnol, et la culture guitare en Espagne, je sais ce que c'est, quoi! Et là je connaissais pas ce pays, ou y'avait une culture aussi forte, finalement. Y'a un jeu … très type, des harmonies, un accordage particulier, tout ça. Donc j'ai dit oui, mais quand j'ai eu le CD, ouais, ouais, j'ai dû bosser – je sais pas – deux-trois mois pour arriver à … [rire]. J'ai appelé tous les copains malgaches que je connaissais pour euh … Voilà, et bon. Et depuis, je me suis passionné pour, pour le pays et tout ça, et puis je suis parti en tournée. Voilà. Ah ouais, et puis donc je suis arrivé à Paris, et j'ai appelé Rachel de suite pour savoir si elle voulait qu'on travaille ensemble, et donc, euh … de là est né cet album. (Meinhof's and Gibert's interview, June 2007, Paris)

25 Et après je suis partie ici. Parce que j'avais des connexions, j'avais des amis qui étaient ici, qui étaient dans la musique, et qui m'ont dit ouais non mais il faut que tu viennes ici, c'est génial … et c'est comme ça que de fil en aiguille j'ai rencontré d'autres musiciens et puis Paris c'est quand même un carrefour où on rencontre beaucoup de musiciens, de toutes les nationalités quand même, et du coup, j'ai rencontré des Brésiliens, j'ai fait de la percussion brésilienne, après j'ai rencontré des Indiens, j'ai fait de la musique aussi indienne, et tout s'est un peu passé comme ça quoi, en France. (Meinhof's and Rasolofondraosolo's interview, April 2009, Paris)

26 C'est ça, c'est cette expérimentation qui m'intéresse. En fait c'est de, de toujours aller à la racine des choses et puis après, après bon ben je pense que voilà,

maintenant je vis, je vis dans un monde, je dirais, c'est urbain. Et même si je m'inspire du terroir, il se trouve que je vis aussi dans un monde urbain, donc c'est de tirer le meilleur de tout ça pour faire quelque chose de personnel en fait. Je, je prétends pas du tout représenter la musique malgache ou le truc malgache par contre oui, je dirais, je représente un coté contemporain de la musique malgache, contemporain, dans le sens aujourd'hui, dans le monde d'aujourd'hui. Même si de toute façon les racines viennent de Madagascar. (Meinhof's and Rasolofondraosolo's interview, April 2009)

Chapter 4

1 Ulrike: Topaka, ça veut dire quoi?
Edgar: Topaka? Topa, c'est les ... c'est le ... le murmure de l'eau.
Ulrike: Aaaah! Voilà ...
Edgar: Topa, topa ... Et ka c'est le bruit de la percussion indienne ... Le plat de la main sur la percussion, c'est le ka ... Et donc, comme les Malgaches ils sont un peu ... indo-européens ... j'ai mélangé Topa-ka. (Meinhof's interview, November 2007, during the TNMundi concert in Tana)

2 J'étais à Saint-Étienne, donc je vivais à Saint-Étienne, et ... je me suis présenté pour représenter la région Rhône-Alpes ... pour le Printemps de Bourges. Le Printemps, le grand festival. Et j'ai fini premier. Donc j'ai représenté ma région – pour moi c'était déjà un grand honneur en tant que être Malgache, de représenter ma région – au Printemps de Bourges. Voilà ... Après Bourges, donc j'ai pu enregistrer un titre. Apres j'ai fait quelques concours, j'ai fini à l'Olympia. J'ai ... gagné aussi. Là c'était un concours national, et j'ai gagné. Et puis après, j'ai fait encore d'autres ... On cherche toujours son chemin! Parce qu'on est loin! Donc on ... on garde toujours la mémoire. La culture aussi, c'est ce qui nous reste quand on a tout oublié! (Meinhof's interview, November 2007, during the TNMundi concert in Tana)

3 Edgar: Je vais à Paris en finale, à l'Olympia. Et j'ai gagné. J'ai gagné le prix, et j'ai enregistré un 45 tours. Mais avec une chanson qui s'appelle 'Sovay'. Est-ce que ça va pas ... vay c'est quoi déjà?
Dama: Vay ... c'est ... comment c'est ... tu vois c'est ... tu grattes et ça se gonfle et ça s'infecte, et il faut vraiment l'enlever.
Edgar: Et j'ai écrit une chanson qui s'intitule 'Sovay'. Donc c'est qui s'infecte tu vois ... Et cette chanson elle gagne ... mais c'est déjà un mélange encore, tu dis ... mais comment ils font ... comment les gens ils comprennent une chanson où il y a deux langues qui se chevauchent, et pas forcément de la compréhension, quoi. C'est-à-dire que ... C'est simplement ... soit ils adhèrent, soit ils adhèrent pas. Mais j'ai concouru, avec des gens qui venaient partout de France, et puis il y avait des chansons bien françaises [rires].
Dama: C'est la différence, la différence.
Edgar: Et moi j'arrive ... la-la-la-la avec des ... tu sais des trucs ... et là je gagne ... et je sors ce 45 tours ... mais toujours pas ... mais déjà

une assise ... et une assise professionnelle c'est-à-dire quelque chose qui s'installe ... donc en fait mon cursus, c'est que les gens que j'ai rencontrés qui m'ont aidé à le faire. Après, donc, que cette école m'a produit, ils me disent, et ben pendant trois ans on va s'occuper de toi. Donc là ils me donnent l'argent ... je deviens professionnel pendant trois ans ... grâce à l'école ... grâce à l'école ... Et ces trois ans, ça passe vite les trois ans parce que, ça passe vite, après ... je fais une émission avec un chanteur ... il y a un grand concours qui est organisé ... dans toute l'Europe, tout l'espace francophone. Ça se passe à Périgueux ... Et ... ma femme elle voit elle dit oh là ... va ... je vais la première fois, je ... je gagne ... je présente 'Je me suis fait tout petit' de Georges Brassens et je gagne. Donc là je pars ... je fais les éliminatoires ... je vais en vacances avec les enfants ... et les enfants ils étaient tous là ... ils regardaient papa chanter ... [rires] après on allait faire les vacances, on revenait, je faisais la finale, je gagnais les sous, hop. (Meinhof's and Rasolofondraosolo's interview, April 2009, at Edgar's home in Roanne)

4 Il me dit je cherche moi un projet. Et je dis: Madagascar. Il dit: Va. Donc voilà ça a donné naissance à cet album. Donc je suis parti à Madagascar, j'ai fait des va-et-viens et puis donc voilà. Donc cet album qui j'espère va sortir un peu plus grand ... un peu plus grandi aussi ... dans les échanges. Et puis j'évolue aussi dans mes rapports ... avec les autres, les autres hommes les ... les gens de ma communauté ... ça reste pas restrictif hein, ma communauté c'est très large, hein. Mais en même temps ma communauté ... avec les Malgaches je rencontre ... je trouve que je rencontre beaucoup plus de Malgaches qu'avant ... beaucoup plus ... c'est un équilibre, surtout que ça rejoint bien mes chansons. Je trouve que c'est bien, maintenant, je peux dire tiens, en français, en malgache ... voilà. Donc, et maintenant, donc, j'attends cette sortie ... j'ai encore un peu ... même dans la difficulté actuelle économique du monde, ben ... je remercie qu'on me permette encore de chanter et de partager avec l'autre. Et je sais que c'est très fragile, que la vie est fragile, la carrière est fragile aussi ... Tu vois, c'est fragile ... Mais bon, ben tout ce que je prends, ben je remercie ... que je le vis au moins pleinement. Voilà. (Meinhof's and Rasolofondraosolo's interview, April 2009, at Edgar's home in Roanne)

5 Elsa: La première fois, en fait qu'ils sont partis, ils ont été invités par la CCF d'Alger, pour la réouverture en fait des centres culturels en Algérie et donc quand ils sont partis, ils ont rencontré entre autres, Nassim dont on parlait tout à l'heure et donc ils ont un peu jammé, ils ont capté qu'il y a vraiment des choses à faire et du coup, l'idée c'est il faut qu'on retourne là-bas pour prendre le temps de vraiment travailler avec les musiciens de là-bas mais je pense que c'est un peu une prise de conscience aussi progressive de, à un moment donné parce que c'était déjà là enfin je veux dire, je sais pas, les mélodies mais après de se dire, vraiment un moment donné oui ben c'est ça ça qu'on veut faire comme projet, ça a pris quand même du temps ... et oui effectivement le premier voyage en Algérie, c'est un peu un moment de prise de conscience.

Karine: Ouais carrément.

Elsa: Que c'est ça qu'on veut faire pour de bon quoi.

Karine: Parce qu'en fait il y a deux trucs, nous, quand on est allé en Algérie, nous, on a pris conscience que nous ... c'était vachement superficiel d'arriver dans un pays, de faire un concert et de partir quoi, on avait envie de connaître les groupes qu'il y avait, ça d'une part et d'autre part, et pour moi c'était 'back to the roots' quoi. J'ai compris que j'étais algérienne alors qu'avant j'en avais pas du tout conscience [...] en fait ça s'est fait dans notre chemin à tous de vie, en fait, ce projet diaspora. (Kiwan's interview with Elsa and Karine, Watcha Clan, June 2007, Marseille)

6 Le diwane en fait, il avait en fait beaucoup plus un rôle social à la base, mais surtout thérapeutique au départ, vraiment, quand je me rappelle, quand j'étais petit, c'est essentiellement social, parce que les gens se rencontrent et se cooptent et puis, mais surtout thérapeutique mais en fait ça s'est étendu quand il s'est développé notamment ces dernières années par le fait qu'il y a des groupes qui l'ont fait connaître – il est devenu quelque chose de culturel on va dire ... mais à Béchar il y a d'autres trucs et c'est ça ... il faut que tu rentres là-dedans ... c'est une marmite parce que c'est une zone frontalière à tout point de vue ... Des frontières naturelles ... le Maroc est tout près ... donc on est un peu marocain ... c'est une terre d'immigration [...] donc il y a aussi ces populations qui viennent de partout mais surtout t'as la population locale depuis très longtemps qu'on appelle les l'Eksouria, l'Eksouria – c'est des arabo-berbères qui pratiquent quatre ou cinq styles très très différents ... alors t'as le Maroc, l'Eksouria – la base mais surtout t'as l'influence du Nord, des hauts plateaux sont pas très loin. Le nord chez nous c'est pas Oran, c'est pas Alger, c'est immédiatement les montages ça s'appelle les Atlas, et il y a des sons de ces Atlas qui sont très très puissants qui ont aussi soufflé sur Béchar. C'est pour ça ces turbulences-là au sens de marmite mais le plus important, la texture, le rythme et le son il vient d'Adrar et Timimoun via le Mali en fait l'Eksouria du sud ont beaucoup beaucoup inspiré ... et t'as une tradition gnawa, diwane mais aussi il y a une tradition Issawa qui est très très fort dans une oasis à coté ... d'ailleurs Ferda ils sont, mettant un peu d'inspiration un peu Issawa ... nous on est plutôt gnawa ... parce que j'ai vécu avec Taieb ... dans un quartier où il y a le gnawa, le mur qui me sépare du diwane c'est mon voisin donc tout le temps, on a entendu le diwane. Le diwane, le diwane ... sans y être, tu y es ... il te passe par la peau quoi ... Aïcha tu vois, elle symbolise Timimoun-Adrar, le Mali ... elle est de Timimoun-Adrar. (Kiwan's interview with Abdelati Laoufi, June 2007, Paris)

7 Ce qui est bien c'est que les cinq, chacun est ... les personnalités musicales chacun ... déjà c'est très intéressant. Les racines des cinq aussi c'est vrai que ... c'est très ... différent. Même les manières de composer la musique, de chanter, de ... et c'est ça qui est intéressant quoi. Pour moi au niveau musical là, musicalement, c'est très très intéressant ... Pour qu'on puisse arriver à jouer ensemble là, les cinq personnalités musicales, même si on est tous Malgaches, il faut souligner que c'est vraiment ... bien vu la composition quoi, que c'est vraiment bien vu par Dama quoi. Et c'est pour cela que je n'hésite pas une seconde quand il m'a téléphoné pour annoncer le projet. Et ... je pense que ça va apporter beaucoup de fruits hein, parce que là on forme un seul arbre maintenant, et là on va avoir beaucoup

de branches et beaucoup de fruits. Il faut que ... c'est vrai que même si c'est pas encore vraiment mûr, les fruits, moi je pense que d'ici quelque temps, on va avoir beaucoup plus de jus! Le jus de fruit, d'orange et tout ça c'est sûr!! (Meinhof's and Rasolofondraosolo's interview, May 2006 after the Traumzeit Festival in Duisburg)

8 Justin: En plus ce qui est vraiment intéressant, vraiment vraiment, tous les timbres vocals des cinq c'est vraiment –
Dama: C'est différent.
Justin: C'est différent. Et ça c'est ... whaou ...!
Ulrike: Comment tu ... tu me dis un peu comment tu le vois? Parce que c'est très différent, tu peux caractériser un peu chacun?
Justin: Ah oui! Par exemple, on trouve chez notre chef Dama, là, c'est ... euh ... une voix très présent, une voix un peu de ... séducteur ... Non non il faut le dire ... je dirais même une voix sexy aussi! Il faut dire la vérité hein. Et une voix qui ... qui porte à l'espoir aussi, à la joie de vivre quoi, à tout ça. Et quand on voit la voix de ... Erick, c'est vrai que c'est, quelque fois on le sent comme une voix ... au milieu de forêt tropicale! Au milieu des cannes à sucre, hein? Y a ... la nostalgie aussi. Et quant au voix de Fenoamby par exemple, Marius, c'est ... une voix qui tue quoi, avec son aiguille, avec sa vibration ... qui vibre le public ... quand on voit Régis là, bourré de spirituel, y a quelque chose qui se forme, qui se dégage ... Quand on voit ma voix je suis un petit peu comme le ... la voiture qui est en train de s'échauffer.
Dama: C'est Erick là! C'est la définition de Erick là!
Justin: Non non c'est ... c'est assez vraiment ... Euh ... étonnant quoi. C'est pourquoi d'ailleurs que c'est très important dans notre ... groupe là, All Stars, c'est que c'est pas ... on va essayer de trouver deux ou trois morceaux, même si on compose ensemble, a cappella, pour montrer cette richesse vocale et harmonique que nous avons quoi, c'est ... il faut exploiter quoi, voilà. (Meinhof's and Rasolofondraosolo's interview, May 2006 after the Traumzeit Festival in Duisburg)

9 Dama: Je suis déjà interpellé ... Tous les cinq on veut aussi donner notre image de Madagascar. En faisant des tournées partout. De plus en plus conscients de ça. Finalement, on s'est pas rencontrés, comme ça, on a notre objectif, c'est donner image bien de Madagascar ... Parce que la route c'est là-bas bien donner une autre image de Madagascar. Une image multiple, et nous on va dans ce sens-là. Chacun de notre côté ... Donc c'est ça, dans cinq ans on aimerait bien que tous les artistes malgaches qui pensent comme ça, vont être sur le même chemin. Pour ... oui, parce que là c'est déjà un grand pas que nous avons pu mettre en place les cinq. Moi je suis à Madagascar, Erick il est à Bordeaux, Justin Vali à Lille, Régis est partout dans le monde! Mais on a fait, parce que on a trouvé que le Madagascar est très important. Donc on a réduit les distances, on a réduit les distances, pour cet objectif. Et là, ça c'est bien. Ça c'est bien ça. Parce que c'est pas facile de faire un groupe quand même, quand même. On a assez de problèmes déjà pour gérer chaque, notre propre, notre propre groupe. Mais encore chercher des problèmes pour être ensemble. Donc on a su dépasser ça grâce a une, une noble

cause, si on peut dire comme ça. Noble cause, oui. (Meinhof and Rasolofondraosolo in conversation with Seheno in Paris, April 2009)

10 Haja: Mais moi, j'ai aimé créer, depuis tout petit. À la cuisine, avec les instruments, et tout. En fait, justement par rapport à la musique, j'ai commencé, on va dire, la musique à l'âge de sept ans. Donc, à part aller chanter avec tout ce qui est traditionnel, j'ai commencé à l'âge de sept ans. J'ai vu mon oncle jouer de la guitare. J'ai vraiment aimé, mais on n'avait pas de guitare à la maison, c'était pas possible, c'était trop cher. Y'avait même pas ... parce que, si tu te souviens, c'était le temps très dur ...

Dama: Pffff ... oui!

Haja: Hein? Années 80, fin 70 début 80, y'avait rien dans les étalages de magasins, y'avait rien! On a fait la queue pour acheter des savons, on devait se réveiller à 4h du matin.

Dama: Pour le riz.

Haja: Pour le riz ... Non, pour l'huile, pour le savon, tout! Et on a joué beau-coup, c'est là qu'on a chanté beaucoup, parce que y'avait rien à faire. De 4 heures jusqu'à 8 heures le magasin était ouvert, on a mis des ...

Dama: Des pierres!

Haja: ... Des pierres pour remplacer les personnes, quoi. Voilà!

Dama: Oui, oui. Pour la queue.

Haja: Pour la queue. Et nous, en même temps, on a joué, on a chanté, on a fait n'importe quoi. Et c'est là qu'on a créé les petites guitares, déjà ... pour passer le temps ... Mais en même temps, on rêve toujours d'une vraie guitare. Donc on jouait comme ça, avec les mains [rires], les six cordes, là. (Meinhof's and Rasolofondraosolo's interview, September 2007, Vienna)

11 Mon petit frère, il aimait comme moi aussi la guitare. Et le grand frère il était tout le temps bon à l'école, donc c'était pas pour lui! [rires] Il était tout le temps premier à l'école, donc c'était surtout pour nous. Donc on s'est dit, avec mon petit frère: 'Ah, OK, on va faire quelque chose, parce qu'apparemment, on pourra avoir une guitare.' Donc, bien sûr, ça a marché, et le jour de Noël, la guitare était là ... Donc là, je me souviens, on a touché les cordes comme ça, une à une. On n'a même pas osé prendre la guitare à corps. On a touché les cordes et on a écouté le son. Touché les cordes ... Donc mon petit frère et moi on a appris la guitare avec ensemble. Seulement comme ça, au pied dans notre escalier, on a joué tout le temps ... Donc on a joué tout le temps dans les escaliers là. C'est là, parce que ça sonne bien. C'est comme dans les douches. (Meinhof's and Rasolofondraosolo's interview, September 2007, Vienna)

12 Et il y en avait qui me voyaient en train de former un groupe, mais sans guitare [rires]. Voilà, on a chanté a cappella, on a fait avec les percussions. J'ai dit: 'Moi, je joue des instruments, mais j'ai pas d'instrument ici.' Donc, il y avait une femme qui m'a donné une guitare. Elle a dit: 'OK, jusqu'au moment où tu en as une à toi-même, ici, je vais te donner ça. Ou si tu veux, tu peux même garder.' Donc j'ai eu cette guitare. Et j'ai voyagé avec cette guitare ... Bien sûr, j'ai amené un kabosy de Madagascar. Ça, c'était toujours avec moi. Et j'ai voyagé donc, avec sac à dos,

le train, dans plusieurs pays en Europe. Et c'était vraiment rigolo, parce que quand j'avais la guitare sur le dos en voyageant, il y a beaucoup de sourires que les gens te donnent sans faire quoi que ce soit. Donc moi j'ai vu que la musique c'est comme une sorte de porte, une sorte d'introduction dans une communication avec un inconnu. Et j'ai entendu beaucoup d'histoires avec les immigrés, avec les Africains. Je me suis dit: 'Ce que je vis en ce moment, c'est un peu différent.' Mais j'ai pas trop compris que c'était en fait à cause de la guitare que j'ai vu les choses différemment. Parce que là, même les flics quand ils te voient avec la guitare, ils te contrôlent, parce qu'ils soupçonnent toujours que vous avez des drogues – ce gars, il vient de l'Afrique, musicien, hum … – Mais, quand les contrôles sont finis, ils commencent toujours à s'intéresser plus. Ils demandent quelle sorte de musique tu fais, elle vient de quel pays, ça va bien? Donc cette suite-là j'ai vu que, pour les copains qui n'étaient pas musiciens, c'était pas là. C'était tout de suite fini. Donc la discussion, c'était toujours plus global et plus intéressante. Donc avec les gens, par exemple, j'étais dans des trains avec des familles, y'a des gens qui demandent: 'Où est-ce que tu vas, qu'est-ce que tu vas faire là-bas?' Et tout ça, ça m'a poussé à faire les deux choses que j'aime vraiment le plus, c'est la musique et voyager [rires]. Donc je me suis dit: 'Ah, en fait c'est possible peut-être de combiner les deux!' Et comme j'ai étudié un peu comment diriger des choses, je me suis dit: 'Peut-être je peux combiner les trois?' Voilà, donc c'est ça qui m'a amené … Au début, c'était vraiment l'amour de la musique, l'amour pour la musique plutôt, l'amour pour le voyage, la découverte des autres, la découverte d'un autre pays. Et en même temps, pouvoir faire ça par soi-même, en quelque sorte, donc gérer sa vie. (Meinhof's and Rasolofondraosolo's interview, September 2007, Vienna)

13 Quand je les rencontre après, ils me racontent: 'Ah! On a vraiment … je me suis rappelé de ce que tu nous as dit par rapport au taxi-brousse …' Parce que moi, ce que j'ai tout le temps évité de faire, c'est de donner une fausse image de Madagascar. Je leur dit tout le temps que c'est un des pays pauvres, un des pays les plus pauvres du monde, économiquement. Voilà, je précise toujours économiquement. Mais si vous voulez voir d'autres choses enrichissantes, essayez de voyager là-bas. Parce que si vous quittez l'Autriche ou la France, vous allez en Grèce, quelque part, c'est encore la même chose, hein? Si vous allez à Madagascar, c'est un autre monde. Et là, il faut pas prendre l'avion, il faut prendre le taxi-brousse, vous allez voir qu'est-ce qui se passe. Et, par exemple, pendant les ateliers, j'ai créé des danses où les enfants sont avec moi dans une voiture, et on roule sur des routes mauvaises [rires]. Ah, les enfants … ils connaissent la réalité, mais en même temps ils s'amusent. En général, c'est ce qu'il y a de mieux pour les enfants. Donc je leur dis la réalité de mon pays, et en même temps, ils apprennent quelque chose et ils s'amusent. Donc, cette diversification, ça m'a donné encore plus de chances de voyager. Voilà. Et en fait, j'ai même … comme j'aime faire la cuisine, je fais ça aussi. Par exemple, une soirée pour écouter, goûter, regarder, toucher des instruments et sentir Madagascar. Voilà, donc les cinq sens. Et c'est une expérience très intense, parce qu'ils vont jamais oublier toute leur vie, parce que c'est très rare d'aller dans un concert, ou un dîner-concert, et on a tout ça en même temps. Donc j'ai des concepts comme ça. Je contacte des entreprises, et je leur propose, OK, si vous voulez quelque chose de spécial, pas seulement les reprises de Beatles et tout ça, voilà, c'est une aventure. Mais vous allez pas voyager, vous allez être

sur place. C'est une aventure. Donc cette diversification, j'aime beaucoup, parce que je peux utiliser beaucoup de mes talents, je peux créer beaucoup, et ça me tient toujours euh ... ça me donne toujours ce lien très fort avec mon pays. (Meinhof's and Rasolofondraosolo's interview, September 2007, Vienna)

14 Je peux pas dire que je suis 100 pourcent campagne. En même temps, je sais que quand je suis dans la campagne, je me sens moi-même. Je peux pas dire non plus que je suis 100 pourcent ville, parce qu'y a des moments ou j'aime vraiment la campagne. Donc, ce mélange-là, je monte sur scène avec: je mets, par exemple, des peintures sur le corps, je me mets torse nu ... La moitié de ma vie, j'étais torse nu: à la maison, c'était torse nu, à la campagne, c'était impossible de mettre quoi que ce soit. Donc j'amène tout le temps ces roots-là, ces racines-là, partout ou je vais. Finalement, au fur et à mesure des voyages, j'ai trouvé que, en fait, je fais la musique que je fais maintenant parce que ça me donne toujours un pied à Madagascar, la possibilité d'avoir un pied à Madagascar et un autre pied à l'étranger. Donc je partage des valeurs malgaches à l'étranger. En même temps, peut-être c'est pas encore assez, en même temps, quand je rentre au pays, en parlant avec mes cousins, oncles, amis, il y a aussi quelque chose que j'amène d'ici. Je leur dis ce qu'il y a ici, qu'est-ce qui se passe. (Meinhof's and Rasolofondraosolo's interview, September 2007, Vienna)

15 Donc ce type-là, Yann Crespel, quittait la Tunisie, je pense le 2 ou le 3 ou le 1er septembre il repartait vers la France ou vers le Maroc, je ne sais pas, et il se trouve que j'étais à Tunis ce jour-là en train de refaire ma carte d'identité pour pouvoir me barrer et rentrer à Paris et j'ai rencontré ce type-là via Khais Ben Mabrouk qui m'a appelé donc j'ai eu 40 minutes pour discuter avec ce Yann Crespel et en gros ce qu'on a fait, c'est qu'on a mis en commun nos réseaux pour se dire 'qu'est-ce qu'on peut faire avec ça?' et en gros à l'issu de ces 40 minutes, deux semaines après j'ai reçu un mail de Yann Crespel qui m'a dit 'très bien, on va partir sur quelque chose', sachant que lui est détaché de la ville de Romans, qui est à 40 minutes de Lyon, et moi j'avais mes entrées qu'il considérait comme le le label associatif qui pouvait être le gros support en France, à savoir Jarring Effects à Lyon, il s'est dit, 'essayons de faire quelque chose' et on a sorti le projet Pitchworks qui est un projet pour le moment en trois étapes [...] donc Pitchworks c'est un projet de résidence créative en trois étapes pour le moment. La première étape s'est passée à Aubenas du 4–10 février en Ardèche dans les cadre de la semaine de la Tunisie ... donc étaient présents toute la semaine Mounir Trudi et son flutiste qui s'appelle Houcine ... Peut-être un des meilleurs musiciens tunisiens que j'ai jamais vu ... une rencontre incroyable avec ces musiciens-là [...] l'idée au départ c'était de faire une résidence pan-arabe [...] ce projet, il y aura encore une autre étape dans la ville de Romans, du 4–10 mai, dans le cadre de la BIS, la biennale de l'international et de la solidarité [...] Et ensuite le dernier épisode ça sera à El-Jem pour le festival, le 21 août, et donc après on est en train de discuter de quels sont les outputs, est-ce qu'on réalise un disque ... il y a déjà des partenaires ... ce qui est sûr ce qui est sorti déjà, c'est le contact ... il y a d'autres personnes qui vont rejoindre cette résidence. (Kiwan's and Gibert's interview with Skander Besbes, February 2008, Paris)

16 C'est vrai qu'à Lyon en fait, ça m'a donné une position de force ... parce que le fait de pas y vivre mais en même temps d'être introduit sur les meilleures

plateformes fait que, que ben j'ai pas l'implication du quotidien [...] pour eux je suis à l'extérieur, je reviens [...] les gens prennent le temps, puisque je suis là qu'une semaine. (Kiwan's and Gibert's interview with Skander Besbes, February 2008, Paris)

17 Solidifier le pont Lyon–La Marsa–Tunis. (Kiwan's and Gibert's interview with Skander Besbes, February 2008, Paris)

18 J'ai cette idée utopiste de communauté, de gens qui font des choses ensemble, qui mettent en commun et du know-how et du matériel. (Kiwan's and Gibert's interview with Skander Besbes, February 2008, Paris)

19 À Paris, la plupart des gens que je vois sont des amis d'enfance [...] on fait tous le ping-pong, l'été on y est tous [in Tunisia] ... Il y a pas vraiment besoin de choisir quand on est à cheval entre la France et la Tunisie ... le rêve de tous les Franco-Tunisiens, moi, je suis franco-tunisien donc j'ai un pied, je suis à cheval, on me prend souvent comme artiste tunisien, on oublie que ma mère est française et j'ai quand même grandi en parlant français à la maison et tout ça mais il y a jamais eu une volonté de choisir entre les deux quoi ... on est bien avec un pied sur chaque rive de la Méditerranée surtout dans deux pays qui sont si proches. (Kiwan's and Gibert's interview with Skander Besbes, February 2008, Paris)

20 Donc Philippe m'a présenté du monde à Paris, et à Avignon, j'ai travaillé sur des morceaux qu'on m'a proposé, qu'il a choisi ... j'ai écrit quelques paroles, parce qu'il y avait certains morceaux qui n'étaient que de la musique ... c'était un peu ma première expérience à l'écrit quoi, euh ... ça a duré deux ans, pendant ce temps-là, bon chaque fois que je revenais ici, bon j'avais commencé à faire une petite place ... j'existais dans la presse, des magazines ... chaque fois qu'il y avait une soirée ou un téléthon ou quelque chose à la télévision, j'étais invitée [...] j'ai beaucoup de chance parce que j'ai pas eu moi-même à aller frapper aux portes, s'il vous-plaît 'donnez-moi des chansons', machin donc franchement on m'a ouvert toutes les portes et tout ... mais je me suis rendue compte que tout ce qu'on me proposait à chanter, ne me correspondait pas forcément. (Kiwan's and Gibert's interview with Oum, April 2008, Casablanca)

21 Oum: Et j'avais déjà une place [in France] ... et puis un jour, alors que je reviens de France, cette une année spéciale ... il se passait tellement de trucs ... bon, il y a les attentas du 16 mai ...

Marie: 2003 alors?

Oum: Voilà, il y a eu la coupe d'Afrique où le Maroc est allé je pense en final ... ou en demi-finales ... quoi ... en bref, il y avait pleins d'émotions en marocanité si tu veux ... et voilà, j'ai été un peu sensible ... et en même temps, j'ai rencontré euh ... voilà, j'ai été sensible, et je me suis dit euh ... ça serait très bien que je fasse des trucs ici maintenant ... mais en même temps ... c'est venu parce que je savais que j'avais pas tout ce que j'ai envie en France. (Kiwan's and Gibert's interview with Oum, April 2008, Casablanca)

22 Voilà qu'on revenait vers les trucs du 16 mai, effectivement, moi j'avais envie en tant que fille de monter sur scène et de chanter ... et danser en disant Hamdoullah et qu'il y a pas de mal, quoi, surtout ... dans ma période ou j'ai mis du temps à accepter que je pouvais être vraiment bien d'ici, et chanter des choses d'ici ... mais que j'ai emprunté à là-bas, tu vois. C'est-à-dire que j'ai jamais compris pourquoi dans le gospel, par exemple ... on chantait l'amour de Dieu, on chantait ... on se mettait en transe et tout ça, et on dansait et tout, alors que moi je veux dire ouais je suis plutôt tendance musulmane, quoi, de culture et tout [...] j'ai une foi énorme, et ça j'avais envie aussi de le dire, comme je m'habille avec mon look ... et en chantant peut-être en anglais, et en dansant ... mais de dire Hamdoullah surtout après ces choses-là, le 16 mai etc., ça a rajouté aussi au fait que ... à l'époque il y avait pas encore de filles, quoi. Bon encore aujourd'hui, mais ... aujourd'hui ça va un petit peu mieux ... donc si tu veux, parce que pour moi on a quand-même une mission ... le truc c'est pas que d'aller s'amuser sur scène et gagner un petit peu d'argent et tout ... le fait c'est qu'il faut qu'on serve à quelque chose, quoi, pas forcément que les gens ils s'identifient à nous, mais qu'on ait une façon de penser, tout ça quoi, qu'on apporte quelque chose ... et je me suis sentie ... je me sens toujours ce rôle-là comme ça quoi. Je suis bien d'ici ... j'ai mes convictions ... j'aime l'Islam, et d'ailleurs pour ici et pour ailleurs, j'ai envie de chanter cet Islam, et de le chanter vraiment librement. (Kiwan's and Gibert's interview with Oum, April 2008, Casablanca)

23. Khansa: J'étais très remplie ... il fallait que je me vide, j'étais très remplie, il fallait que je me vide et puis après on cessait pas de me dire 'Khansa, Khansa, Khansa', on me réclamait, des gens dans la rue, des trucs comme sur les blogs ou des trucs ou conneries comme ça ... et puis quand je faisais des allers-retours tout le temps ... je voyais l'évolution de loin ... je voyais comment ça se passait ... puis après j'ai eu la proposition de cette boîte Click, et je me suis dit why not, allez, pourquoi pas? Et puis au fond, j'avais envie aussi. J'avais envie d'être ... cette fois-ci j'ai passé trois ans à être derrière la camera, j'avais envie d'être devant la camera un peu.

Nadia: Tu dis que tu observais l'évolution de loin ... dans quel sens? Au niveau média ... je sais pas ... infrastructure?

Khansa: Tout. La mentalité des gens qui sont à la tête du Maroc, et les medias, ce boom avec la libération du paysage audiovisuel, surtout les radios ...

Nadia: Qui date de 200–?

Khansa: 2005. 200–6. 2006.

Nadia: Là où il y a la libéralisation des ondes?

Khansa: Oui. Puis après tous les festivals, toutes les manifestations culturelles qui ont commencé à naître ... festival de Dakhla, festival de ça, festival de ci. (Kiwan's interview with Khansa Batma, April 2008, Casablanca)

24 Nadia: Mais malgré tout ça, quand même si tu es revenue, si tu continues, si tu enregistres, ça veut dire que toi tu vois, tu restes optimiste par rapport à ce qui se passe ici?

Khansa: Bien-sûr, parce que je reste optimiste, parce que c'est mon pays, merde. Non, pas ça, je vais pas tenir le discours 'c'est mon pays', bla

bla bla nationaliste à fond et tout, chose que je suis, mais patriotique, si je le suis, c'est normal, mais en même temps ... c'est ... j'ai compris quelque chose que quel que soit le succès qu'on peut avoir ailleurs, celui de là où tu viens n'a pas de prix. Il n'a pas de prix. Et puis après il y a tout à faire au Maroc. Il y a tout un public à mener derrière ... tu vois, à venir comme ça. Il y a tout à faire. C'est dur. C'est difficile. Ça demande une grande volonté. Beaucoup de patience ... des nerfs solides, se casser la gueule, être solide et se relever ... plein de choses comme ça, parce qu'il y a tout à faire et à apprendre ... et à réapprendre. Il y a tout à faire. Il y a un système ... tout un système culturel qu'il faut changer. Qu'il faut réadapter ... il faut réécrire. On est en train d'écrire l'histoire du Maroc, culturelle. Notre jeunesse, nous notre génération, nous sommes en train d'écrire l'histoire de la culture musicale marocaine. Je parle de la musique marocaine. Et on est en train de le faire. Mais cette fois-ci, cette fois-ci, la tâche, elle est dure. (Kiwan's interview with Khansa Batma, April 2008, Casablanca)

25 J'ai quitté Paris en '93, on riait plus quoi ... on avait été à place de la Bastille en '81 avec Mitterrand, et en '93 ça riait plus du tout à Paris donc ... en même temps il y avait le son qui s'ouvrait ici [...] et ça s'ouvrait au niveau de la pub au Maroc, ça s'ouvrait un petit peu et tout, et donc j'ai dit bon ben je vais rentrer dans mon bled ... et je suis revenu au Maroc. (Kiwan's and Gibert's interview with Ali Faraoui, April 2008, Casablanca)

26 On a l'impression ouais que Darga c'est le super groupe, machin etc., mais on est super fragile, quand même. On essaie bien sûr de structurer cà au maximum, mais c'est super dur quand on sait que pendant six mois on avait zéro dirhams, et que là on est totalement déficitaire, quoi. Donc oui bien-sûr c'est bien beau, bien-sûr ouais il y a toutes ces radios, machins etc., mais pour moi c'est rien de sérieux ... on n'a rien vraiment bâti quoi ... même le Boulevard qui existe pendant dix ans et sur lequel tout le monde compte, ben du jour au lendemain il peut ne plus exister, quoi. Et on sait même pas est-ce que il y aura les moyens ... qu'est-ce qu'il va faire etc. ... alors donc là c'est clair que là pour Darga, déjà ça fait depuis deux ans qu'on le sait ... ce qui a sauvé Darga, c'est qu'on a pu commencer à jouer à l'étranger, et qu'il y a eu cette tourneuse espagnole qui a tout de suite fait confiance au groupe, qui a vu que ça pouvait marcher, et qui a beaucoup investi ... mais il y aurait pas eu cette tourneuse espagnole, aujourd'hui on n'aurait rien du tout. (Kiwan's and Gibert's interview with Amel Abou el aaazm, April 2008, Rabat)

Chapter 5

1 Le Goethe-Institut allemand, ou Cercle germano-malgache depuis 1975, plus connu sous l'appellation de CGM, a la réputation d'être le plus convivial des lieux culturels à Antananarivo. Dès sa création en 1960, il a été un lieu d'échanges artistiques, de découverte musicale et d'études linguistiques. Aujourd'hui, le Cercle

propose différentes activités de formation dont la langue allemande naturellement, le dessin et la musique. Sa petite salle de concert est le lieu de rendez-vous de mélomanes notamment lors du festival Madajazzcar. Le CGM favorise aussi la musique du terroir. De grands noms de la musique malgache doivent beaucoup à ce centre culturel. L'on peut citer Ricky, Rossy, Dama, Silo, Rakoto Frah, Feo Gasy, Solomiral ... Le CGM offre aussi une plate-forme d'expression aux poètes malgaches réunis dans le cadre du 'Faribolana Sandratra'. À part ses activités didactiques et culturelles, il est devenu un véritable centre d'information sur l'Allemagne. (www.madanight.com/articles/diplomatie/783-madagascar-allemagne-une-cooperation-bilaterale-epanouie.html, accessed 16 May 2010)

2 Moi je peux même dire que Olszowski était pour beaucoup, je peux même dire un peu plus que 50 pourcent, dans l'orientation finale du parcours de Salala. Parce que lui dans le temps, il m'a dit, parce que moi, j'ai mélangé, je faisais des choses a cappella, je faisais des choses avec accompagnement instrumental, mais Olszowski m'a dit tu choisis, tu choisis parce là tu te sous-estimes mais tu as une certaine carrure, ton groupe, mais il faut que tu optes pour une voie, et c'est pour ça que tu donnes plus de visibilité aux gens par rapport à ton groupe. Dans le temps, j'étais pas du tout convaincu. Mais je, parce que en fait on se dit dans le temps, on ne pensait pas encore que un jour on fera en quelque sorte carrière dans la musique, donc on se dit, on tentait tous les voies possibles. Mais Olszowski m'a dit, voilà tu arrêtes les chansons à l'eau de rose, t'arrêtes les trucs avec guitare et tout ça, arrête d'introduire comme ça des femmes, des cœurs de femmes dans ton groupe. Travaillez à vous trois. Et donc, j'ai essayé. J'étais pas convaincu mais lui. Il était convaincu. Et donc il m'a emmené voir des gens qui étaient du même avis que lui. Donc je me suis dit, donc de toute façon donc l'issue c'est quelqu'un du genre d'Olszowski. Si la voix, si Le Goethe me dit que c'est ça qui l'intéresse, ce serait idiot de le contrarier. Au départ, donc c'était ça. Et puis ben voilà, il nous a organisé ce concert avec Ricky. Et puis les gens sont enthousiasmés mais dans le temps, dans le temps on pouvait même pas remplir la petite salle du CGM. Mais bon c'était un travail mais dans le temps qui était relativement professionnel dans le temps. Et le CGM dans le temps, surpassait le ministère de la culture de très très loin, en matière de promotion, de la culture surtout de la musique malgache. Moi je pense qu'il y a pas mal de groupes, dont Salala qui auraient, cela ferait déjà longtemps que ce groupe aurait disparu si il n'y avait pas des structures comme CGM. (Meinhof's interview, April 2009, Nantes)

3 Font bouger un peu la culture au Maroc. (Kiwan's interview with Badre Belhachemi, April 2008, Rabat)

4 C'est quand même une opportunité de faire des échanges très très enrichis-sants [...] Donc c'est des choses comme ça aussi ... des nouveaux réseaux sociaux apportent des nouvelles couleurs musicales, culturelles, artistiques. (Gibert's interview with Skander, May 2007, London)

5 Le souci c'est vraiment de réussir les rencontres et de ne pas tomber dans des rencontres anecdotiques [...] sinon on peut appeler ça jam session, il y a pas de problème. (Kiwan's interview with Majid Bekkas, April 2008, Rabat)

Chapter 6

1 Domi: À cinq ans ... Pendant un moment, je ne voulais pas parler du tout Malgache. Mais les parents ont toujours insisté pour qu'on parle Malgache, et je le comprenais très bien de toute façon, donc y'avait pas de problème là-dessus. Ils ont insisté et, je sais pas, à un moment donné c'est ... On se pose pas la question pourquoi on a envie de, de, de, de se rapprocher de Madagascar. Vers l'adolescence, ça s'est rapproché, on avait envie. On habitait à Auch – donc c'est à 70 kilomètres de Toulouse – et on n'était pas du tout dans la communauté malgache, on évoluait vraiment dans la communauté très intégrés chez les Français, mais à un moment donné, de toute façon les parents, enfin mon père surtout, il est, il est ... il a toujours gardé les traditions malgaches et le côté malgache, il l'a jamais perdu. Donc c'est revenu ... Naturellement, à un moment donné, on avait envie d'être avec les Malgaches, d'aller dans des soirées malgaches, d'écouter de la musique malgache, de redécouvrir Madagascar ...

Ulrike: Et tu te rappelles ... les amis que tu avais, c'était d'abord des Français ou c'était d'abord des gens d'autre part?

Domi: Non, surtout des Français ... [Nous étions] vraiment intégrés dans la société ... Euh, on maîtrise parfaitement la langue, euh ... On se sentait pas autres qu'eux, on était vraiment bien intégrés, mais, mais y'a un côté malgache qui appelle à un moment donné – je sais pas, moi je l'ai ressenti comme ça – où on a besoin de savoir d'où l'on vient. Ça nous intéresse d'un coup, Madagascar, et ... et voilà! (Meinhof's interview, Castelginest, December 2006)

2 Domi: En fait ça a commencé parce qu'on était dans une association qui s'appelait Taredy tous: ma sœur, donc elle en était présidente, moi je suis passée par secrétaire etc. dedans. Et au départ, donc, c'était une association avec des jeunes Malgaches. On a fait du sport etc., et puis on a fait de la danse ... [et on s'est demandé] pourquoi ne pas faire un premier concert? Parce qu'on a toujours été attirés par les artistes malgaches etc. Donc, euh, ça faisait un moment qu'on ... on avait fait des organisations, on va dire de petite envergure, sur Toulouse, et on était prêts à passer à la vitesse supérieure où il fallait plus de moyens, plus d'implication etc. Donc on a fait le premier concert ... Et bon, ça a eu du succès. Nous aussi on avait bien organisé donc euh, on avait eu beaucoup de plaisir à le faire. (Meinhof's interview, Castelginest, December 2006)

3 Domi: Ah oui! Pourquoi on avait fait une deuxième association? Oui, parce qu'à l'intérieur de Taredy tout le monde, on était assez nombreux, et tout le monde ne voulait pas continuer sur ce chemin artistique parce que c'était beaucoup de moyens financiers, beaucoup d'implication, beaucoup de temps euh ... à dépenser dedans, donc euh ... à un moment donné y'a eu une

scission. Bon, bé, Taredy voulait pas continuer là-dedans, donc nous on va créer notre propre association ... On fait pas que ça, enfin, on fait pas que des organisations d'artistes, mais notre approche est toujours artistique, que ce soit exposition de peinture, que ce soit concert, que ce soit ... Ça peut être du théâtre, de la littérature ... mais tout ce qui touche de, enfin, approche Madagascar de façon artistique. (Meinhof's interview, Castelginest, December 2006)

4 Hangotiana: On voulait insister aussi, comme elle a cité dans le journal, c'était la mixité raciale. On voulait vraiment appuyer là-dessus. C'est-à-dire que les habitants de Castelginest, on voudrait vraiment qu'ils soient nombreux avec nous, les Malgaches. Mais pas que nous, les Malgaches. Nous, notre objectif c'est pas que la diaspora. C'est vraiment s'ouvrir aux gens. Et c'est plus intéressant quand on explique aux gens qui ne connaissent pas que les Malgaches qui disent 'Bon, c'est bon, je connais, tu vas pas m'apprendre le pays.' C'est plus intéressant ... Donc avec le maire, la mairie d'ici, on a travaillé pour qu'on mette des affiches partout dans le village. Et le maire espère aussi que ça marche, parce que moi j'ai dit 'Mon objectif, c'est pas de faire quelque chose de communautaire, rester entre nous. Pas du tout. C'est vraiment de s'ouvrir. On habite ici, on siège ici, donc que les habitants de Castelginest viennent nous rencontrer, et faire tomber des a priori. Qu'ils découvrent, parce qu'il y en a plein qui ne connaissent pas.' Y'en a beaucoup qui ne connaissent pas, c'est pas médiatisé Madagascar, hein? C'est pas surmédiatisé, on va dire. Y'a d'autres endroits qui sont bien médiatisés, mais Madagascar, c'est encore ... Petit à petit, parfois on voit, puis on ... Pas trop. Et puis on voit toujours, souvent on voit toujours les mêmes images. De la misère, de la pauvreté. Et c'est vrai qu'on hésite entre s'énerver après ça en disant 'Mais y'a pas que ça! On a des richesses énormes! ... Y'a une joie de vivre.' (Meinhof's interview, Castelginest, December 2006)

5 Hangotiana: Alors, en fait c'est un projet donc Voajanahari qu'on a ... Le jour où on a vraiment commencé à parler avec Dama, en fait, il nous a fait voir une vidéo. C'est vrai que, sur le coup – on avait vu, y'avait ma sœur, y'avait moi, y'avait ma maman – sur le coup, personne n'était vraiment intéressé. C'est pas pas intéressé, mais on regardait. C'était comme un film qu'on regardait. Moi, c'était particulier, parce que c'était une réponse à quelque chose que j'attendais. Parce que jusqu'à présent, on a fait des concerts. On a posé des artistes sur scène, et on chante, et c'est des chansons qu'on aime. Mais là y'avait quelque chose de particulier sur Voajanahari, qui me touchait. J'étais très émue. Je sais pas, c'était ma terre. Y'a quelque chose qui faisait que je voulais absolument, absolument être du voyage. Donc on en a parlé tous, on en a parlé avec Dama: qu'est-ce que c'est exactement,

qu'est-ce que vous avez, est-ce que c'est un mouvement, c'est quoi exactement Voajanahari? On a demandé à Dama, qu'est-ce que c'est exactement? Et puis il nous a expliqué ce que c'était. Ils se disent 'On connait Dama, on connait Ricky, mais c'est quoi? Qu'est-ce qui va se passer? Pourquoi ça a l'air, euh ...?' Ben, tout simplement, on a dit, que – pour que le plus grand nombre comprenne – on a dit qu'on sensibilise les gens sur la protection de notre environnement. Mais environnement culturel, aussi, nos traditions. Pas seulement l'environnement, la nature, mais aussi la relation entre ces deux mondes qui doivent absolument cohabiter, mais pas ... De toute façon aujourd'hui, avec ce qui se passe à Madagascar, même à Madagascar c'est très difficile aussi de faire passer le message. Les gens ont besoin de vivre, de manger ... Si on a faim, on s'en fiche que l'arbre brûle ... Donc, comment faire cohabiter tout ça? Parce que sinon, si on fait que philosopher, ça n'intéresse pas les gens. Eux, ils ont besoin de concret ... Donc, ce qui a été très difficile pour nous, c'est de faire en sorte que les gens soient quand même accrochés. Alors on a quand même utilisé le marketing pour pouvoir les accrocher, c'est-à-dire, essayez de vous raccrocher au wagon Voajanahari. Pour leur dire que c'est dynamique, qu'on s'endort pas. (Meinhof's interview, Castelginest, December 2006)

6 Voilà, donc, Mosaik Production existe depuis 2005, c'est en fait moi et deux autres personnes, on râle qu'il se passe rien à Geneve ... donc l'idée est de toujours, parmi nos actions, euh ... culturelles et artistiques, on est toujours en lien avec les différentes communautés ici, en général africaines et maghrébines, et on s'est dit qu'on allait euh ... ben, essayer de créer une association, mais dès le départ, l'objectif était de faire un lien avec l'Afrique. Parce que nous, on est imprégnés de l'Afrique, on sent ça ... ben on a besoin de ce lien, pour pouvoir survivre dans la jungle urbaine [rires] ... voilà, quoi. C'est un lien très fort, quoi. (Kiwan's interview with Amina, July 2009, Geneva)

7 Mais la première des choses c'est que moi, ça fait 30 ans que j'ai quitté le Maroc, donc je vis à Genève, donc le Maroc actuel n'a plus rien à voir avec le Maroc que j'ai laissé ... donc. Voilà, c'est là où je découvre, moi j'ai laissé, je suis partie en '79, à peu près, et à l'époque c'était Nass el Ghiwane, et toute cette mouvance [...] mais c'était là où ça s'est arrêté, voilà, on a fermé à clé ... et on a fermé et on a jeté les clés en fait, et que ça s'est arrêté là. Culturellement il se passait plus rien au Maroc. Bon moi étant ici ... donc voilà. Je repartais au Maroc de temps en temps, mais avec aucun lien culturel ... j'allais voir mes parents ... et je revenais ... donc ça fait à peu près maintenant un peu plus de dix ans que j'ai renoué avec le Maroc, avec le nouveau état gouvernement, un nouveau roi, de nouveautés avec une ouverture ... une tolérance, une entre guillemets une démocratie qui se met en place, enfin, voilà quoi. Et donc avec tout ça ... donc ce qui était intéressant, c'est qu'on a quand-même ... l'ouverture est venue des jeunes, qui se sont imposés petit à petit, avec leurs différences, avec leurs références musicales, et culturelles, voilà, le Maroc c'est un pays de contradictions, il y en a qui regardent vers l'orient, et d'autres qui

regardent vers l'occident ... et ... mais ça marche, et voilà! C'est un rapport en connaissance de cause donc ça marche. (Kiwan's interview with Amina, July 2009, Geneva)

8 Parce qu'ici ah, le Maroc, l'Afrique ... c'est quand même, il y a beaucoup de préjugés ... et donc moi, j'avais un peu marre de ces préjugés, et j'avais pas envie non plus d'être ghettoisée étiquetée ... oui euh ... c'est une association culturelle, donc une association d'intégration, donc tout ce que ça implique ... voilà ... j'en ai marre de cette étiquette ... donc je refuse ça, et donc je me suis dit euh ... voilà, on fait une association culturelle, effectivement, qui cible l'Afrique, qui cible les arts urbains, parce qu'on est en plein dedans quoi ... on ne peut pas renier ça ... et ras le bol de cette étiquette aussi de l'Afrique traditionnelle ... pagne, boubou, couscous machin ... voilà. On va changer les choses ... on va essayer de voir les choses différemment et ... donner quelque chose de différent. Il n'y a jamais eu cette dynamique ici ... donc nous on va la créer ... on va donner ... et depuis que nous on est actifs ... beaucoup de choses ont changé. (Kiwan's interview with Amina, July 2009, Geneva)

9 C'était l'année 2007 en fait ... moi j'étais là avant, pour le Tremplin, donc j'ai été moi donner un coup de main ... sur le Tremplin ... j'étais là ... j'ai pu voir, si tu veux ... je connais un peu les festivals sur différentes cultures et ... mais à chaque fois je suis là, et euh ... vraiment c'est difficile si tu veux pour ... je trouve incroyable qu'un festival comme ça ... de cette envergure euh ... puisse me faire confiance ... qu'il y ait cette ouverture et puis que ... voilà, c'est pas toujours dit, hein, si ... mais ici voilà si tu connais pas des gens, tu peux pas être backstage ni même en tant qu'artiste ... voilà quoi. Donc, voilà ... ça il y a eu ... une confiance qui s'est établie petit-à-petit [...] Mais ce qui est sympa, c'est qu'il y a vraiment ... que je reconnais qui est très, qui est mérité enfin pour les organisateurs c'est que jamais on nous a demandé quoi que ce soit, quoi. L'objectif c'est pas ... 'ouais il y a des Suisses qui arrivent, on va leur demander' ... non, jamais! ... et ça a été un rapport d'égal, qui étais magnifique pour nous. C'était vraiment très important ... c'est ça qui nous a en plus impliqué en disant ... mais attends, c'est des gens, nous demandent absolument rien ... on est là, on est dans un autre contexte et tout ... on amène un peu ... donc voilà, le lien ... il s'est tissé c'est vraiment des forts liens ... il y a des gens qui restent en contact ... des artistes ... qui voilà avec Facebook avec internet, c'est plus facile quoi ... et chaque fois on arrive, avec les bras grands ouverts des tous les gens qui gravitent autour du festival quoi. (Kiwan's interview with Amina, July 2009, Geneva)

10 Ulrike: Wie kommt ein Erich Raab aus Muenchen zu Madagaskar?
Erich: Ja der Erich Raab hat mit seiner Frau den Kilimandscharo bestiegen und zur Belohnung hat er sich dann mit seiner Frau eine Woche Urlaub auf Mauritius gegoennt, und da sind wir ueber Madagaskar hinweggeflogen, ham runtergeschaut und ham gesagt, ach da gehn wir auch mal hin und schaun uns dieses Land an und das ham wir dann ein paar Jahre spaeter gemacht, das war 1987, unsere erste Reise nach Madagaskar, mit dem Rucksack ohne Plan durch das Land gereist und uns in das Land verliebt und haengengeblieben, Leute kennengelernt, und im naechsten Jahr gleich wiedergekommen und so seit fast 20

jahren jetzt regelmaessig in Madagaskar, einmal im Jahr, manchmal auch zweimal im Jahr ... Ich hab, glaub ich beim letzten Mal meine alten Reisepaesse nach den Visastempeln durchgeforstet und ich glaub das war jetzt unsere 22. Reise ...

Also wir sind, nachdem wir zum wiederholten Male unser Visa bei einem Konsul beantragt hatten, beim Honorarkonsul von Madagaskar, hat uns dieser Konsul mal angerufen und hat uns darauf hingewiesen, dass es die deutsch-madagassische Gesellschaft gibt, eine Organisation auf Bundesebene. Und ob wir nicht Lust haetten – wir seien so oft in Madagaskar – ob wir nicht Lust haetten, da Mitglied zu werden. Wir sind dann zu der naechsten Mitgliederversammlung dieser deutsch-madagas-sischen Gesellschaft gegangen – sie war damals in Koblenz glaub ich – und bei dieser Mitgliederversammlung berichtete ein junger Kollege aus Muenchen ueber einen gerade gegruendeten Madagaskarverein in Muenchen, und da sind wir natuerlich hellhoerig geworden, haben sofort Kontakt aufgenommen und sind auch diesem Verein dann gleich beigetreten. Und der Verein kam so zustande, dass einige andere Leute aus Muenchen, direkt aus Schwabing, wo wir auch wohnen auch nach Madagaskar gereist waren und den Schulleiter der Grundschule in Belo Tsirihibina kennengelernt haben und der hat ihm die Schule gezeigt und eben die aermlichen Verhaeltnisse, unter denen die Kinder da unterrichtet werden, und diese Menschen haben beschlossen, diese Schule zu unterstuetzen durch Sachspenden, die sie bei der naechsten Reise mitgebracht haben oder auch durch Sachspenden, die sie hinges-chickt haben. Und wir haben uns dann diesem Verein angeschlossen und dieses Projekt dann von Anfang an mit aufgebaut. (Meinhof's interview, Munich, July 2007)

11 Einmal hattem wir anlaesslich eines Nationalfeiertags in Berlin Kontakt mit einem madagassischen Musiker, der da aufgetreten ist ... und ueber den, ueber diesen Kontakt sind wir dann mit seinem Bruder Ricky in Tana in Kontakt gekommen, das hat sich dann so ergeben, und Ricky trat dann einmal in, ich glaub das erste Mal wars in Bergisch Gladbach auf mit dem Projekt Voajanahari zusammen mit Dama und Hajazz, da sind wir hingefahren, haben nach dem Konzert uns angefreundet, ein bisschen Wein getrunken, ja und so hat sich das so entwickelt und nun hatten wir zweimal schon das Projekt Voajanahari in München einmal auf der Buga, einmal im Eine Welt Haus in Muenchen einmal im Buergerhaus in Eching und letztes Jahr ein zweites Mal ein zweites Mal in Muenchen am Ampere in der Moffathalle. (Meinhof's interview, Munich, July 2007)

12 Und dann haben wir Dama und Ricky gefragt, ob sie nicht auch mal Lust haetten nach Belo mitzukommen und dort ein Konzert zu geben und sie haben eingewilligt und haben dann ein wunderbares Konzert in Belo organisiert was ganz schwierig zu organisieren war weil es da keine Anlage gibt, das mussten wir alles aus Tana mitschleppen, das hat alles Dama mit seinem Pick-up nach Morondava gebracht, dort hat unser Adolpho es dann uebernommen und nach Belo ueberfuehrt und das groesste Problem was Adolph dann bei diesem Konzert in Belo hatte, war an diesem Abend wenn das Konzert stattfindet darf der Vertreter von Gerama von der Energiebehoerde den Strom nicht abschalten ...

Weil sonst immer abends der Strom abgeschaltet wurde ... Und das hat dann geklappt. Na wenn so grosse Prominenz Wie die Leute gesagt haben, das war das groesste Kulturereignis in der Geschichte der Stadt, dass so jemand Prominenter wie Dama und Ricky da ein KONZERT GEBEN, dann muss der schon fuer den Strom sorgen ... Das Publikum war im Sonntagsgewand, das war richtig ein Konzertpublikum, die Prominenz der Stadt war da und am Ende waren 500 Leute drin. (Meinhof's interview, Munich, July 2007)

13 Bei einem der letzten Besuche, das war auch im Zusammenhang mit einem Konzert, das von Dama und Ricky, das wir in Belo organsiert hatten, da kamen die Vertreter der Bauernverbaende ins Hotel auf Dama zu und Dama musste einen ganzen Vormittag mit den Bauern ihre Probleme diskutieren, und wir hatten dann eben auch gemerkt, dass unsere Beschraenkung auf die Zielgruppe Schule Lehrer und Kinder eigentlich auf Dauer nicht haltbar ist, sondern dass wir ein breiteres Spektrum hier ansprechen muessen, weil die 90–95 Prozent der Bevoelkerung dort sind Bauern und wir koennen davon nicht absehen und dass da eben die Problematik der Landwirtschaft ganz wichtig zentral wird auch was die Bildung der Kinder mit angeht, das ist inzwischen klar geworden und wir versuchen jetzt auch staerker das mit einzubeziehen, dass auch in unserer Bibliothek die Angebote gemacht werden fuer die erwachsene Bevoelkerung der Stadt. (Meinhof's interview, Munich, July 2007)

14 Unser Satzungszweck sind die Kinder von Belo, aber da steht auch dabei, das Projekt kann aber auch auf andere ausgeweitet werden, allerdings koennen wir das erst machen, wenn wir genuegend Resourcen dafuer haben. Und das haben wir im Moment noch nicht, dafuer ist unser Verein zu klein. Wir haben jetzt noch eine neue Zusammenarbeit begonnen, die Zusammenarbeit eben mit der Oeko-farm von Dama, und haben auch dieses Projekt von Dama jetzt unterstuetzt und wollen das auch beibehalten und noch weiter ausbauen, die Zusammenarbeit mit diesem Zentrum von Dama, weil das ja auch naheliegt, das liegt in der Region, wir kommen da direkt vorbei, und wir haben auch Dama gewonnen dass er auch als Berater fuer unser Projekt agiert, und das ist schon eine neue Perspektive. (Meinhof's interview, Munich, July 2007)

15 Also die ersten Jahre gab es eigentlich nur die Zusammenarbeit ueber die Musik, ueber die Kultur, weil die Mitglieder von Mahaleo auch immer wieder betonten ihr erstes Anliegen ist sowas wie eine Globalisierung der Freundschaft herzustellen und die muss ohne Geld und ohne Abhaengigkeiten funktionieren. Wir haben dann im Laufe der Zeit auch angeboten, also wir sind auch eine Organisation, die Projekte finanziert und dass, wenn sie etwas vorschlagen koennen sind wir gerne bereit, das naeher anzusehen. So hat sich dann so langsam auch ein Kontakt ueber Entwicklungszusammenarbeit ueber Entwicklungsprojekte konkret ergeben. (Meinhof's interview, Linz, September 2007)

16 Lorsque on a commencé à travailler sur le festival, on s'est vraiment ouvert à tous les arts de la rue ... mais avec une tendance vraiment locale et africaine. L'idée c'est pas d'importer la façon qu'on a de concevoir les arts de la rue ... en France et en Europe ... c'est vraiment de se laisser ... de ... d'explorer ce qu'il y a ici ... ce qui existait et ce qui existe encore ... de le faire ... de le relier à ce qui

existe en Afrique, et voilà, de faire revivre un peu tout ça, de faire remonter tout ça … Donc l'objectif du festival, c'est exactement ça, c'est de faire, de provoquer des rencontres … entre la création contemporaine européenne et méditerranéenne et puis ce qui existe en Afrique et au Maroc. (Kiwan's and Gibert's interview with Claire Le Goff, Éclats de lune, April 2008, Marrakesh)

17 Nadia:　Et la musique … le groupe […] vous pouvez en dire un peu plus?

Claire:　Alors, donc eux ils ont fait … ils font partie des fondateurs d'Éclats de lune. Et donc … c'est avec eux qu'on a commencé à travailler sur justement, sur insertion professionnelle … euh donc en gros, c'est composé de percussionnistes, dont un nombre va et vient … et de jongleurs. Bon en fait c'est pas vraiment structuré et la plupart du temps ils travaillent essentiellement dans des … les boîtes de nuit, quoi. Donc nous, ce qu'on a essayé de faire, c'est de travailler avec eux et de les emmener sur un processus de … création, processus beaucoup plus artistique, euh … mais on n'a pas réussi […] Ça fait partie de … voilà, ça fait partie du processus de création du centre de formation ici, c'est-à-dire, on peut pas … en gros, on s'est rendu compte à travers le travail qu'on a fait avec eux, qu'on peut pas imposer à des jeunes, un processus dans lequel ils sont pas […]

Marie:　Et du coup ça vous a fait remettre en question un certain nombre de choses dans la construction de ce centre et …

Claire:　Oui, complètement. Voilà, on s'est dit qu'il fallait, qu'il fallait vraiment faire attention avec quel public on travaille … il fallait faire attention au processus au … comment on engendre le processus quoi, c'est-à-dire […] et là on s'est dit je pense que c'est important qu'on travaille avec un public jeune, c'est pour ça je parlais de 16–25 ans … et encore 25 c'est presque trop vieux déjà, en gros c'est vraiment pour les prendre au départ, de leur démarche artistique quoi. Pour les vraiment les accompagner depuis la base. Et lorsqu'on travaille avec des jeunes qui sont plus formés déjà … là il faudra vraiment prendre plus de précautions … et à la rigueur faire des phases de sélection que ce soit vraiment des jeunes qui sont en demande … plutôt que l'inverse, quoi. (Kiwan's and Gibert's interview with Claire Le Goff, Éclats de lune, April 2008, Marrakesh)

18 En gros, l'idée c'est de former des artistes euh … qui sont capables de monter eux-mêmes leur structure […] les amener à prendre conscience de leur rôle en tant qu'artiste dans un territoire. (Kiwan's and Gibert's interview with Claire Le Goff, Éclats de lune, April 2008, Marrakesh)

19 Nadia:　Et vous êtes combien de personnes dans l'équipe?

Claire:　L'équipe pour le moment est vraiment réduite … elle est en train de se construire donc … alors il y a quatre artistes, médiateurs culturels, on va dire, donc eux ils sont … sur le festival, par exemple, ils en charge toute l'action culturelle … et c'est les responsables des sites de spectacle … c'est-à-dire qu'ils sont en lien avec les associations qui sont partenaires avec nous sur le festival, et ils préparent avec eux pendant genre trois ou quatre mois avant le festival, ils préparent l'arrivée du festival quoi. Ils mobilisent les équipes, ils construisent les équipes ... ils font en sorte que les responsables des associations sont en connexion avec et les pouvoirs publics pour qu'on ait tout ce qu'il nous faut pour le festival ... voilà, c'est ce qu'on appelle l'action culturelle. Ils préparent l'arrivée des festivals ... à travers sur plusieurs choses et là ça dépend vraiment des associations avec lesquelles on travaille ... sur chaque site c'est différent, quoi. Par exemple, Aghmat, on travaille avec une asso qui veut valoriser le patrimoine matériel du village ... donc l'artiste travaille sur l'aménagement de la place publique. Voilà, il travaille en ce moment sur ça. Et ce biais-là permet de mobiliser les troupes, en fait. Comme ça au moment où le festival arrive, on a toute une population qui est à fond dedans ... qui est mobilisée ... et l'idéal à terme ... l'idée c'est que ce soit eux ... enfin que ce soit ces associations-là qui soient organisatrices locales du festival. (Kiwan's and Gibert's interview with Claire Le Goff, Éclats de lune, April 2008, Marrakesh)

20 Nadia: Et du coup, les ateliers qui ont lieu dans les villages-là, est-ce que les enfants-là, est-ce qu'ils parlent français, ou ça se passe avec les formateurs ils sont ... qui parlent en *darija*?

Claire: Dans ce cas-là on fait de binômes, on met un artiste de chez nous qui lui vraiment parle ... soit le berbère, soit l'arabe, et voilà ... et un intervenant en français ou alors, si c'est pas un artiste de chez nous, c'est un membre de l'association de référence, quoi. C'est intéressant, parce que si ... enfin ... tout moment est un moment de formation aussi ... celui qui va faire justement le binôme, la traduction ... on va le choisir de façon ... à ce que ce moment-là soit pour lui un moment formateur, ça peut etre un jeune, par exemple, qui a envie de développer des compétences en termes d'animation, et donc qui va au contact des artistes ... voilà, il va apprendre ce que c'est qu'un atelier ... ce que c'est qu'un processus pédagogique. (Kiwan's and Gibert's interview with Claire Le Goff, Éclats de lune, April 2008, Marrakesh)

21 À Tassemmitt c'est devenu un endroit, enfin une deuxième, une sorte de petite planque, c'est devenu un peu notre maison, on connaît pratiquement toutes les familles de cette région-là – c'est pas, en fait il y a pas de village c'est des maisons séparées sur un grand espace, il y a un hameau voilà donc les musiciens montaient régulièrement. (Hicham Bahou speaking at a panel at the TNMundi conference in Rabat, 'Music and Migration: North African Artists' Networks across Europe and Africa', Rabat, 13–14 November 2008, Faculty of Letters, Mohammed V University, Agdal, Rabat, Morocco)

22 Mais le but de l'association, le but de ASIDD c'est pas seulement construire une école, ou d'assister, ou de ramener des fonds, de faire des petites opérations d'urgence, en ramenant des vêtements avant l'hiver ou, le but c'est vraiment de penser à long terme à ce que les gens puissent travailler sur place et avoir un revenu, et se prendre en charge eux-mêmes sans chercher à descendre à Beni Mellal ou aller, traverser le détroit parce que c'est en fait la région est dans le fameux

triangle de la mort [...] qui fournit la majorité des candidats à l'émigration ... vers l'Italie essentiellement et l'Espagne et le but c'était de convaincre les habitants, de leur dire, 'écoutez, c'est un très bel endroit, c'est un petit paradis, c'est vrai qu'il y a la misère mais c'est ici là où vous pouvez vous pouvez faire des choses ... vous n'avez pas besoin d'aller ailleurs'. (Hicham Bahou speaking at a panel at the TNMundi conference in Rabat, 'Music and Migration: North African Artists' Networks across Europe and Africa', Rabat, 13–14 November 2008, Faculty of Letters, Mohammed V University, Agdal, Rabat, Morocco)

23 Donc ces habitants, il a fallu aider à une prise de conscience justement de la potentialité de la région ... c'est très simple vaut mieux que ça soit les habitants qui en profitent ou d'autres et les autres il y a en beaucoup [...] maintenant il y a une coopérative qui existe qui est sortie de l'association et qui est gérée entière-ment pas les habitants, donc président c'est un habitant de justement, c'est quelqu'un de la région qui habite à côté de Beni Mellal donc maintenant ils sont autonomes et voilà la région est en cours de, enfin c'est prétentieux de dire en cours de développement et ... mais je pense il y a une partie des objectifs réalisés ... Amale Samie développe un petit gîte là-bas – et le but, justement on parlait de tourisme culturel, c'est que ce soit aussi une porte pour les artistes ... un lieu pour les artistes ... et on travaille sur connections, avec disons, tous nos connections communs au Boulevard, c'est un certain moment que ce soit un lieu où on monte avec les les artistes où on peut travailler, où on peut développer des choses là-bas euh il y a un groupe de Hindouss, local ... et justement cette année on vise de tra-vailler ensemble sur un projet de résidence de création artistique. (Hicham Bahou speaking at a panel at the TNMundi conference in Rabat, 'Music and Migration: North African Artists' Networks across Europe and Africa', Rabat, 13–14 November 2008, Faculty of Letters, Mohammed V University, Agdal, Rabat, Morocco)

Notes

Notes to Introduction

1. For reasons that we will explain in Chapter 1, we specify transnational movements as those between nations, and translocal movements as those within a nation. But see, among others, Smith (2001) and Bennett and Peterson (2004) for alternative versions of these concepts.
2. As will be shown later, the term African is not a term used as self-identification by either North African or Malagasy people. When used by us in the context of grouping both under the same heading it is a purely geographic and not an identification marker.
3. For further discussion of Mauss's concepts in relation to our work see Gibert and Meinhof (2009).
4. Raoul suddenly died on 3 September 2010 at the age of 59 of a heart attack. His passing was mourned in Madagascar and Europe alike. His last journey from Tamatave to Tana to Antsirabe to Ambositra and finally to the family grave in Ambatofinandrahana was accompanied by thousands of people who visited his coffin where he lay in state and along the road-sides of the long journey. The remaining Mahaleo gave concerts at all the towns on the way, accompanied by many other musicians, including the many young artists whom Raoul had tirelessly supported. In France, too, several commemoration concerts were held, including a tribute concert in Paris at the New Morning venue on 3 October, where Dama and Bekoto from the Mahaleo group were joined by Régis Gizavo, Edgar Ravahatra, and many other young and old Malagasy musicians resident in France. Mahaleo have since confirmed that they will continue their preparations for their 40th anniversary concert just as Raoul would have wanted them to.
5. The numbers within square brackets at the end of quotations refer to the original French or German text in the Appendix.
6. 'Je fais de la musique pour plusieurs pays. J'aime la Terre de mes ancêtres, le salaire c'est une réalité. Je retourne en Europe pour les salaires. "Mitady ravina-hitra" (chercher des bonnes herbes), c'est le titre de notre 1er album. Pour moi, je dois partager au monde mon talent. Comme ça je ne perds pas ma culture. Le tsapiky vient de la campagne de Tuléar. C'est pour cela que je ne reste pas là bas. J'ai besoin de me sentir ici et d'aller là bas.' ('I make music for several countries. I love the earth of my ancestors, but money is a reality. I return to Europe for the money. "Searching for the Good Grass", that's the title of our first album. I need to share my talent with the rest of the world. That way I won't lose my culture. Tsapiky comes from the countryside of Tulear. That's why I won't stay over there [in Europe]. Over here I need to feel who I am and then go over there.')

    (Meinhof's and Rasolofondraosolo's interview with Rakapo, Fort Dauphin, December 2009)
7. By contrast, Madagascar as a *country* is identified either positively through its extraordinary natural diversity and beauty – 80 per cent of its plants and

animals are endemic to Madagascar – or negatively, as a country where this natural diversity is under threat. But apart from a few well-known Malagasy musicians, both from within the diaspora and in Madagascar itself, who have gained international recognition, little is known in Europe about the cultural and especially the musical diversity of Madagascar and its diaspora, a situation that is a cause of much debate and worry among transnational Malagasy musicians (see also Fuhr forthcoming).

8. The convention of referencing the first world as 'West' as in 'Western music' makes no sense in the context of our focus on an Indian Ocean island, North Africa and their respective interrelation to Europe. We use North <> South as geographical denominators even though neither 'west' nor 'north' is used by the artists in the 'South' that we interviewed, who prefer to talk about Europe or France or Paris or simply abroad.

Notes to Chapter 1

1. Our team of researchers consisted of Ulrike Meinhof, Nadia Kiwan and Marie-Pierre Gibert. Meinhof's work concentrated on Malagasy networks with the support of the project consultant Dama, the eponymous member of the group Mahaleo. Kiwan worked on the North African links supported by Gibert. Since this book is co-authored by Meinhof and Kiwan we will always use plural pronouns even where the fieldwork was only conducted by one of us. Where we use extracts from interviews we will always reference the name(s) of the interviewer(s).

2. After the referendum the province of Toliara and its provincial governor were replaced by four regions as the highest administrative division with 22 sub-regions headed by regional chiefs directly responsible to the President: (1) Menabe (comprising Morondava as sub-region), (2) Atsimo Andrefanana (comprising Toliara I and Toliara II), (3) Androy and (4) Anosy (comprising Fort Dauphin).

3. 'Taxi brousse' is the name of the legendary mini-buses that criss-cross Madagascar on the most unlikely roads, packed full of people, animals and goods, and carrying mountains of luggage on their roofs. They are the key transport facilities of the population. Mahaleo's song 'Taxi Broussie' celebrates this colourful means of travelling in one of their most popular songs.

4. The air distances were calculated with Google Earth ruler, the road distances by adding together the kilometres indicated on the map of Madagascar published by the Institut géographique national.

5. RN35 (Malagasy text and music by Dama Mahaleo; retranslated from the authorized French translation by Meinhof):

> **RN35**
> There it is, road number 35
> Still an A road, but forgotten by the people
> Travelling from Antananarivo to Morondava
> All the villages on the way have their stories that made them famous
> At the height of Ambatofinandrahana we take a break
> We pass Itremo, then Amborompotsy

Once arrived at Mandrosonoro we can't go to bed on an empty stomach

The restaurant of Mandrosonoro – that has not been forgotten by the people

Mama Sera she's called, the woman who knows how to receive guests

The taste of your angivy soup [a reputedly healthy slightly bitter vegetable stock] lingers in my mouth

Especially when mixed with the taste of the greens, that's a taste that I love to keep in my mouth

The restaurant of Mama Sera it's a place to meet

The travellers are satisfied, the drivers are happy

The restaurant of Mama Sera it's a meetings place

The drivers are happy, the travellers are satisfied

Tell me Mama Sera: What dishes will you serve to the drivers?

I'll serve them *henankisoa* [pork] and *ravintoto*

[minced manioc leaves; the reference here is to a heavy meal that makes people a little bit sleepy, so that the drivers remain calm and stop often to give travellers a chance to pee]

So that they will not rush too much

She is unique, Mama Sera

She preserves the life of the travellers

She also knows how to advise the drivers

Not to drive too fast and not cause an accident

And tell me Mama Sera

What dishes will you serve to the travellers?

I've prepared them the house of the eel

And I'll serve it with my heart

But the house of the eel

That's just an infusion made from the left-over rice

[Malagasy *Ranon'ampango* is water heated in a marmite with the remainders of the rice stuck against the inside of the cooking pot. It is usually drunk at the end of a meal. Because of its golden or brown colour it is also called *ranovola* (lit. golden water)]

The travellers are left speechless

The drivers are full of joy

Yes, she is really unique, Mama Sera

She preserves the life of the drivers

For people are no chicken, olombelon-tsy akoho

[olombelon-tsy akoho = literally 'men are no chicken' is the request made by travellers in a taxi brousse when they want to stop for a pee]

And that's what she wants, Mama Sera

That the drivers stop often on their journey

That restaurant of Mama Sera, no one ever forgets it

Mama Sera, that's the name of someone who knows how to welcome people

The restaurant Mandrosonoro won't be forgotten

We continue our journey on the A road 35

After Mandrosonoro we pass through Janjina

A village reputed to have spirits

We pass through Malaimbandy

> A village reputed to dislike lies
> We pass through Ankilizato
> A village reputed to have one hundred tamarind trees
> We pass through Mahabo
> A village famous for being high up on a hill
> We arrive at Morondava
> The beach there is long, very long
> But the sea risks swallowing it
> Luckily there are the Baobab trees, the pride of Morondava
> That was the story of road number 35
> Still an A road, but forgotten by the people.

6. The extent to which dialectal variation impedes mutual comprehensibility, especially between the dialects of the south and the standard Malagasy variety based on the Merina dialect of the Hauts Plateaux, is disputed. See the discussion in Bouwer (2003, 2007), juxtaposing Rajaonarimanana (1995), who argues that dialectal variation is insignificant, with Tsimilaza's view (1992) and Bouwer's own view that the variation between southern dialects is substantial and needs to be acknowledged by educators.

7. There are distinctive cultural forms of expression between the Sakalava in the north-west of the province, the Morondava region spreading much further north as well, the Vezo and Mahafaly in and around Toliara, and the Antandroy and the Antansoy in the south and south-east (Fort Dauphin region). These complement the highly divergent climactic conditions, a highly varied animal species, flora and fauna, and different forms of local agriculture and fishing of these regions.

8. Ilmenite, also known in colloquial speech as 'black sand', is the source of titanium dioxide, a white pigment that has replaced the dangerous lead additions in white paint. Because of its opacity and pure whiteness it is added as colour to a vast number of industrial products.

9. Edited by the Andrew Lees Trust and Panos London in 2009, downloadable from www.andrewleestrust.org/hepa.htm.

10. www.riotinto.com/whatweproduce/517_17790.asp; or in a more elaborated form www.riotinto.com/documents/Library/Review89_March09_A_promise_fulfilled.pdf, accessed 7 June 2010.

11. See also Mallet (2009: 29) who calls the theft of songs one of the 'leitmotifs' of the tsapiky musicians.

12. This is not just a 'third country' phenomenon. In one of Meinhof's previous collaborative works, similar phenomena were observed in isolated communities along the former East–West European borders (see Meinhof 2003, especially the article by Wastl-Walter *et al.*).

13. Jijy is a form of rap, a recitative practised in Madagascar long before the arrival of modern-style rap music.

14. Charlie Gillett's blog www.charliegillett.com/bb/viewtopic.php?f=60&t=9353

> posted by andry » Tue Dec 09, 2008 5:55 pm:
> The mangaliba rythm is, like most of the malagasy rythm, a ternary beat.

ok let's play a little bit:
count 1,2,3,4,5,6
mark the 1 and 4 with your feet and clap your hands on the 5.
this is the basic ternary.
Now mangaliba:
still count 1,2,3,4,5,6
Mark the 1, 4 and 5 with your feet and clap your hands on the 2 and
    the 6.
It is the way people in Madagascar do the rythm (two people: one claps
    his hands on the 1, 4 and 5 and the other one claps on the 2 and 5)
This way of clapping hands is call the rombo.
All the rythm still play this way in traditional ceremony.
When using percussion (traditionnal), the rythm is played with aponga
    vilany (small drums use with a stick) and sticks (on the 2 and 5).
If the rythm is used during traditional ceremony, the name is katrehaka
    (or katrehaky).
his use for recreationnal purpose make it changes name (and sometimes
    forms with the addition of solos who don't exist in the katrehaka).

15. We were intrigued to find that the vocabulary of migration as used by all
    our Malagasy informants does not differentiate between national or inter-
    national movements. European nationals resettling from, say, southern
    Bavaria to Berlin, from Yorkshire to London, from Burgundy to Paris would
    hardly conceive of themselves or be perceived by others as 'migrants'. By
    contrast, Malagasies who move from the more remote regions to the capital
    city are already 'des migrants'.
16. Ankatso is one of the university districts of Antananarivo.
17. Their fear of being rejected by audiences when they play back home is
    founded on the bad experiences of others. Answering our question whether
    they were the first Morondavan band ever to return to play back home they
    answer as follows:

Tsiliva:	Non, euh, c'est pas la première fois, mais ils ont échoué, hein [...].
Jules:	Y'a deux artistes, y'a Tsivery.
Tsiliva:	Tsivery.
Jules:	Et Tropical Music. Mais les deux ont échoué.
Tsiliva:	Ils ont échoué.
Marie:	Et quand vous dites qu'ils ont échoué, c'est-à-dire que quand ils sont revenus à Morondava, personne n'est –
Tsiliva:	Personne ...
Marie:	Personne n'est venu?
Tsiliva:	Ouais.
(Tsiliva:	No, it's not the first time, but they failed [...].
Jules:	There were two artists, Tsivery.
Tsiliva:	Tsivery.
Jules:	And Tropical Music. But both failed
Tsiliva:	They failed.

Marie:	And when you say they failed, does that mean that when they came to Morondava, nobody –
Tsiliva:	Nobody
Marie:	Nobody came?
Tsiliva:	Yeah.)

18. A so-called 'cabaret' in Madagascar has little to do with its European namesake other than that it, too, refers to an indoor live performance by artists. Malagasy cabarets are ticketed events, where the public sits at tables, allowing the consumption of food and drink during concerts which usually comprise some 'sing-along' sequences.
19. We are enormously grateful to Dr Markus Verne, anthropologist from the University of Bayreuth in Germany, who during his own fieldwork with metal musicians in Tana during 2009 and 2010 was able to follow up links to Anna on our behalf. His notes and interview recordings helped us to fill in the missing gaps of Anna's story after Meinhof had left Tana.
20. 'Tremplin' means 'springboard' in English and thus this competition is concerned with 'discovering' new and emerging musical talent in Morocco's 'underground' scenes.
21. The *ribab* is a monochord fiddle. See Schuyler (1985).

Notes to Chapter 2

1. Various interviews by Meinhof, and Rasolofondraosolo and Meinhof, as well as unrecorded conversations and discussions between 2003 and 2009.
2. Hegasy (2007) makes these comments in the broader context of a study of youth attitudes towards youth culture and state power in contemporary Morocco. The 'youth' category mainly refers to individuals aged between 18 and 34 years old.
3. The hosting of the 2010 FIFA World Cup in South Africa has further reinforced this dynamic.
4. See Rasolofondraosolo and Meinhof (2003) for a discussion of the range of dialects in Mahaleo lyrics.
5. The lyrics of Mahaleo have only recently been made commercially available as a result of the 35th anniversary concert, the professional organization of a Tana-based firm, Media Consulting, the booklets for the *Mahaleo* film soundtrack by Laterit, and the live concert recordings of the Olympia concert by Laterit. Before then they were lovingly transcribed and passed around by afficionados in handwritten booklets which were exhibited as part of the Mahaleo exhibition in Antananarivo in 2007. Yet in spite of that absence of written records, audiences often remember the words of older songs better than some members of the group themselves, and audiences step in to fill memory-gaps by the singers.
6. In one of the two Olympia concerts in 2007, Dama had to plead with the audience to let him first complete the opening guitar solo and stanza for his song 'Samba la guerra', so that he could enjoy himself with his music, before the audience should join him, thus reversing the more traditional role of audiences needing to be animated by the artists to clap or to sing along.

7. Since 2002 we were able to collaborate with Dama on several research projects. Hence he appears in this book with two quite separate functions: one as a consultant advisor to our research project, acting as mediator between us and some of the musicians we researched, and occasionally as co-interviewer or interpreter. But quite independently of his role as advisor, by giving us access to his own career paths he enabled us to observe independently the workings of an extensive network of musicians in their professional and personal lives. Dama thus became a supporter and a subject of our research in his own right. This collaboration has undoubtedly influenced the development of our field-work, just as Julien Mallet's close collaboration with the musician Damily in Toliara had opened many paths for him (Mallet 2002, 2009). However, just like Mallet and others in similar positions (for example Baily 2001, 2008) we took great care to retain a great deal of variation in our research methods, and to treat all data – whether with or without Dama's direct involvement – with reflexivity and analytical rigour. But see also our reflections on researchers as 'accidental hubs' in the Introduction.

8. The connection between NGOs and music will be explored in detail in Chapter 6. But see also Gibert and Meinhof (2009) for a discussion of the 'inspirational triangle' of music, tourism and development.

9. Marius Meinhof, student of ethnology and nephew of Ulrike, expressed his astonishment after having attended the 2007 anniversary concert in Tana, that a crowd of that size would be so relatively well behaved in comparison to the Western rock and pop music concerts he normally attends (Meinhof's interview with her family about their impressions about the concert, May 2007, Tana).

10. *L'Kounache* means 'the notebook' in Moroccan Arabic.

11. See www.ambafrance-ma.org/maroc/population.cfm, accessed 12 August 2010.

12. *Metropolis*, Un reportage de Rim Mathlouti, Samedi 15 septembre 2007 à 20h00, Rediffusion le 16 septembre à 12h45, Coproduction: ARTE France, Ex-Nihilo.

13. *L'Espoir citoyen* and *Nichan* ceased to be published in 2009 and 2010 respectively. On the topic of *Nayda*, especially its socio-linguistic dimensions, see the work of Dominique Caubet and in particular her documentary film entitled *Casa Nayda*, written by Dominique Caubet, directed by Farida Benlyazid, co-directed by Abderrahim Mettour (2007, Sigma Technologies, Morocco).

14. This is how Justin described to us his introduction to the valiha: 'Je suis de la famille de fabricants de la valiha ... depuis mon grand-père. Mon père est lui-même fabricant de la valiha et aussi un très grand joueur de valiha qui est très connu dans toutes les régions à l'époque des foires ... donc c'est grâce à lui ... que je joue de la valiha quoi en quelque sorte ... et ma mère est une chanteuse de temple ancestral, qui est leader vocal, dans le temple ancestral où toutes les femmes chantent a cappella.' ('I come from a family who has been making valihas ever since my grandfather. My father was already build-ing valihas and he was also a great valiha player who was well known in all the regions during the fairs [...] so it's thanks to him that I play the valiha [...] and my mother is a singer in the ancestral temple, she is the leading voice in the ancestral temple where all the women sing a cappella.) (Meinhof and Rasolofondraosolo's interview, May 2006, following the concert by the Madagascar All Stars at the Traumzeit Festival in Germany)

15. For a most amusing account of how Justin bought his first taxi brousse ticket to Tana by selling his hen who had laid an enormous egg, see Meinhof (2009: 157).

Notes to Chapter 3

1. Donald McNeill also argues that many scholars have also been guilty of portraying the New York or Los Angeles experiences as characteristic of *all* global cities, with little attempt being made to nuance and pay attention to non-American, that is, European contexts. See McNeill (1999).
2. On this topic, see Portes (2000).
3. See Kiwan (2005).
4. See Kiwan (2005).
5. See Kiwan (2005).
6. Bled – which has now become a French word meaning town/village – is derived from the Arabic *bilad*, meaning country/homeland. It is used by North African immigrants to refer to their home country (and not necessarily in the 'nostalgic' sense).
7. www.croissance.com/ and http://sobika.com/ are both transnationally oriented Malagasy sites. Croissance is more French-based communitarian, whereas Sobika is based in Madagascar. Both are widely consulted by the diaspora.
8. Erick Manana lives in Bordeaux but has for decades enjoyed the support of the Malagasy diaspora. The group Lolo sy ny Tariny goes back nearly as long as Mahaleo, and apart from Lolo himself, who lives in Paris, also includes Erick Manana. After many years of silence they have regrouped and recommenced to perform, sharing a platform with Mahaleo in Antananarivo, as well as appearing in Paris and beyond.
9. Ulrike: Mais tu n'as jamais essayé de travailler avec des institutions par exemple les CGM ou L'Alliance française ou ... les choses comme ça?

    Lova: En fait c'est ... je fais des initiatives privées donc là je travaille avec le CCAC mais je ne suis pas dans l'organisation même, mais plus dans la communication, mais le but c'est ça en fait, c'est de travailler avec eux, le CGM, le CCAC mais euh ... on est plutôt indépendants en fait. Oui, c'est ça, on aime bien faire nos choses et pas dépendre des autres. On fait en sorte que ce qu'on veut faire, qu'on nous soutienne ou qu'on ne nous soutienne pas, il faut que ça se fasse. Donc, après on va voir les institutions, tant mieux si ils nous suivent, et tant pis s'ils nous suivent pas, on le fait quand même. Donc, c'est au moins la philosophie qu'on a, mais, non non, on nous demande quand même de, de ... mais ça viendra, nous on est ouverts.

    (Ulrike: But you never tried to work with institutions such as the GCM or the Alliance française, or something similar?

    Lova: In fact, it is ... I'm taking private initiatives, so I'm working with CCAC, not in terms of organization but rather in terms of communication. The goal is to work with them, the CGM and the CCAS, but we are ... we are rather independent. We like to do our things and not to be dependent on others. We make sure that we can do what we want to do, whether people support us or not. Having said that, we always go and talk to the institutions afterward and it is great if they come along. And if not, we will do our project anyway. Well at least, it is our philosophy, but it could come.)

10. For an account of Justin's branching out into the world music scene through the intervention of UK pop singer Kate Bush and her brother Paddy Bush, and a connection to Peter Gabriel, see Meinhof (2009).
11. RNS is an annual event that attracts many thousands of Malagasies and stands for Rencontre nationale sportive et activités culturelles de la communauté malagasy en Europe.
12. The fieldwork with North African musicians in London was carried out by the TNMundi research fellow Dr Marie-Pierre Gibert and the authors are grateful to her for her contribution to our project's findings.
13. For a full account and analysis of the London 'international jam sessions', see Gibert (2008a and 2008b).
14. See Gibert (2010).
15. Gibert's interviews with Seddik Zebiri, July 2007, Karim Dellali, July 2007 and Tahar El Idrissi and Farid Nainia, January 2008, London.
16. Meinhof's interview for the Cultural Cooperation website, 2005, London, and Gibert's interview in April 2007, London, French original.
17. Meinhof's interview for the Cultural Cooperation website in 2005 at her home in Sussex, English original.
18. Kiwan's and Gibert's interview with Khalid, Kasba, July 2008, Boxtel, the Netherlands.
19. Kiwan's and Gibert's interview with Salah Edin, June 2008, Amsterdam.

Notes to Chapter 4

1. In their analysis of the discourses of migrant musicians, Meinhof and Triandafyllidou (2006) have suggested that diasporic, neo-communitarian and cosmopolitan identifications should be seen as the variable registers in identity construction of individuals rather than as alternatives.
2. Elsa also assists the group in finding funding for residencies/tours via Watcha Clan's association *Vai la Botte*.
3. This biographical information was drawn from the following newspaper article: 'Aïcha Lebga, "la fille du désert" au Zénith – Nantes', *Ouest France*, 14 March 2009, www.ouest-france.fr/2009/03/14/nantes/Aïcha-Lebga-la-fille-du-desert-au-Zenith—55628453.html, accessed 25 January 2010.
4. See the film *Casa Nayda*, written by Dominique Caubet, directed by Farida Benlyazid, co-directed by Abderrahim Mettour (2007, Sigma Technologies, Morocco).
5. Khansa Batma ended her contract with Click records and her third album is self-produced.
6. Many of the artists and groups active within the contemporary urban music scenes in Morocco adopt nationalist/patriotic tropes and motifs in their lyrics and aesthetics, to the extent that this movement can be described as

engaging with a sort of alternative nationalism. For further discussion on this topic, see Chapter 2.

7. Previously Khansa Batma had been talking about Moroccan musicians who feel compelled to leave Morocco in order to be able to make a living from their art.

Notes to Chapter 5

1. www.diplomatie.gouv.fr/fr/actions-france_830/culture_1031/un-reseau-etranger_11309/index.html, accessed 23 April 2010.
2. Kiwan's interview with Hicham Bajjou, March 2008, Casablanca.
3. *Matbakh* is an Arabic word meaning kitchen, hence Music Matbakh is getting at the notion of mixing different musical cultures and experiences together.
4. The following section on Music Matbakh draws on the TNMundi research fellow Marie-Pierre Gibert's ethnography of the residency in London, Cambridge and Newcastle, and the report she produced for the British Council and TNMundi team summing up her observations. The authors are grateful to her for her valuable research collaboration throughout the TNMundi project.
5. Nevertheless, the Music Matbakh group did enjoy very positive receptions in other countries, especially in Jordan; see for instance http://khobbeizeh. blogspot.com/2007/07/perfect-flavors-in-music-matbakh.html, accessed August 2010. The authors extend their thanks to Marie-Pierre Gibert for bringing this website to their attention.
6. The Changing City Spaces cultural event, *Music Matters: Cultural Flows in Changing City Spaces*, Paris, 7–9 April 2005, was held at Mains d'oeuvres, Saint-Ouen and was co-sponsored by the Ministry of Culture and Communication, the Délégation interministérielle de la ville, the Association for the Study of Modern and Contemporary France, the Mairie de Paris, the British Council, the Fondation Evens and the FASILD (Fonds d'action et de soutien à l'intégration et à la lutte contre les discriminations).
7. The second event in Rabat was also co-produced with the Centre for Cross Cultural Learning and the School for International Training, Rabat.

Notes to Chapter 6

1. For a discussion of the ways in which the experience of the diaspora enters Malagasy song lyrics, see also Meinhof and Rasolofondraosolo (2005).
2. For a discussion of African diasporic networks as safe spaces see for example Ellerbe-Dueck (2011).
3. Carstensen-Egwuom and Holly (2011) show that Vietnamese migrants in Chemnitz in Germany have similar desires to introduce and 'integrate' Germans into their cultural traditions thus reversing the usual perspective on 'integration' as one where migrants 'integrate' into majority society.
4. *Madagascar* (2005), *Madagascar: Escape 2 Africa* (2008).
5. The film *Mahaleo* by Laterit, made in close collaboration with the musicians, tackles this dilemma of representation head-on, in showing contrasting and conflicting scenes from everyday life in Madagascar. To give just one example: supplying water to a village is shown not only as one of the projects

which Dama as an independent MP embarks on and finally succeeds with, but also links to other scenes of the film. One scene in particular focuses on the different ways of transporting water downhill from a river. It shows a tiny boy dressed in a pair of shorts hardly held together by a safety pin who is nearly keeling over by the weight of the water he's carrying in two enormous buckets, a truly touching image that together with that of another young man already malformed by years of doing just that could easily have reconfirmed the sense of the deprivation of the local people. However, without diminishing the viewer's sense of the difficulty of everyday life, any purely 'miserabilist' reading is counteracted by the liveliness of a whole lot of different people of all ages going or riding down that path together – from the mutual support rendered by a bigger girl part of the way, who carries his bucket for a while, to the giggling teenagers holding hands who are clearly having an excellent flirtatious time. Scenes such as these precisely avoid the 'miserabilist vision' of Madagascar, while not falling for any sentimentalizing or exoticizing depictions either. Marie-Clemence Paes and the Laterit team are fully aware of the balancing act that is required and have frequently addressed these issues when introducing their film (for example during the round-table discussion at Saint-Ouen in 2005 and the Brighton Festival in 2005).

6. For a discussion of a successful transformation of an 'audience' wishing to be entertained to a more informed public by Mahaleo members Dama and Charle at the Brighton Festival in 2002, see Meinhof (2005).
7. Source: www.cia.gov/library/publications/the-world-factbook/geos/mo.html, accessed 27 May 2010. For comparison, the GDP (PPP) of the United Kingdom for 2009 is estimated at $35,200.
8. The third part of the 'triangle' in the article is 'tourism'. This is to capture the fact that, on the one hand, either visits as tourists by members of these associations had prompted their subsequent engagement as 'developers' or that their role as developers led to their becoming visitors to Madagascar. Hence tourism, development and music have come together to form this mutual cycle of support.
9. See Cérise Maréchaud, 'Asidd Rock', *L'Kounache Magazine*, June 2005.
10. This perspective is echoed by Barry Ferguson, a natural scientist working in the region of Fort Dauphin on the preservation of the natural environment, who also underlines the need for a 'cultural turn' in his own forthcoming PhD thesis, based on a ten-year engagement in the region: Ferguson (forthcoming). See also Ferguson (2009), Ratsimbazafy *et al.* (2008) and Gardner *et al.* (2008).

Bibliography

Ager, D. E. (2005) 'French cultural, languages and telecommunications policy towards sub-Saharan Africa', *Modern and Contemporary France*, 13:1, 57–69.

Aksoy, A. (2006) 'London and the project of urban cosmopolitanism', in U. H. Meinhof and A. Triandafyllidou (eds), *Transcultural Europe: Cultural Policy in a Changing Europe*. Basingstoke: Palgrave Macmillan.

Appadurai, A. (1996) *Modernity at Large: Cultural Dimensions of Globalization*. Minneapolis: University of Minnesota Press.

Armbruster, Heidi (2008) 'Introduction: the ethics of taking sides', in H. Armbruster and A. Laerke (eds), *Taking Sides*. New York and Oxford: Berghahn.

Armbruster, Heidi and U. H. Meinhof (2011) *Borders, Networks, Neighbourhoods: Negotiating Multicultural Europe*. Basingstoke: Palgrave Macmillan.

Baily, John (2001) 'Learning to perform as a research technique in ethnomusicology', *Ethnomusicology Forum*, 10:2, 85–98.

Baily, John (2008) 'Ethnomusicology, intermusability, and performance practice', in Henry Stobart (ed.), *The New (Ethno)musicologies*. Chicago: Scarecrow Press.

Bash, L., N. Glick Schiller and C. Szanton Blanc (1994) *Nations Unbound: Transnational Projects, Postcolonial Predicaments, and Deterritorialized Nation-States*. New York: Gordon and Breach.

Beck, U. (2000) *What is Globalization?* Cambridge: Polity Press.

Becker, H. (1982) *Art Worlds*. Berkeley and Los Angeles: University of California Press.

Belghazi, T. (2005) 'Festivalisation of urban space in Morocco', in D. Richards, T. Agoumy and T. Belghazi (eds), *Urban Generations: Post-Colonial Cities*. Casablanca: Faculty of Letters of Rabat.

Bennett, Andy and Richard A. Peterson (eds) (2004) *Music Scenes: Local, Translocal, and Virtual*. Nashville: Vanderbilt University Press.

Bergenholtz, H. *et al.* (eds) (1991) *Malagasy Alema. Madagassisch-Deutsches Wörterbuch*. Moers: Aragon.

Bergenholz, H. *et al.* (eds) (1994) *Deutsch-Madagassisches Wörterbuch*. Moers: Aragon.

Böse, M., B. Busch and M. D. Sesic (2006) 'Despite and beyond cultural policy: third and fourth sector practices and strategies in Vienna and Belgrade', in U. H. Meinhof and A. Triandafyllidou (eds), *Transcultural Europe: Cultural Policy in a Changing Europe*. Basingstoke: Palgrave Macmillan.

Bourdieu, P. and L. D. Wacquant (1992) *An Invitation to Reflexive Sociology*. Chicago University Press.

Bouwer, Leoni E. (2003) 'The viability of official Malagasy in the language ecology of southern Madagascar, with special emphasis on the Bara speech community', Phd thesis, University of South Africa, Pretoria.

Bouwer, L. (2007) 'Intercomprehension and mutual intelligibility among southern Malagasy languages', *Language Matters*, 38:2, 253–74.

Bunnell, T. (2007) 'Post-maritime transnationalization: Malay seafarers in Liverpool', *Global Networks*, 7:4, 412–29.

Carstensen-Egwuom, Inken and Holly Werner (2011) 'Integration, identities, no-go-areas: everyday experiences and public discourses of neighbourhood-building in a German region', in H. Armbruster and U. H. Meinhof (eds), *Borders, Networks, Neighbourhoods: Negotiating Multicultural Europe*. Basingstoke: Palgrave Macmillan.

Castells, M. (1996) *The Rise of the Network Society*. Oxford: Blackwell.

Chafer, T. (2005) 'Chirac and la "Françafrique": no longer a family affair', *Modern and Contemporary France*, 13:1, 7–23.

Charbonneau, B. (2008) 'Dreams of empire: France, Europe, and the new interventionism in Africa', *Modern and Contemporary France*, 16:3, 279–95.

Cherti, M. (2007) *Paradoxes of Social Capital: A Multi-Generational Study of Moroccans in London*. Amsterdam University Press.

Clifford, J. and George E. Marcus (eds) (1986) *Writing Culture: The Poetics and Politics of Ethnography*. Berkeley: University of California Press.

Cohen, R. (2008) *Global Diasporas: An Introduction*, 2nd edn. London and New York: Routledge.

Cohen, S. and J. Larabi (2006) *Morocco: Globalization and its Consequences*. London and New York: Routledge.

Collins, R. (1998) *The Sociology of Philosophies: A Global Theory of Intellectual Change*. Cambridge, MA: Harvard University Press.

Collyer, M. (2004) *Profile of the Algerian Population in the UK*. London: The Information Centre about Asylum and Refugees in the UK.

Daoud, Z. (2007) *Maroc: les années de plomb 1958–1988: chroniques d'une résistance*. Houilles: Éditions Manucius.

Daoudi, B. and H. Miliani (2002) *Beurs' mélodies: cent ans de chansons immigrées du blues berbère au rap beur*. Paris: Éditions Séguier.

Derderian, R. (2004) *North Africans in Contemporary France: Becoming Visible*. Basingstoke: Palgrave Macmillan.

Dirlik, A. (1996) 'The global in the local', in R. Wilson and W. Dissanayake (eds), *Global/Local: Cultural Production and the Transnational Imaginary*. Durham, NC and London: Duke University Press.

Durrschmidt, J. (2000) *Everyday Lives in the Global City: The Delinking of Locale and Milieu*. London and New York: Routledge.

Dwyer, K. (2007) 'Moroccan cinema and the promotion of culture', *Journal of North African Studies*, 12:3, 277–86.

Ellerbe-Dueck, Cassandra (2011) 'The networks and "safe spaces" of black European women in Germany and Austria', in H. Armbruster and U. H. Meinhof (eds), *Borders, Networks, Neighbourhoods: Negotiating Multicultural Europe*. Basingstoke: Palgrave Macmillan.

Erlmann, V. (1993) 'The politics and aesthetics of transnational musics', *The World of Music*, 35:2, 3–15.

Featherstone, D., R. Phillips and J. Waters (2007) 'Introduction: spatialities of transnational networks', *Global Networks*, 7:4, 383–91.

Ferguson, Barry (2009) 'REDD comes into fashion in Madagascar', *Madagascar Conservation and Development*, 4:2, 132–7.

Ferguson, B. (forthcoming) 'The political ecology of forests and Tandroy communities in southern Madagascar', PhD thesis in progress, University of East Anglia.

Fisher, Michael M. J. and George E. Marcus (eds) (1986) *Anthropology as Cultural Critique*. University of Chicago Press.

Fuhr, J. (2006) 'Malagasy roots musicians in contemporary Antananarivo', MA dissertation, SOAS, London University.

Fuhr, Jenny (forthcoming) 'Experiencing rhythm: contemporary Malagasy music and identity', PhD thesis, expecting viva 2011 University of Southampton.

Gardner, C. J., B. Ferguson, F. Rebara and A. N. Ratsifandrihamanana (2008) 'Integrating traditional values and management regimes into Madagascar's expanded protected area system: the case of Ankodida', in J.-M. Mallarach (ed.), *Values of Protected Landscapes and Seascapes*, vol. 2: *Protected Landscapes and Cultural and Spiritual Values*. Gland: IUCN World Commission on Protected Areas.

Gazzah, M. (2008) *Rhythms and Rhymes of Life: Music and Identification Processes of Dutch-Moroccan Youth*. Amsterdam University Press.

Geertz, Clifford (1990) *Works and Lives: The Anthropologist as Author*. Stanford University Press.

Gibert, M.-P. (2008a) 'Migrant and artist: Moroccan musicians in the UK, between professional aims, personal experiences, and creative memory', Paper presented at the conference on 'Moroccan Migration in Europe: Identity Formation, Representation and Memory', University of Sussex, November.

Gibert, M.-P. (2008b) 'Ancrage local et réseaux transnationaux d'artistes d'origine nord-africaine au Royaume-Uni: la "jam session" comme point nodal des réseaux', Paper presented at 'Music and Migration: North African Artists' Networks across Europe and Africa' Conference, Université Mohammed V-Agdal, Morocco, 13 November.

Gibert, M.-P. (2010) 'Re-enchanting Britain through a musical idealised multi-cultural past: "Al Andalus" in the UK', Paper presented at the 11th EASA Biennial Conference on 'Crisis and Imagination', Maynooth, Ireland, 24–27 August.

Gibert, Marie-Pierre and Ulrike Hanna Meinhof (2009) 'Inspiration triangulaire: musique, tourisme et développement à Madagascar', Numéro spécial des *Cahiers d'études africaines: mise en tourisme de la culture: réseaux, représentations et pratiques*.

Gilroy, P. (1993) *The Black Atlantic: Modernity and Double Consciousness*. London: Verso.

Goedefroit, Sophie (2007) 'La restitution du droit à la parole', *Études Rurales*, 178, 39–63.

Goedefroit, Sophie and Jean-Pierre Revéret (2007) 'Quel développement à Madagascar? Introduction', *Études Rurales*, 178, 9–21.

Grillo, R. D. and R. L. Stirrat (eds) (1997) *Discourses of Development: Anthropological Perspectives*. Oxford and New York: Berg.

Guilbault, J. (1993) *Zouk: World Music in the West Indies*. University of Chicago Press.

HAJAMadagascar and August Schmidhofer (eds) (2003) *Worldmusic – Madagascar*. Vienna: Universal Edition.

Halpern, D. (2005) *Social Capital*. Malden, MA: Polity.

Hegasy, S. (2007) 'Young authority: quantitative and qualitative insights into youth, youth culture, and state power in contemporary Morocco', *Journal of North African Studies*, 12:1, 19–36.

Hoffman, K. E. (2002) 'Generational change in Berber women's song of the Anti-Atlas Mountains, Morocco', *Ethnomusicology*, 46:3, 510–40.

Holton, R. J. (2005) *Making Globalization*. Basingstoke: Palgrave Macmillan.

Holton, R. J. (2008) *Global Networks*. Basingstoke: Palgrave Macmillan.

Hopper, P. (2007) *Understanding Cultural Globalization*. Cambridge: Polity.

Hymes, Dell (ed.) (1999) *Reinventing Anthropology*. Ann Arbor: University of Michigan Press.

International Crisis Group (2010) 'Madagascar: sortir du cycle de crises', *Rapport Afrique* No. 156 (18 March).

Kalb, Don, Marco van der Land, Richard Staring, Bart van Steenbergen and Nico Wilterdink (eds) (1993) *The Ends of Globalization: Bringing Society Back In*. Lanham, MD: Rowman and Littlefield, 253–70.

Kapchan, D. (2007) *Traveling Spirit Masters: Moroccan Music and Trance in the Global Marketplace*. Middletown, CT: Wesleyan University Press.

Kiwan, N. (2005) '"Maghrebi music" in and beyond the post-colonial city', in D. Richards, T. Agoumy and T. Belghazi (eds), *Urban Generations: Post-Colonial Cities*. Rabat: Faculty of Letters.

Kiwan, N. (2009) *Identities, Discourses and Experiences: Young People of North African Origin in France*. Manchester University Press.

Kiwan, N. and K. Kosnick (2006) 'The whiteness of cultural policy in Paris and Berlin', in U. H. Meinhof and A. Triandafyllidou (eds), *Transcultural Europe: Cultural Policy in a Changing Europe*. Basingstoke: Palgrave Macmillan.

Kosic, Ankica and Anna Triandafyllidou (2006) 'Urban cultural policy and immigrants in Rome: multiculturalism or simply "paternalism"?', in U. H. Meinhof and A. Triandafyllidou (eds), *Transcultural Europe: Cultural Policy in a Changing Europe*. Basingstoke: Palgrave Macmillan.

Lacroix, T. (2005) *Les Réseaux marocains du développement: géographie du transnational et politiques du territorial*. Paris: Presses de la Fondation Nationale des Sciences Politiques.

Landolt, P. (2001) 'Salvadoran economic transnationalism: embedded strategies for household maintenance, immigrant incorporation, and entrepreneurial expansion', *Global Networks*, 1, 217–42.

Latour, B. (1999) 'On recalling ANT', in J. Law and J. Hassard (eds), *Actor Network Theory and After*. Oxford: Basil Blackwell.

Latour, B. (2005) *Reassembling the Social: An Introduction to Actor-Network Theory*. Oxford University Press.

Lemanski, C. (2007) 'Global cities in the South: deepening social and spatial polarization in Cape Town', *Cities*, 24:6, 448–61.

Levitt, P. (1998) 'Social remittances: migration driven local-level forms of cultural diffusion', *International Migration Review*, 32, 926–48.

Levitt, P. (2001) *The Transnational Villagers*. Berkeley and Los Angeles: University of California Press.

Levitt, P. and Deepak Lamba-Nieves (2011) 'Social remittances revisited', *Journal of Ethnic and Migration Studies*, 37:1, 1–22.

Levitt, Peggy, Josh DeWind and Steven Vertovec (eds) (2003) 'International perspectives on transnational migration: an introduction', *International Migration Review*, Special Issue on Transnational Migration, 37:3, 565–76.

Li, W. (1998) 'Anatomy of a new ethnic settlement: the Chinese ethnoburb in Los Angeles', *Urban Studies*, 35, 479–501.

Lortat-Jacob, B. (1981) 'Community music as an obstacle to professionalism: a Berber example', *Ethnomusicology*, 25:1, 87–98.

Mallet, J. (2002) 'Histoire de vies, histoire d'une vie: Damily, musicien de "tsapik", troubadour des temps modernes / Story of lives, story of a life: the tsapiky musician Damily-Troubadour of modern times', *Cahiers-de-musiques-traditionnelles*, 15, 113–32.

Mallet, Julien (2009) *Le Tsapiky, une jeune musique de Madagascar*. Paris: Éditions Karthala.

Marcus, G. E. (1995) 'Ethnography in/of the world system: the emergence of multi-sited ethnography', *Annual Review of Anthropology*, 24: 95–117.

Marcus, G. E. (1998) *Ethnography through Thick and Thin*. Princeton University Press.

Massey, D. (2005) *For Space*. London: Sage.

Mauss, Marcel (1997 [1923–24]) 'Essai sur le don: forme et raison de l'échange dans les sociétés archaïques', in Marcel Mauss, *Sociologie et Anthropologie*, Paris: PUF, 143–280.

McNeill, D. (1999) 'Globalization and the European city', *Cities*, 16:3, 143–7.

Meinhof, Ulrike Hanna (ed.) (2003) 'Bordering European identities', Special Issue, *Journal of Ethnic and Migration Studies*, 29:5.

Meinhof, Ulrike Hanna (2005) 'Initiating a public: Malagasy music and live audiences in differentiated cultural contexts', in Sonia Livingstone (ed.), *Audiences and Publics: When Cultural Engagement Matters for the Public Sphere*. Bristol and Portland, OR: Intellect.

Meinhof, Ulrike Hanna (2009) 'Transnational flows, networks and "transcultural capital": reflections on researching migrant networks through linguistic ethnography', in Stef Slembrouck, Jim Collins and Mike Baynham (eds), *Globalization and Languages in Contact: Scale, Migration, and Communicative Practices*. London: Continuum.

Meinhof, U. H. and H. Armbruster (2008) *Cultural Diasporas*, European Parliament Policy Department B, Structural and Cohesion Policies (PE389.600).

Meinhof, Ulrike Hanna and D. Dariusz Galasinski (2005) *The Language of Belonging*. Basingstoke: Palgrave Macmillan.

Meinhof, Ulrike H., Nadia Kiwan and Marie-Pierre Gibert (2010) 'Transnational musicians' networks across Africa and Europe', in K. Knott and D. McLoughlin (eds), *Diasporas: Concepts, Intersections, Identities*. London: Zed Books.

Meinhof, Ulrike Hanna and Zafimahaleo Rasolofondraosolo (2005) 'Malagasy song-writer musicians in transnational settings', *Moving Worlds*, 5:1, 144–58.

Meinhof, Ulrike Hanna and Anna Triandafyllidou (eds) (2006) *Transcultural Europe: Cultural Policy in a Changing Europe*. Basingstoke: Palgrave Macmillan.

Njoh, A. J. (2006) 'African cities and regional trade in historical perspective: implications for contemporary globalization trends', *Cities*, 23:1, 18–29.

Pizzorno, A. (1991) 'On the individualistic theory of social order', in P. Bourdieu and J. S. Coleman (eds), *Social Theory for a Changing Society*. Boulder, CO: Westview Press.

Portes, A. (2000) 'Globalization from below: the rise of transnational communities', in Don Kalb, Marco van der Land, Richard Staring, Bart van Steenbergen and Nico Wilterdink (eds), *The Ends of Globalization: Bringing Society Back In*. Lanham, MD: Rowman and Littlefield.

Portes, A., L. E. Guarnizo and P. Landolt (1999) 'The study of transnationalism: pitfalls and promise of an emergent field', *Ethnic and Racial Studies*, 22:2, 217–37.

Pottier, J., A. Bicker and P. Sillitoe (eds) (2003) *Negotiating Local Knowledge: Power and Identity in Development*. London and Sterling, VA: Pluto Press.

Putnam, R. (2000) *Bowling Alone: The Collapse and Revival of American Community.* New York: Simon & Schuster.

Rabenilaina, R.-B. (1993) *L'Intégration des différents parlers, signes manifestes de l'unicité de la langue malgache.* Oslo: Novus Forlag.

Rajaonarimanana, N. (1995) *Grammaire moderne de la langue malgache.* Paris: L'Asiathèque.

Rasolofondraosolo, Zafimahaleo and Ulrike Hanna Meinhof (2003) 'Popular Malagasy music and the construction of cultural identities', in S. Makoni and U. H. Meinhof (eds), *Africa and Applied Linguistics. AILA REVIEW,* 16, 127–48.

Ratsimbazafy, J., L. J. Rakotoniaina and J. Durbin (2008) 'Cultural anthropologists and conservationists: can we learn from each other to conserve the diversity of Malagasy species and culture?', in J. C. Kaufmann (ed.), *Greening the Great Red Island: Madagascar in Nature and Culture.* Pretoria: Africa Institute of South Africa.

Rice, Timothy (2003) 'Time, place, and metaphor in musical experience and ethnography', *Ethnomusicology,* 47:2, 151–79.

Robertson, R. (1992) *Globalization: Social Theory and Global Culture.* London: Sage.

Robertson, R. (1994) 'Globalisation or glocalisation?', *Journal of International Communication,* 1:1, 33–52.

Robertson, R. (1995) 'Glocalization: time-space and homogeneity-heterogeneity', in Mike Featherstone, Scott Lash and Roland Robertson (eds), *Global Modernities.* London: Sage.

Robertson, R. and K. E. White (eds) (2003) *Globalization: Critical Concepts in Sociology,* vol. 1. London and New York: Routledge.

Robins, K. (2001) 'Becoming anybody: thinking against the nation and through the city', *City,* 5:1, 77– 90.

Robins, K. (2006) 'Towards a transcultural policy for European cosmopolitanism', in U. H. Meinhof and A. Triandafyllidou (eds), *Transcultural Europe: Cultural Policy in a Changing Europe.* Basingstoke: Palgrave Macmillan.

Russell, G. and C. Tuite (2002) 'Introducing Romantic sociability', in G. Russell and C. Tuite (eds), *Romantic Sociability: Social Networks and Literary Culture in Britain 1770–1840.* Cambridge University Press.

Safran, W. (1991) 'Diasporas in modern societies: myths of homeland and return', *Diaspora,* 1, 83–99.

Sassen, S. (1991) *The Global City: New York, London, Tokyo.* Princeton University Press.

Sassen, S. (2002) 'Global cities and diasporic networks: micro-sites in global civil society', in H. Anheier, M. Glasius and M. Kaldor (eds), *Global Civil Society.* Oxford University Press.

Sassen, S. (2007) *Sociology of Globalization.* New York and London: W. W. Norton.

Schmidhofer, A. (1994) 'Kabosy, mandoliny, gitara. Zur Entwicklung neuer Populärmusikformen in Madagaskar', in A. Schmidhofer and D. Sch"uller (eds), *For Gerhard Kubik, Festschrift.* Frankfurt am Main and New York: Peter Lang.

Schuyler, P. D. (1985) 'The Rwais and the Zawia: professional musicians and the rural religious elite in southwestern Morocco', *Asian Music,* 17:1, 114–31.

Smith, M. P. (1999) 'Transnationalism and the city', in S. Body-Gendrot and R. Beauregard (eds), *The Urban Moment: Cosmopolitan Essays on the Late 20th Century City.* London: Sage.

Smith, M. P. (2001) *Transnational Urbanism: Locating Globalization.* Oxford: Blackwell.

Smith, M. P. and L. E. Guarnizo (eds) (1998) *Transnationalism from Below.* New Brunswick, NJ: Transaction Publishers.

Tsimilaza, A. (1992) 'La notation de l'accent en malgache: réflexions sur quelques questions de transcription et d'orthographie', *Études Océan Indien*, 15, 33–48.

Van de Veer, P. (2002) 'Colonial cosmopolitanism', in S. Vertovec and R. Cohen (eds), *Conceiving Cosmopolitanism.* Oxford University Press.

Vermeren, P. (2006) *Histoire du Maroc depuis l'indépendance.* Paris: Éditions La Découverte.

Vertovec, S. (2003) 'Migration and other modes of transnationalism: towards conceptual cross-fertilization', *International Migration Review*, 37:3, 641–66.

Vertovec, S. (2004) 'Migrant transnationalism and modes of transformation', *International Migration Review*, 38:3, 970–1001.

Vertovec, S. (2009) *Transnationalism.* London: Routledge.

Wastl-Walter, D., M. Varadi and F. Veider (2003) 'Coping with marginality: to stay or to go', *Journal of Ethnic and Migration Studies*, 29:5, 797–817.

Wimmer, A. and N. Glick Schiller (2002) 'Methodological nationalism and beyond: nation-state building, migration and the social sciences', *Global Networks*, 2:4, 301–34.

Wimmer, A. and N. Glick Schiller (2003) 'Methodological nationalism, the social sciences, and the study of migration: an essay in historical epistemology', *The International Migration Review*, 37:33, 576–610.

Winders, J. (2006) *Paris Africain: Rhythms of the African Diaspora.* Basingstoke: Palgrave Macmillan.

Zhou, Y. and Y. Tseng (2001) 'Regrounding the "ungrounded empires": localization as the geographical catalyst for transnationalism', *Global Networks*, 1, 131–53.

Films cited

Casa Nayda, written by Dominique Caubet, directed by Farida Benlyazid, co-directed by Abderrahim Mettour (2007, Sigma Technologies, Morocco).

Mahaleo, directed by Cesar Paes and Raimond Rajaonarivelo (2005, Laterit Productions, Paris) www.mahaleo.com.

Index

Note: bold entries refer to illustrations.